C000088559

FUSE™

**FORESIGHT-DRIVEN UNDERSTANDING,
STRATEGY AND EXECUTION**™

FUSE™

FORESIGHT-DRIVEN UNDERSTANDING, STRATEGY AND EXECUTION™

MOVE THE FUTURE™

DEVADAS KRISHNADAS

© 2015 Future-Moves Group Pte. Ltd.

FUSE™ Foresight-driven Understanding, Strategy and Execution and ≫**Future-Mo>es™** move the future are trademarks of Future-Moves Group Pte. Ltd.

Published by Marshall Cavendish Business
An imprint of Marshall Cavendish International
1 New Industrial Road, Singapore 536196

All rights reserved

No part of this publication may be reproduced, stored in a retrieval system or transmitted, in any form or by any means, electronic, mechanical, photocopying, recording or otherwise, without the prior permission of the copyright owner. Request for permission should be addressed to the Publisher, Marshall Cavendish International (Asia) Private Limited, 1 New Industrial Road, Singapore 536196. Tel: (65) 6213 9300. Fax: (65) 6285 4871. E-mail: genrefsales@sg.marshallcavendish.com Website: www.marshallcavendish.com/genref

The publisher makes no representation or warranties with respect to the contents of this book, and specifically disclaims any implied warranties or merchantability or fitness for any particular purpose, and shall in no event be liable for any loss of profit or any other commercial damage, including but not limited to special, incidental, consequential, or other damages.

Other Marshall Cavendish Offices:
Marshall Cavendish Corporation. 99 White Plains Road, Tarrytown NY 10591-9001, USA • Marshall Cavendish International (Thailand) Co Ltd. 253 Asoke, 12th Flr, Sukhumvit 21 Road, Klongtoey Nua, Wattana, Bangkok 10110, Thailand • Marshall Cavendish (Malaysia) Sdn Bhd, Times Subang, Lot 46, Subang Hi-Tech Industrial Park, Batu Tiga, 40000 Shah Alam, Selangor Darul Ehsan, Malaysia

Marshall Cavendish is a trademark of Times Publishing Limited

National Library Board Cataloguing-in-Publication Data
Krishnadas, Devadas, author.
FUSE : foresight-driven understanding, strategy and execution: move the future / Devadas Krishnadas.
- Singapore: Marshall Cavendish Business, [2015]
pages cm
Includes bibliographical references.
ISBN: 978-981-4721-12-7 (hardcover)
Strategic planning. 2. Business planning. 3. Management. I. Title.

HD30.28
658.4012 — dc23   OCN913438846

Printed in Singapore by Craft Print International Ltd.

FOR MY PARENTS

CONTENTS

AUTHOR'S NOTE

Every book represents a series of journeys. These journeys are mental, emotional and physical. None of these journeys would have been possible for me without the support of friends and family.

FUSE is not only about an idea, it is also the story of Future-Moves Group (FMG), the company I founded in 2012. The people who work at FMG and the clients we have had the privilege to work with on amazing projects have all played a part in developing FUSE.

The FMG Team—Eunice Leong, Daniel Ho, Shawn Teow and Mabel Ang—have been a source of support and inspiration. Particular mention must go to Isabel Chew, a Senior Associate Consultant at FMG, who acted as Principal Research Assistant. She helped flesh out ideas, verified data and information and challenged my thinking as we worked together to produce the book. This book is as much hers as it is mine.

I wish to thank Mr Peter Ho for his kind endorsement of the book and his support over the years I have been involved in the foresight scene in Singapore.

My good friends, Tan Kiat How, Tan Tin Wee, Gerard Pennefather, Thomas Sass, José Manual Fonseca, Calvin Cheng, Nizam Ismail, Max Everest-Phillips, Lee Swee Siong and Tan Ling Yin were instrumental in supporting me with their friendship and advice.

My family often paid the price for the long hours and strain of a husband and father challenged by the demands of establishing a business in as competitive an environment as strategic consulting. I am forever in their debt. They remain the motivation, when all else fails, which keeps me going.

Notwithstanding the support and advice of the many mentioned, any mistakes or errors are mine alone.

Devadas Krishnadas

Singapore, August 2015

LIST OF FIGURES

SECTION 1
INTRODUCTION

CHAPTER 1
A TALE OF TWO COMPANIES
NETFLIX VERSUS BLOCKBUSTER

In 2000, Reed Hastings, co-founder of online DVD rental company Netflix, made a proposition to John Antioco, then-CEO of the video-rental company Blockbuster: buy over Netflix for $50 million and leverage on Netflix's online rental service.

At that time, Netflix was only into its third year of operations. Although it enjoyed reasonable success in its nascent years, like many other start-ups it now faced a cash flow problem. Blockbuster, on the other hand, commanded 7,700 stores. It had just entered the New York Stock Exchange a few months earlier with a respectable IPO of $4.7 billion.[1]

As Netflix's former CFO Barry McCarthy reminisces, "[Blockbuster] just about laughed us out of their office."[2] Despite Netflix's persistent efforts, Blockbuster doggedly refused to bite, congratulating itself on avoiding what it thought was a revenue-haemorrhaging liability.[3] Yet in the aftermath of the dot-com crash of 2000, it was Blockbuster that fatally misdiagnosed the shifting technological landscape.

Fast forward to 2014. Blockbuster has since been liquidated. Its 60,000 employees, 9,000 international stores, and $5 billion market value—all widely vaunted figures at its peak in 2004—have disappeared,[4] replaced by a bankruptcy order and a buyout by satellite TV provider DISH Network for a measly $320 million in 2010.[5]

Meanwhile, Netflix has morphed from its origins as a DVD-by-mail rental service to become the biggest on-demand streaming service provider in the United States. It is also setting its sights on global domination: In September 2014, Netflix added six European countries—including Germany and France—to its ever-growing roster of global sites.[6]

The numbers continue to tell the story. Netflix's current market value stands at $28 billion, just $2 billion shy of the market valuation of CBS Network, the most watched TV network in the US.[7] From its subscription base of 300,000 in 2000,[8] Netflix's American subscribers crossed the 30 million mark in October 2013, exceeding HBO's 28.6 million online subscribers for the first time.[9]

But what happened? Why did the curtains fall on what had seemed to be a rising star? And how did the underdog go from being a fledging business to becoming an industry leader?

BEING TECHNOLOGICALLY MINDED: IT'S NOT JUST ABOUT TECHNOLOGY

In 1985, in Dallas, Texas, David Cook, a database enthusiast, was watching his oil equipment company flounder amidst plunging oil prices. Eager to cut his losses, Cook abandoned the business and started scouting around for new ideas.

By that time, the VCR was fast becoming a mainstay in America's living room, and the VHS was emerging as the standard format for the viewing of videos. Sandy Cook, Cook's ex-wife, disappointed by the limited selection of titles in her neighbourhood store, suggested that Cook open a chain of "superstores" that could capture the booming video rental industry.

On 19 October 1985, the first Blockbuster store opened at the corner of a busy intersection along Northwest Highway.[10]

From the onset, Blockbuster was a success. Lines of excited customers snaked around the store and the cash registers rang nonstop. Soon, investors wanted in. Blockbuster hit all the right notes. Customers wandered in wide-eyed at the large expanse of selection displayed openly; until then, VHS tapes had been traditionally kept in the backroom, brought out only when a customer made a request. Parents embraced with open arms Blockbuster's family-friendly policy of refusing to stock adult films by bringing their entire brood to the store. Teenagers hung out at Blockbuster late at night when other businesses were already closed for the day.

Cook's background in computing came in handy. He developed a computer system that scanned bar codes to access key data from the rental tapes and member cards. This accelerated retail operations as it bypassed the time-consuming process of manually recording differentiated rental charges and late fees. The system also allowed store managers to keep track of the burgeoning inventory; the inventory system would eventually allow Blockbuster to expand at a phenomenal rate of a new store every 17 hours.[11]

Yet for all of Blockbuster's adoption of technology, it was never a technologically disruptive company. At its heart, Blockbuster was a brick and mortar business that adopted existing technology as a means to achieving greater efficiency within the current framework of doing business. It was not interested in advancing technology further, nor did it did seek to revolutionise business models as technology made new strides.

Just two years after Blockbuster opened, it was already on the fast track to expansion. However, as it was with Netflix in 2000, Blockbuster faced a cash flow problem in its embryonic years.

In 1987, Wayne Huizenga, an American businessman with a reputation for consolidating fragmented industries, bought over the company. Huizenga was old-school and ruthless in his tactics: he simply bulldozed his way through the competition by buying them over. One by one, Blockbuster forced its competitors out of the game. By the late eighties, its market share had also expanded proportionately.

Yet this was a business strategy based solely on muscle power, without any attempts at innovation. Revenue was generated through physical expansion—Blockbuster was opening up one new store a day at its height in 2004. It also squeezed customers dry by demanding exorbitant late-return fees: in 2000, late charges contributed nearly $800 million to the company, accounting for a whopping 16% of total revenue.[12]

Importantly, Blockbuster did not use technology to disrupt existing business models: while Cook may have been a front-runner in the development of the inventory system, the technological potential of this invention was never fully realised. Although this system allowed consumer analysis reports to be generated—which would have facilitated better strategic decisions—Blockbuster never took advantage of this technological function until many years later, when it was no longer at the top of its game.[13]

This lack of technological drive was underpinned by an overbearing focus on the present at the expense of the future. There was no larger vision, no overarching purpose that could push the company to greater heights —the singular focus on profit margins ironically compromised Blockbuster's value to customers.

Netflix's beginnings were triggered by a lacklustre customer experience at Blockbuster. In 1997, Reed Hastings rented a copy of *Apollo 13* at his neighbourhood Blockbuster store. He was late in returning the title and was slapped with a $40 fine.

"It was six weeks late and I owed the video store $40. I had misplaced the cassette," Hastings recounts. "It was all my fault. I didn't want to talk to my wife about it. And I said to myself, am I going to compromise the integrity of my marriage over a late fee?" As he headed to the gym to exercise, a thought came to his mind: what if there was a better business model than Blockbuster? What if he provided a flat-rate rental service with unlimited due dates and no late fees?

This marked the beginning of the Netflix journey.[14]

From the start, Netflix adopted a disruptive business model in the way it went about making its business decisions. The choice to rent out the more technologically-advanced DVD was a strategic one: even though DVDs were just appearing on the market at that time, they provided superior viewing quality compared to the older VHS formatting. They were also less bulky, thereby reducing postage costs. Importantly, Netflix completely did away with a physical storefront. It mobilised the power of the Internet by setting up an online rental site where people could reserve their videos and have them delivered to them by post.

At the time, the mechanics of the Internet were still rather rudimentary: compared to today's high-speed wireless connectivity, the only way to access the Internet then was through a dial-up connection via one's phone line. Nonetheless, such a business model retained certain irreducible advantages over the traditional bricks-and-mortar store: Netflix saved on rental and operational costs, enjoyed reduced personnel requirements, and ran into fewer limiting factors when it came to scalability. The few advantages that Blockbuster initially possessed quickly receded into the background.

First, Blockbuster's leverage with its sizeable selection of titles was immediately negated by Netflix's virtual inventory. Whereas Blockbuster's ability to expand its selection was ultimately limited by considerations of space, the infinite expanses of the Internet made this a moot consideration for Netflix. Similarly, the snowball effect created when customers discovered new titles by browsing the open racks at Blockbuster paled in comparison to Netflix's technological alternative. By tracking customers' browsing and rental history through computer algorithms, Netflix could generate personalised recommendations of titles to watch.

Importantly, throughout its lifespan as a company, Netflix has constantly sought to push the envelope on technological innovations in the interest of disrupting the industry and creating new markets that had not existed previously. These efforts were not limited to its in-house research team—Netflix never shied away from jumping onto the technological bandwagon of other tech-savvy firms and adapting these technologies for its own use.

Even as the DVD-rental business took off, Reed Hastings was consistently looking for new ways to disrupt his business. As early as 2000, the same year that Netflix tried to get Blockbuster to purchase a partnership stake in it, the Netflix team was already busy trying to figure out a way to deliver movies directly to the home via the Internet.

The idea wasn't new. In September 1995, ESPN SportsZone streamed the first live radio broadcast of a baseball game between the Seattle Mariners and the New York Yankees to an audience comprising thousands of listeners spread across the globe.[15] Media streaming was hovering on the edge of a breakthrough, although it would be years before the battle between technology companies such as Microsoft and RealNetworks yielded any kind of credible results. In an era where bandwidth was both expensive and miserable, the best the Netflix team could muster in 2000 was an unimpressive delivery time of 16 hours for a *single* movie.[16]

Hastings knew, however, that Netflix had to be one step ahead of the technological curve if it wanted to survive. He persisted with efforts to deliver movies via the Internet and poured even more resources into these endeavours.[17] In late 2003, these efforts culminated in the development of a hardware that would download movies according to your movie queue. An average movie, however, would still need six hours for it to completely load. It didn't look as if this was going to be sufficient enough to disrupt the market. Hastings himself was not entirely keen on relying on hardware either; his ultimate aim was to develop software that customers could use without the hassle and fuss of purchase and installation.

14 February 2005 heralded the dawn of a new era in online media —it marked the founding of YouTube, a video-sharing website that allowed viewers to "click and play". Hastings knew right away that this was the disruptor he was looking for. Netflix got to work on incorporating this new technology into its online services, and by 2007 officially rolled out its on-demand streaming services. The future of television was forever changed.

For all of its emphasis on computer engineering and software development, Netflix is inherently a video streaming company. It is not a technology company, nor is it a software developer. Yet in an increasingly open economy where change is being driven by technology, Netflix has grown its market share by being technologically minded. Whereas Block-buster simply adopted ready-made technology as a means of increasing its share of a diminishing market pie, Netflix continuously pushed the boundaries of technological change in order to disrupt the market and expand the size of the entire pie.

Being technological has allowed Netflix to be an industry mover and shaker. It is not simply about being ahead of the curve: it is about creating the next wave.

ACTIVELY CREATING THE NEXT WAVE

In February 2013, John Farrell, Director of YouTube Latin America, made this bold statement: "Online video will reach 75% of consumers by 2020. Within seven years, it could overtake broadcast TV and even pay TV."[18] Clearly, the future of home entertainment is changing.

Before online streaming became part of our everyday vocabulary, however, Blockbuster completely missed the ball in anticipating just how ubiquitous the Internet would become. In fact, it never quite understood the value of the Internet. Instead, it insisted on a growth strategy that was woefully outdated: even as property and manpower costs continued to climb, Blockbuster persisted in channelling its funds into securing its physical presence. By the time it tried to salvage the situation by pumping in hundreds of millions of dollars in a new online service to rival Netflix —eight whole years after Netflix had established the service—Blockbuster was already antiquated.

Netflix, on the other hand, has consistently sought to stay ahead of the game. It has invested much time and effort in keeping abreast of developments within the technological spectrum: by being a pioneer in the early adoption of online streaming and cloud computing, and subsequently working on developing the incipient infrastructure, Netflix has effectively become a leader within the industry.

Importantly, Netflix has also paid much attention to the way technology intersects with entertainment, focusing on how these interactions have changed the face of consumer behaviour. Such observations are not simply passive; as the Internet revolutionises the way the world works, Netflix has embarked on a mission to actively shape viewers' behaviour. In this way, it doesn't have to worry about staying ahead of the curve. It now creates the curve.

From the very beginning, Netflix operated on a subscription model where customers paid a flat fee to watch an unlimited number of shows. Its introduction of on-demand services changed the way people thought about television: In the past, viewers had to be content with waiting each week for a new episode to come out on broadcast TV. With on-demand streaming however, entire seasons of older series became available for viewing, allowing marathon-viewing of multiple episodes, or what has become more popularly known as binge-watching.[19] As viewers got accustomed to consuming an entire season in a single sitting, the rules and expectations surrounding television production also changed.

In 2013, Netflix released its first original production, a remake of the television series *House of Cards*. Unlike traditional TV series, Netflix made the unconventional decision of premiering an entire season of the show on its site. Producer of the show Beau Willimon joked that "[the] goal [was] to shut down a portion of America for a day" as audiences binge-watched the show.[20]

With the expectation that viewers would be consuming the series in huge gulps, the creative team at *House of Cards* did away with several traditional features of network TV, including the use of flashbacks that served as a device to remind viewers of the previous week's episode. Writers could weave in greater plot twists as well, since an event that happened four episodes ago, was also more likely to have been watched by the viewer four hours ago.[21]

Netflix could make such a radical break from traditional programming because it had the data to back it up. By analysing users' habits on the site, Netflix was able to come to the conclusion that a political drama starring Kevin Spacey would appeal to its millions of subscribers. While Netflix has refused to release viewership numbers, a pilot survey conducted among 3,000 USA video on-demand subscribers places it as the top-ranking online streaming show in the US, underscoring the popularity of the show.[22]

Beyond television, Netflix has also set its sights on the movie industry. In 2014, Netflix made waves when it announced that it was going to bring new movie releases to its streaming platform. Users can expect to catch the sequel to Ang Lee's 2000 blockbuster hit, *Crouching Tiger, Hidden Dragon*, on Netflix in 2015, even as the movie simultaneously debuts in IMAX theatres. Netflix has revealed as well that it will be financing the production of four Adam Sandler movies to be rolled out over the next few years on its online platform.[23] As home entertainment systems continue to evolve, it is evident that Netflix is trying to shape and disrupt the way viewers are consuming movies.

It is important to anticipate changing trends when making decisions in the present—Blockbuster did not: perhaps it was a fear of the future or complacency that drove it to denial and paralysis. This culminated in its redundancy and subsequently, failure.

In this fast-moving world, staying ahead of the curve is no longer enough. A company might possibly hope to survive in the increasingly competitive economy by staying one step in front of its rival. However, if it wants to be sustainable, it is not enough to be ahead of the curve, one has to invent the curve.

Reed Hastings says it best himself: "I've always thought trying to change consumer behavior is scary, and most companies that promote that fail. But when it works, like iPod, it works big."[24]

Netflix has been able to enjoy growth over the last decade because it set its goal higher: be ahead of the curve, but better yet, invent the curve.

LEADERSHIP MATTERS

While technology and innovation contributed to Netflix's success, they are insufficient. Ultimately, without leadership that is bold and focused on a clear vision, these factors count for nothing.

In Blockbuster's case, the video-rental chain lacked a strong leader. Its leadership read like a revolving slate of managers whose visions were often muddled, short-sighted and incoherent. Wayne Huizenga, Blockbuster's first CEO after David Cook left the company, pursued a strategy of aggressive buyouts and expansion. In 1994, after Huizenga left the firm, Steven Berrard took over his position. Under his leadership, Blockbuster stepped up its rate of expansion. But Berrard was only at his seat for a year and a half, and by 1996, amidst fledging sales, yet another CEO, Bill Fields came on board. In his short one-year tenure, Fields attempted to diversify Blockbuster's business by bringing in other merchandises to the store. All of a sudden, Blockbuster was not only renting out videos, it was also selling T-shirts, toys, snacks, books, magazines and CDs. By the time John Antioco took over the role in 1997, Blockbuster was in over its head.[25]

Antioco immediately set about trying to streamline operations. He moved the business back to its original core—video rentals—while reviving its old tag line, "Make it a Blockbuster Night". He scaled back on Blockbuster's expansion plans, and also moved to cut personnel by a third. However, Antioco missed Blockbuster's golden opportunity when he slammed the door shut in Netflix's face in 2000. He quickly realised his mistake and moved to implement Blockbuster's online operations.[26] But by that time, it was too late.

Infighting led to Antioco's removal at the helm in 2007. James Keyes, the previous president and CEO of 7-Eleven, was installed as CEO.[27] Keyes halted Blockbuster's unprofitable online service and tried to buy over rival Circuit City. But he could not steer the large ship that was Blockbuster away from the impending iceberg it was heading towards. In 2010, Blockbuster was finally declared bankrupt.

On the other hand, Netflix's founder and CEO Reed Hastings had a clear vision about the direction that he wanted his company to head towards from the very beginning. This conviction provided him with the ability and sharpness to sift through what was less important and to focus instead on what was truly crucial. This in turn gave him the boldness to make decisions that were difficult and genuinely painful.

Even as Netflix begun as a DVD-rental service in 1997, Hastings already knew that he wanted to build an Internet-based company that would provide streaming services. When asked about Netflix's move into the streaming business in 2009, Hastings replied, "Eventually in the very long term, it's unlikely that we'll be on plastic media. So, we've always known that. That's why we named the company Netflix and not DVDs by Mail."[28]

This clarity in vision and farsightedness has led to Hastings making some incredibly bold and radical business decisions.

In 2000, engineers at Netflix were racing against the clock to develop a technology that would allow movies to be streamed online. In 2003, they came up with a hardware that could stream movies onto the computer, but at a price—$300 and a lengthy wait of six hours. It wasn't what Hastings wanted.

When YouTube made its premiere in 2005, Hastings did not hesitate. Despite all the hours, effort and manpower that went into making the device, Hastings pulled the plug. The device was quickly dropped and the engineering team shifted its focus to developing its online streaming services. Two years later in 2007, Netflix's had its on-demand streaming service up-and-running.

As Netflix transited to becoming a fully-fledged, on-demand streaming company, its R&D team continued to work on innovating technology. The same year that on-demand streaming was introduced, the team at Netflix was making the final preparations to release a Netflix-branded device that could stream movies and TV shows on television by connecting it to the Internet.

A few weeks before the device was due to be publicly released, Hastings aborted the project. Jaws dropped. Anthony Wood, then-VP of Internet TV at Netflix remembers: "We built our own streaming player and hardware, which was a bold step for an Internet company. And the whole time, we had been showing demos at company meetings. Everyone was really excited. Everyone really wanted to ship the Netflix player."[29]

Hastings, however, had realised that a Netflix hardware would place it in direct competition with hardware providers such as Apple and Sony. This would threaten potential partnerships with existing market leaders. According to a high-level insider, "Reed said to me one day, 'I want to be able to call Steve Jobs and talk to him about putting Netflix on Apple TV. But if I am making my own hardware, Steve's not going to take my call.'"[30] If this happened, Netflix would not be able to promote its streaming services as effectively across different device providers. In the end, Hastings decided that Netflix's identity was first and foremost a video streaming software company.

The Netflix team responsible for the development of its earlier streaming hardware was quickly re-constituted as a separate company known as Roku. This kept the hardware development component distinct from the core business of the firm.[31] Today, Roku is a leading device maker for digital media. Not only has it produced hardware for Netflix, it also counts other leading digital media providers, such as Amazon and Hulu, among its clients. Netflix, meanwhile, avoided the potentially devastating conflict of having both a hardware and software arm.

This was not the only time that Hastings stepped up to make a difficult decision. After Netflix introduced streaming, it was faced with the task of persuading its subscribers to switch to streaming from DVD rentals. Unwilling to go down the same path as AOL, which was unable to retain its dial-up customers when it switched to offering broadband services, Hastings knew that he had to find a way to capture his 10 million subscribers before another company beat him to it. Together with a small team, Hastings decided they would give streaming away.[32] For no additional cost to the existing subscribers, Netflix would offer them unlimited streaming.

The set-up was thorough: Netflix approached networks for older TV shows and films that were cheaper to acquire. Employing Netflix's personalised recommendation engine, they directed customers to these older shows based on their preferences. This way, Netflix was able to keep the initial costs of streaming low to prevent the free streaming services from becoming a fiscal burden.[33] The strategy worked, and today, Netflix has more than tripled its subscriber numbers from the 10 million it had in 2007.

Of course, Hastings hasn't always been right. The 2011 disastrous separation of Netflix into its on-demand streaming and DVD rental components was a mistake that Hastings has readily admitted to. In addition, Hastings also tripped up on the sudden introduction of an increase in subscription price. This became a huge public relations failure that led to the loss of 600,000 subscribers and a drop of 50% in stock prices.[34] Since then Netflix has bounced back, and importantly, learned from its mistakes.

Netflix and Blockbuster started out in the same industry. Both showed keen signs of becoming the next big thing. At their core, however, they couldn't be any more different. Blockbuster took an existing business model and scaled up. For a while it prospered under the illusion of expanding storefronts, but unable to sustain this inefficient way of doing business, it was forced to pull down its shutters.

Netflix, meanwhile, started out by disrupting the business model Blockbuster had championed. Had it simply assumed that business would continue as usual, it could easily have gone down the same path as Blockbuster. However, the leadership had the foresight to imagine a larger vision for the future, driven by a strong sense of identity and value.

OVERVIEW OF THE SECTION

In a complex and uncertain world, it is no longer enough to merely survive. There is a need to get better at making strategic decisions—decisions that will place you in an advantageous position for sustained success. You want to emulate Netflix's strengths while learning from Blockbuster's mistakes.

This book is designed to introduce you to a decision-making framework that was developed at FMG. We call this methodology **F**oresight-driven, **U**nderstanding, **S**trategy and **E**xecution, or FUSE.

There are four core principles to this approach:

First, people matter.

While technology has the potential to bring about huge advances in the development of society, it takes its cue from the social, cultural and political intelligence of human beings. Technology by itself is merely a tool; it only gains purpose when people inject meaning into it.

Human intelligence is not the only requisite component, however. Leadership is key to navigating this world. We need leaders who have imagination and vision, who dare to go beyond the thinkable, who commit resources in a distinct and coherent direction.

Second, ideas matter.

How we think about the world shapes the way we react to events happening around us. Ideas are thus powerful. They have the ability to frame facts in a way that influences your actions.

Third, data matters, but not as much as we may think.

Even as we rely on ever-increasing amounts of knowledge to inform our decisions, the uncertain nature of our world means that we can never assume perfect knowledge of anything. How many times have we extrapolated present trends into the future, only to be proven otherwise?

While you should always be in the habit of substantiating your claims and assertions with cold, hard data, you need to recognise that nothing is set in stone. Facts change, and you need to retain the flexibility to change your mind accordingly.

Furthermore, we often lack the relevant data to make an informed decision. This is where imagination and ideas fill that knowledge gap. An over-reliance on data can result in an unhealthy 'crutch' mentality, where we cling on to what we know at the expense of embracing that which is unknown but may well produce positive and concrete differences in performance —what we in FMG refer to as a "delta".

Finally, action determines outcomes.

Foresight is not passive. It is meant to effect positive change in the future by taking action in the present. That is also why the FUSE framework does not end at strategy formulation. Execution of the strategy is necessary to bring about the desired outcomes.

In this book, I will bring you through four key processes driven by these core principles—Foresight, Understanding, Strategy and Execution. Each subsequent section is devoted to one specific process, and is intended to introduce you to the philosophies underpinning the FUSE methodology. I will also break these processes down into smaller steps to facilitate effective action.

The next chapter in this section will provide a broader context for this conversation.

The intellectual premises for FUSE did not emerge in a vacuum; it drew on two competing approaches of strategic planning in history—Operations Research and Scenario Planning. While Operations Research employs a highly planned process of scientific methods and principles to derive solutions, Scenario Planning is a narrative-driven approach that embraces uncertainty to produce insightful perspectives of the future. Decisions are made by using these scenarios as a backdrop.

FUSE integrates the key ideas driving both processes, along with other crucial components, to provide a systematic way of undertaking foresight, strategy formulation and operational execution. By situating FUSE within the broader context of existing approaches, you will be able to better appreciate the delta that FUSE contributes to the decision-making process.

The final chapter of this section provides an overview of the entire FUSE process. I draw on a famous example of a battle that happened in the straits of Salamis, an island off mainland Greece, to illustrate how FUSE works. I will break FUSE down into its components and briefly explain how they fit together.

CHAPTER 2

APPROACHES TO STRATEGIC PLANNING

OPERATIONS RESEARCH AND SCENARIO PLANNING

The desire to make better decisions in order to manage uncertainty and complexity is not new. As society progresses and technology advances, human beings have also come up with numerous analytical tools and devices to better deal with the complexities of our environment.

Two prominent approaches to strategic planning that have emerged over the last 50 years include Operations Research (OR) and Scenario Planning. While they have each acquired a significant following within the military and business worlds, their underlying philosophies lie in opposing directions.

Operations Research is highly steeped in quantitative data; it relies on scientific and mathematical methods to arrive at solutions that maximise the efficiency of existing operations. The goal is to pursue managerial excellence with precision and effectiveness.

Scenario Planning, on the other hand, is less concerned with number-crunching than it is with developing coherent and internally consistent narratives of plausible futures. Unlike Operations Research, it actively sets its sights on the future: Scenario Planning aims to better guide decision-making in the present to positively influence the future.

At FMG, we believe in the value of both processes. Neither approach is sufficient on its own, especially in an environment that is fast-paced and fraught with uncertainty. We need to actively anticipate the future so that we will not be caught unprepared when external conditions change—but we also need to possess the managerial competence to execute strategies effectively.

FUSE offers an integrated approach that incorporates both foresight and management into a seamless end-to-end decision-making process. In addition to looking at foresight and execution, FUSE also emphasises introspection and strategy formulation. These individual processes become part of a sequential chain, where the outputs from one process become the inputs for subsequent steps.

In short, FUSE is a systematic and rigorous methodology aimed at creating "delta".

To better appreciate and understand the value of FUSE, it is useful to first recognise how strategic planning has been traditionally considered. The next two sections in this chapter will look at the competing approaches of Operations Research and Scenario Planning in greater detail, with particular interest in their origins and intellectual roots.

The third section, meanwhile, brings FUSE back into the picture. I will show how FUSE drew inspiration from these conventional approaches. Importantly, I will demonstrate how FUSE adds value to the existing toolkit of decision-making methodologies.

OPERATIONS RESEARCH (OR)
History of OR

OR has its roots in World War II, as advances in technology dramatically changed the face of warfare. The scale and magnitude of warfare was recalibrated upwards: war was no longer confined to overland hostilities —the introduction of the fighter plane and battleship extended the battleground to the infinite reaches of the sky and ocean, while improvements in telecommunications enabled military communications across vast distances.

Such technological developments represented a fundamental shift in the way war was conceived: with technology advancing in huge strides, the limiting factor shifted from technology to strategic and tactical advantages.

The recognition that the defining delta would come not just from technological superiority alone, but from better tactical and strategic planning, eventually laid the groundwork for the development of OR during World War II.

Radar and the Development of OR

More than any other single event, the invention of radar in Britain contributed to the development of the discipline that would come to be known as OR.

The use of radar was not exclusive to the British military; by the time World War II broke out, other nations had independently discovered the technological features of radar. What distinguished Britain in its use of radar, however, was not just the technology involved but the way in which radar became integrated into a larger *system*.

The use of radar in tandem with OR gave the British military the leverage it needed to secure a narrow victory in the Battle of Britain. In the wider scheme of things, the confluence of the two contributed to the Allied victory over the Axis powers. In fact, at the end of the war, Sir Stafford Cripps, Minister of Aircraft Production, wrote: "I do not hesitate to say that without [the Operations Research team] we should certainly not be celebrating the victory in Europe—yet—and probably never."[1]

As early as the 1920s, the British military had already recognised the need to bolster its air defences by developing an early warning system that could detect incoming aircraft. This system was unveiled at a demonstration in 1934 —an acoustic system that depended on concrete "mirrors". Nothing could have made for more conspicuous targets off the southern coast of England.

A.P. Rowe, a young physicist trained in air navigation and meteorology, was a member of the audience at the 1934 demonstrations. At the time, Rowe was attached to H.E. Wimperis, the Director of Scientific Research at the British Air Ministry. After listening to the demonstration, Rowe concluded that the acoustic system was ultimately doomed to failure. Convinced of the urgency of the problem, he wrote a memorandum to his boss, arguing that the most pressing problem facing the British military was the lack of an effective early-warning system, and proposed that an alternative approach be taken.

Wimperis agreed and put together a high level independent Committee for the Scientific Study of Air Defence. H.T. Tizard, a Nobel-prize winner with experience in both scientific and military operations, was tasked to lead it. Other members of the committee would include distinguished members of the scientific community, such as P.M.S. Blackett—who would also go on to win a Nobel Prize in physics after the war—as well as Rowe himself.

In 1935, Tizard met with Robert Watson-Watts, Superintendent of the National Physical Laboratory's Radio Research Station, to discuss the possibility of employing electromagnetic power to affect the performance of an aircraft. In response, Watson-Watts suggested a detection device that employed radio waves. Tizard took a gamble and started channelling research efforts into the development of this new detection device. On 26 February 1935, the first rudimentary workings of the radar system debuted.

While radar was independently introduced in the US and Germany in the years leading up to World War II, no efforts were made to develop operational tactics that could augment the use of this new technology. In Britain, however, there was an acute awareness that the effectiveness of radar hinged on a rethink of matters such as fighter control and interception tactics. Far from studying the uses of radar in silos, the entire air defence system, with its adoption of this new technology, had to be rethought.

Having successfully engineered a breakthrough in radar technology, the Tizard Committee, as it became known, turned its attention to achieving operational efficiencies in the use of radar in military operations. As prewar air defence exercises were carried out between 1937 and 1938, it became apparent that the technology was insufficient on its own to be wielded as an effective device. New military tactics, such as the remote-controlled air interception, needed to be developed.

In addition, the initial limitations of the incipient radar system demanded a careful reading of the signals emitted. These signals had to be integrated into a coherent plot that could be read and understood by defence pilots. As a result, the radar development team had to figure out a system of computing vectors that would allow the fighter planes to effectively locate and intercept their unseen targets.

Adding to this deluge of operational requirements was the need to figure out how to better coordinate and correlate the influx of data that was pouring in from the different radar systems.

Harold Larnder, a communications engineer on the team of scientists and engineers tasked with the use of radar, explained: "Although the [prewar defence exercises] had again demonstrated the technical feasibility of the radar system for detecting aircrafts, its operational achievements fell far short of requirements. [A.P. Rowe, head of the research group involved,] therefore proposed that research into the operational—as opposed to the technical—aspects of the system should begin immediately."[2]

As head of the radar unit, Rowe would send the first official OR team into the operations rooms of Fighter Groups to investigate how officers dealt with information coming out of the radar systems. Research was carried out on the techniques for daytime and night operations, and appropriate recommendations made.[3]

These recommendations were implemented during the final prewar defence exercise. The improvements were so obvious that the OR team was transferred to the Royal Air Force's headquarters. Subsequently, other OR divisions were set up in the different military services.

After the war, Sir Charles Goodever, then-Assistant Controller for Research and Development in the Admiralty, estimated that the rate of success for fighter interception improved by a factor of 10 after the introduction of radar. With the employment of OR, the rate of improvement was further doubled. Taken together, these improvements effectively boosted the British Fighter Command's power by a factor of 20.[4] As Air Officer Commanding RAF Fighter Command Hugh Dowding commented at the outbreak of World War II, "The war will be won by science thoughtfully applied to operational needs."[5]

OR and the US

Just as the invention of radar became synonymous with the development of OR in Britain, the development of OR in the US was to become closely associated with its efforts in anti-submarine warfare. At the heart of these developments was a young American physicist by the name of Philip Morse.

While Morse was initially part of the effort to develop wartime equipment, he became curious as to how scientists could better contribute to the war effort by shifting their expertise from a purely technical standpoint to thinking about the operational aspects of war. That meant moving away from an exclusive focus on the design of weapons to studying how these weapons could be used more effectively.

Specifically, Morse was concerned about the proper exploitation of the relationship between technological and military requirements. He asked himself, "Wasn't there a place for one trained to find a pattern in a heap of data, an opportunity, for example, to work out the optimal tactics for new weapons?"[6]

Morse's opportunity did not come until 1942, when the German submarines, or what were more popularly known as U-boats, started attacking the east coast of the US. In March that year, a new unit—the Anti-submarine Warfare (ASW) Unit—was set up to counter this growing threat. It was led by Captain Wilder Baker, a highly-decorated naval officer who would go on to become a Vice-Admiral.

The close relationship between the US and Britain meant that Captain Baker had plenty of opportunities to become well acquainted with his

British counterparts. On one such occasion, Captain Baker met P.M.S. Blackett. The latter shared with Baker how the experience with civil scientists in the military had improved operational decisions and Britain's overall effectiveness in battle.

Baker eventually spent some time in Britain, where he studied how scientists were able to help the British navy by discerning enemy tactics and evaluating the adequacy of British defences. The effectiveness of the approach impressed him. Convinced by the utility of OR, Baker returned to the US with the intention of mobilising scientific personnel in the war effort.

Unsurprisingly, the traditionally tight-lipped military administration baulked at the thought of allowing civilians access to the top-secret world of military operations. But Baker was convinced that traditional policies were no longer adequate for dealing with the complexity of anti-submarine warfare. Putting his career on the line, Baker set about persuading the old-liners within the navy. He succeeded, and Morse got the job of heading this new committee of civilian scientists.

The initial team drew some of the nation's top brains, including mathematicians and physical scientists from schools such as Harvard, MIT, Cal Tech, Princeton and Berkeley. Alienated from the highly hierarchical and Machiavellian nature of the military, the academics quickly formed a tight-knit community, bonded together by their common language of science. As the war effort accelerated, the group quickly got to work.

Their first project was to figure out how to detect enemy submarines more effectively. A surfaced submarine could be detected from the air, but one that was submerged could only be found by underwater sonar, which at the time remained a relatively uncommon device.

Bearing in mind that the German U-boats tended to stay on the surface, except when attacking underwater, the OR team looked at the way aircraft search efforts were being conducted to find enemy vessels. They asked themselves: from how far away could a surfaced submarine be seen? Were they always seen? What percentage of the time were they missed?

By finding the answers to such questions, the team could calculate how many square miles of ocean a plane could cover in an hour. This, by extension, allowed them to calculate how many planes would be needed to cover a fixed part of the ocean with a given rate of success.

At the same time, using the data collected, the team of scientists could devise the most efficient search pattern that would allow planes to locate submarines in the shortest time possible. This same process could be mapped onto the underwater operations using sonar-equipped destroyers.

Morse's team's adoption of quantitative analysis to improve the operationalisation of anti-submarine warfare yielded quick results. The number of submarine sightings per week dramatically increased. Having improved the rate at which enemy submarines were sighted, the team swiftly returned to the drawing board to focus on the real goal—the destruction of the German U-boats.

At the time, planes could only use a depth charge to destroy submarines. A depth charge was an anti-submarine weapon that destroyed its submarine target by generating a powerful hydraulic shock. The airplane would drop this depth charge close to the target, where it would sink slowly before exploding at a predetermined depth.

Making use of the data collected from the operations rooms, operational analysts observed that the depth charges were being dropped at a depth that was too deep to sufficiently maim the German U-boats, which remained on the surface most of the time. By inputting the necessary quantities, the team was able to compute the optimal depth at which the depth charges should be programmed to explode at. In the short span of two months, the number of successful hits rose by five times.

This cemented the validity of OR in the war effort, and very soon, the OR team found itself overseeing the entire record-keeping process for the anti-submarine war effort. As testament to the military's newfound respect for mathematical modelling and scientific techniques, an IBM data processing system was purchased and installed, thereby speeding up the time taken to compute and analyse the massive amount of data that was coming in each day.

As the war continued, both the US and Britain continued to utilise OR in their strategic planning of warfare techniques to great success. By the time the war drew to an end, operations managers outside of the military realm had begun to take an interest in OR.

OR today

When the war ended, many who had worked in wartime OR moved into industry. They brought along with them their expertise and conviction that OR was the way to go. One of the first industrial groups to embrace OR was the National Coal Board in Britain, followed by the nationalised electricity and transport industries. Soon, the private sector started experimenting with OR. By the 1950s, OR had permeated much of industrial thinking in Britain.[7]

The same thing happened in the US. More and more industry executives began taking note of the utility of OR as a decision-making tool for operational processes, including areas such as equipment procurement and logistics management.

Questions that OR sought to answer in a corporate setting included: how can scarce resources be optimally allocated under tight constraints? What is the most efficient solution among competing options? How can inventories be best maintained in light of fluctuating inputs and outputs? How would complex economic and physical systems behave when subject to varying parameters and conditions?

As OR continued to develop and evolve as a discipline, its practitioners lauded its scientific nature of using quantitative methodology to solve problems. The unrelenting advances in technology also meant that more and more sophisticated mathematical modelling programmes could be developed. This simultaneously shortened the time taken to generate solutions, while increasing the numbers of variables that could be computed.

Today, OR remains widely used within the corporate world. Large businesses such as IBM continue to design initiatives based on OR to improve the efficiency and productivity of its operations.

The next section looks at another approach to decision-making that stands in stark contrast to the highly planned and quantitative nature of OR.

SCENARIO PLANNING

Whereas OR is concerned primarily with the improvement of operational processes in the here and now, Scenario Planning takes the future as its starting point. This is called "Foresight". In particular, Scenario Planning is interested in applied foresight, where scenarios of the future help to shape decisions in the present.

The beginnings of Scenario Planning owe the most to two remarkable individuals: Herman Kahn, an American military strategist, and Pierre Wack, a Frenchman most notable for his work at Royal Dutch Shell.

Herman Kahn and Thermonuclear War

People who knew Kahn described him as being loud, gregarious and boisterous. However, underneath his cheery nature concealed a depth of intelligence and imagination that was rarely seen except in the most brilliant of individuals.[8]

Kahn was born in New Jersey in 1922. He moved to Los Angeles when his parents divorced. There, he attended college at UCLA, majoring in Physics, before embarking on a PhD programme at CalTech that he never completed due to financial issues. At the age of 25, he started work as a physicist and mathematician at RAND (Research ANd Development), the R&D arm of the US Air Force. During his time there, Kahn was involved in the development of nuclear weapons, including the hydrogen bomb.

The period was the 1950s, and it was at the height of the Cold War. The Eisenhower administration had adopted a doctrine of massive retaliation against the Soviet Union: should the US be provoked, they would not hesitate to use the hydrogen bomb against their enemies. While this was meant to serve as a deterrence, many analysts believed it to be ultimately destabilising.

Kahn was intrigued by this problem. He went beyond the conventional fear that a nuclear war would spark off the annihilation of mankind. He imagined several future scenarios in which nuclear war had broken out between the US and the Soviet Union. In doing so, he surmised that nuclear exchange was not only possible, but it did not necessarily mean the end of civilisation. The question was, to what extent were the American people willing to accept the consequences?

If the doctrine of massive retaliation was to be effective in deterring the Soviet Union, then the US had to put on a credible show of demonstrating its seriousness about nuclear retaliation. Using these scenarios as a testing ground, Kahn proposed strengthening the nation's civil defence to drive home the point to the Soviets.

Kahn was not an advocate of nuclear war. But by daring to "think the unthinkable", he was able to highlight the faulty assumptions inherent in Eisenhower's "massive retaliation" policy. By correcting for these, Kahn could better steer the policy towards a positive outcome, thereby reducing the probability of a nuclear war happening.[9] In the words of Kahn himself, "We draw scenarios and try to cope with history before it happens."[10]

Kahn went on to start a think tank called the Hudson Institute. The institute was focused on futures thinking, and combined the expertise of individuals who came from various disciplinary backgrounds. While he made numerous important contributions to the field of foresight thinking, it was his use of scenarios that changed the way people contemplated the future. Kahn influenced a whole generation of foresight practitioners. One of them, a Frenchman by the name of Pierre Wack, was to further enhance and refine the methodology of Scenario Planning within the business sphere.

Royal Dutch Shell and Pierre Wack

In the 1960s, many large companies, particularly in the oil and gas industry, engaged in forecasting methods, using linear modelling to guide their day-to-day decisions. This was no different at Royal Dutch Shell, where they employed a computer system they called the Unified Planning Machinery, or UPM for short. Using UPM, managers would input the current year's sales and budget in order to produce an estimate of the revenue and expenditure expected the following year. Senior management would then make planning decisions on the basis of these projections.

In other words, it was a business-as-usual, or BAU scenario.

In a high-risk and high-capital industry, this was possibly the worst thing a company could do. Given the high profits that oil companies were raking in, it almost appeared as if the UPM was specially designed to tell oil managers what they wanted to hear.[11] Ted Newman, who headed the planning department at the time, had his doubts about the method. He had previously attended a few of Kahn's lectures in New York and thought that there might be some value to the latter's use of scenarios and narratives.

Newman recruited Pierre Wack, who had been working as the director of economics for Shell France at the time, into his team. Like Newman, Wack was familiar with Herman Kahn's work on scenarios, and thought the UPM system ineffectual and pointless: there was no way of ensuring that the current trajectory would continue, as there were simply too many uncertainties and instabilities for forecasters to get it right. Wack could not understand why the company was investing in such a method.

In the early 1970s, such wisdom acquired increasing saliency as the geopolitical situation in the Middle East started to shift. In a period of ever-increasing oil demand, the first cracks hinting at an impending oil crisis emerged. Yet the UPM system was failing to pick up any of these signs. Wack decided to adopt a different tack. Instead of shunning uncertainty, he argued that a more profitable method would be to embrace, understand, and incorporate uncertainty in thinking about the future.[12]

Wack and his team identified and analysed the primary drivers influencing change in the oil industry. In doing so, they were able to unearth the relationships and interactions between different variables. This eventually led them to locate pre-determinants—factors that were inevitable—and uncertainties that would shape the future.

Using these predetermined elements and uncertainties as building blocks, Wack and his team generated plausible scenarios about the future. These sounded warning bells about a looming energy crisis. He presented these scenarios to the management team. The use of narratives appealed to the cognitive faculties of the senior management in a way that numbers could not, and effectively challenged previous assumptions about the future. Convinced by the coherency and plausibility of the scenarios that Wack was presenting, the senior management revised the overall planning direction for the company.

When the oil crisis occurred in 1973, Royal Dutch Shell was the only Western oil company that was prepared. They were able to weather the storm because its management had the foresight to execute salient decisions. From being the "ugly sister" of the seven sisters—the term given to the top global oil companies at the time—Royal Dutch Shell emerged from the oil crisis stronger and better. Applied foresight played its part.

Scenario Planning today

Today, Scenario Planning continues to be widely used in the military and corporate world as well as by governments.

One of the more prominent Scenario Planning exercises completed over the last two decades was the 1994 Mont Fleur scenario project conducted in South Africa, right after the abolishment of apartheid. The next section on Foresight will illustrate how these scenarios had a transformative effect on the mind-sets of the participants: assumptions were identified and addressed, and possibilities about the future considered.

Importantly, in a country that experienced deep-reaching divisions in its immediate past, these scenarios had the vital function of pushing a diverse group of stakeholders towards the realisation that certain action-steps had to be taken in order to attain their desired vision of the future.

It is not only countries that have benefitted from the use of scenarios in their strategic planning exercises. Businesses have also adopted Scenario Planning as a way of making better decisions for the future. The New

York Board of Trade (NYBOT) was an example of an entity that engaged regularly in Scenario Planning exercises throughout the 1990s. During one such exercise, it identified the possibility of a disaster that could affect its main trading floor in the World Trade Center. In order to pre-empt this possibility, NYBOT invested in secondary trading floors in the Queens section of New York City to be used as a substitute office. Although the secondary trading floors sat empty for years, costing the company $300,000 annually in maintenance fees, it saved the Board millions of dollars in recovery fees when the 9/11 attacks happened.[13]

Through the use of narratives, Scenario Planning challenges conventional thinking about the future in order to better anticipate the changes that will occur.

FUTURE PLANNING

Operations Research and Scenario Planning stand in opposition to each other. Where OR is about crunching numbers, Scenario Planning is about constructing stories. While the former tries to pin down certainty, the latter embraces uncertainty. OR is concerned about optimising current operational processes, but Scenario Planning is more interested in shaping the future. OR emphasises planning right down to the minute detail; Scenario Planning, on the other hand, promotes flexibility and adaptability.

Yet neither one of these approaches is sufficient in and of itself when it comes to attaining sustainable results with a clear delta.

The increasing privileging of data

In our world today, this dichotomy between the two approaches has acquired particular salience as the advent of technology continues to accelerate; in fact, OR's highly quantitative and planned approach is pulling ahead to reign supreme.

There are two reasons why this is happening. At an operational level, the ever-increasing processing power of computers has made collecting huge amounts of quantifiable data cheaper, faster and easier than ever before. In the emergent era of big data, it has never been more convenient for managers to generate numerical outputs and representations to justify decisions.

We now generate more data in two days than we did from the beginning of civilisation up till 2003.[14] To cope with this incredible spin rate, the global market for big-data related software, hardware and professional services is booming: sales are projected to hit $30 billion in 2014,[15] and the entire industry is growing at a rate six times faster than the rest of the Information Technology (IT) industry.

Increasingly, the decision-making framework in fields as diverse as advertising, media, financial services and public health is being informed and advised by a set of quantitative data that is seen as precise, accurate and scientific. Its uses range from processes such as enhancing customer experience, innovating new business models, increasing operational efficiency, promoting precise marketing and aiding real-time analysis and decision-making.[16]

Take advertising, for example. Whereas the advertising executive of the past may have relied on instinct, creativity and a fundamental understanding of the human psyche, the advertising executive of today is more likely to make decisions based on computer algorithms that churn out consolidated reports of customers' activities. An ad is pulled off air if no significant statistical correlation is shown between its promotion and the product's sales numbers. A rebranding campaign may be rolled out based on quantitative data highlighting customers' preferences.

Gary King, director of Harvard's Institute for Quantitative Social Science remarks, "It's a revolution. [...] The march of quantification, made possible by enormous new sources of data, will sweep through academia, business and government. There is no area that is going to be untouched."[17]

There is also a second reason why the quantitative approach has gained so much traction over the last few years. The technological advances of our modern world have secured the triumph of scientific empiricism and mathematical logic as the ultimate governing paradigm for human society.

This has led to the rise of positivism, a philosophical ideology that argues that all knowledge can only be authenticated by empirical experiences verifiable through logical and mathematic treatment.

According to this perspective, the world exists under a set of fixed rules and relationships that are discoverable by science. Quantitative methodology then, with its easily traceable legacy to scientific principles and rationality, wears the cloak of authenticity and legitimacy.

Why data is necessary but insufficient

There are certainly benefits to adopting a quantitative and scientific methodology to decision-making. This helps to make the process more robust and provides greater empirical grounding in support of your choices.

However, an overreliance on data and quantification is dangerous. In mathematical modelling, reality is stimulated by reducing phenomena to key variables whose relationship with one another can be accurately mapped out and explained.

While this sounds simple, reality is rarely that straightforward. We live in a world that is complex. It is often difficult to entangle causal factors, much less pinpoint the exact nature of relationships between variables. Sometimes, it is not even possible to isolate the key variables that influence the environment. When this happens, mathematical models can no longer work.

Quantitative data also has the misleading effect of reducing nuances to meaningless numbers. Take the case of NBC News as an example. In February 2014, the news organisation revamped their website based on output from big data feature sets and small, statistically invalid focus groups. Without any qualitative exploration relating to the user experience, the website flopped majorly, with a devastating loss of 7 million viewers within a month.

The company quickly went back to the drawing board. While continuing with its utilisation of technology and quantitative methods, NBC also recalibrated its focus to allocate more weightage to qualitative feedback from its audiences.[18] Insights that would have otherwise been lost amidst the onslaught of numbers were successfully captured and effectively mobilised. Six months later, NBC re-launched its new website to an improved reception.

Another problem with the philosophy underlying OR is that it leads to the tendency to overplan. This may sound strange—after all, isn't strategic planning supposed to result in well-developed plans for organisations to follow? Yet in an uncertain world, the tendency to want to follow a detailed list of instructions can lead to organisational inertia.

We cannot be sure of the future. Even as you try your best to anticipate the future, unexpected events are still bound to take you by surprise. By over-planning, you become tied down to your plans. It is important not to lose sight of the bigger picture and to maintain the agility to react accordingly when events change.

Do not be afraid of uncertainty. Rather, embrace uncertainty by accepting it, accounting for it and trying to understand it. This will help you to anticipate and "rehearse the future", thereby better positioning you to deal with the complexities of our world.

The limitations of Scenario Planning

While Scenario Planning helps us to make sense of the complexity and uncertainty in the world today, like OR, it is insufficient in and of itself.

One problem with Scenario Planning is its tendency to remain mere thought experiments. While a lot of time and resources may be poured into Scenario Planning exercises, it is often difficult to translate these insights into real actionable steps.

Unlike OR, where the goal is to arrive at concrete solutions for the operationalisation of activities in the immediate present, Scenario Planning may yield scenarios that are too abstract or remote for participants to effectively act upon.

Scenario Planning also needs to be backed up by data. Even as future scenarios are generated, these have to be plausible. They have to find their basis in empirical evidence. Such evidence need not be quantitative—

although this is where data can come in—but they should be rigorous and robust in their analysis.

THE NEED FOR FUSE

Operations Research and Scenario Planning are strategic planning tools that have withstood the test of time. While they are useful, their effectiveness, when used in isolation, is limited by their inherent weaknesses.

FUSE presents a systematic and intentional methodology of decision-making that draws upon the strengths of these two approaches while recognising and mitigating their inadequacies. The future is used as a tool to better understand the present: it seeks out and identifies hidden assumptions while clarifying existing assumptions.

FUSE also allows you to go beyond your external environment to obtain clearer insights into yourself and your organisation. Using these insights, you will be able to formulate strategies that are better tailored towards your circumstances and conditions.

However, the decision-making process does not stop here. FUSE's ultimate goal is to create a sustainable delta. This requires effective execution, to ensure that strategies are translated into real and tangible outcomes.

In the final chapter of this introductory section, I will use an example of a battle that happened in ancient Greece to illustrate the core precepts of FUSE.

CHAPTER 3
THE BATTLE OF SALAMIS
FUSE IN ACTION

The Battle of Salamis in 480 BCE is a historical illustration of FUSE in action. Salamis represents one of the most significant battles in human history, having marked a major turning point in the Greco-Persian Wars. It was the start of a decisive swing in the balance of power toward the Greeks.

The battle finds its origins in desperate circumstances and grave uncertainty. The Athenians, fearful of invasion by the Persians, consulted the Greek Oracle at Delphi. In seeking the wisdom of the Oracle, the Athenians were trying to manage the uncertainty that they felt threatened their future. Their consultations were made with a view to action.

Those who sought the wisdom of the Oracle had to deliberate carefully on what to ask and how to phrase the question they would pose to the scared oracle. This was a serious business—such queries had to be accompanied by substantial payment and any pronouncements were regarded as divine.

The three-part forecast the Athenians received was hardly comforting.

First, they were told that there would be a "wooden wall" that would remain unconquered.

Second, the Athenians were told to flee their city.

Third, it was pronounced that many young men would die near the island of Salamis.

The Athenian leaders were dejected with the prophecy, which seemed to conclusively portend their defeat. However, rather than despair, they engaged in debate on what to make of this news. Finally, one of their statesmen, Themistocles, made the case that the "wooden wall" referred not to the city walls but to the massed wooden ships of the Athenian navy. He pointed out that the prophecy that "many young men will die" did not necessarily mean many Greek men. He took the view that in the face of a larger opposing army, it was only sensible for the people to flee the city: the Athenians would fight the Persians at sea in the narrow straits off Salamis and cut off their lines of communication.

By combining the Delphic pronouncement and Themistocles's strategic thinking, the Athenians reframed their perspective from one of despair to one of initiative. But the Athenians also followed through this strategic process with decisive action. They proceeded to fight the Persians at sea and the Persians were subsequently defeated in the ensuing battle.

Three lessons in foresight-driven strategy can be gleaned from the Battle of Salamis.

Strategic inquiry

An organisation seeking to think strategically should be clear about its strategic priorities and concerns. In considering the impending threat, the Athenians had to be clear about their strengths and weaknesses as well as their objectives: this is called "In-sighting". This calculation allowed them to arrive at a decision to temporarily sacrifice their city for the greater strategic result of decisively defeating the Persians. Management must have some normative sense of direction for the organisation. Clear questions must be considered. Muddy or ambiguous scoping will almost certainly lead to vague or irrelevant strategic products.

Strategic debate

Organisations sometimes expect "turnkey" solutions or recommendations. Foresight-driven processes can lead to rethinking, strategic reframing or fresh insights, but not prescriptions for action. Instead, the task of interpreting and analysing futures is the job of management. The Athenians struggled to interpret Delphi's pronouncements, but ultimately, it was by reframing their analysis through debate and lateral thinking that they arrived at a more promising strategic perspective than the bleak outlook they had originally envisioned.

Strategic decision & action

The Athenians, beyond combining the Delphic pronouncement and Themistocles's strategic thinking, followed through this strategic process with decisive action. Decision encompasses action, but management also needs to take responsibility for the consequences of their actions. The longevity of the Delphi Oracle was not because its prophecies always led to positive results, but because its clients accepted that they were owners of the eventual outcomes.

FUSE

The FUSE approach can be broken down into four key aspects.

Foresight

Like the Athenians who sought the counsel of the Delphi Oracle, foresight requires making a conscious and deliberate effort to think about the future in order to make better decisions in the present. The next section will demonstrate how to effectively develop a set of scenarios that can be used to better understand the changing external environment while mapping out the options available to you and your organisation.

Understanding

The Athenians needed to know what their strengths and weaknesses were in relation to their external environment. The third section of this book will illustrate how understanding the external environment is only one singular component to the formulation of effective strategies. I will show how you can systematically obtain valuable and accurate insights into your organisation to better generate strategies that are optimised to your organisation's unique characteristics and circumstances.

Strategy

Having obtained a deeper understanding of both the external and internal environment, the Athenians were able to come up with an effective strategy to defeat the militarily stronger Persians. In the fourth section on Strategy, I will demonstrate how strategies tailored to your specific organisation can be better formulated.

Execution

Finally, the Athenians were able to turn their strategy into real concrete action. In the same way, the best thought-out strategy means nothing if it is not executed effectively. The final section of this book will illustrate how the abstract can be translated into actionable results while keeping track of the desired outcomes.

Fig. 1 on pages 52–53 maps out the entire process pathway of FUSE.

The Foresight process begins by locating a focal question for decision-making. What is the critical decision that needs to be made in order to better safeguard and secure the future? This focal question forms the boundaries of strategic inquiry, and guides the scenario-building process.

The focal question is also used to map out the conventional view of the future. This view is tested for assumptions. What are the fundamental premises supporting this view? Do they hold true, or do they require revision? The clarification of assumptions allows the driving forces influencing your external environment to be identified.

The final stage in the Foresight process revolves around the construction of scenarios. There are two main ways of doing this: the inductive method generates scenarios by projecting forward using trend-lines and patterns, while the deductive method begins from a desired future and works backwards to figure out the steps needed to get there. In either case, this scenario-building process helps to better illuminate some of the key forces shaping the future.

From here, the various outputs from the Foresight process are fed into the Understanding process. Unlike Foresight, which focuses on the external environment, the Understanding process takes an introspective look at the internal environment.

First, biases are confronted. Biases are internal blind spots that hinder a clear view of yourself and of the world around you. Because assumptions are frequently underpinned by biases, it is important to be aware of these biases and to take active steps towards correcting them.

The In-sighting process then follows. This involves developing a shared desired vision, where the ideal end-point is mapped out to provide a set of guidelines for decision-making. Along with the external scenarios constructed earlier, these form the backdrop against which the internal enablers and derailers are identified. This will give you the strategic perspective.

The strategic perspective is used to develop strategy. It helps to identify the core principles that should guide your strategy. Principles alone, however, are not enough. Good leadership is vital.

A third and final ingredient in the formulation of effective strategy is stress-testing. The strategy must be able to withstand exogenous shocks and unexpected variations in parameters. To make it more robust and resilient, run your strategy through a sensitivity analysis and wind-tunnelling process.

Finally, execute the strategy. Execution begins with implementation. This requires five key components: credibility, consultation, communication, coordination and commitment.

Implementation does not represent the end of the Execution process, however. In a non-static world where things are constantly in flux, you need to review and adjust your strategies accordingly. To do so, evaluate and adapt your strategies to effect a clear and sustainable delta.

The next section begins with the Foresight process.

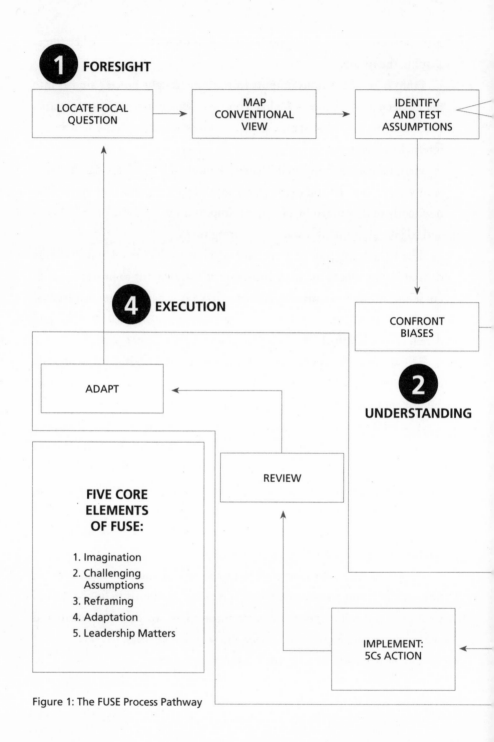

Figure 1: The FUSE Process Pathway

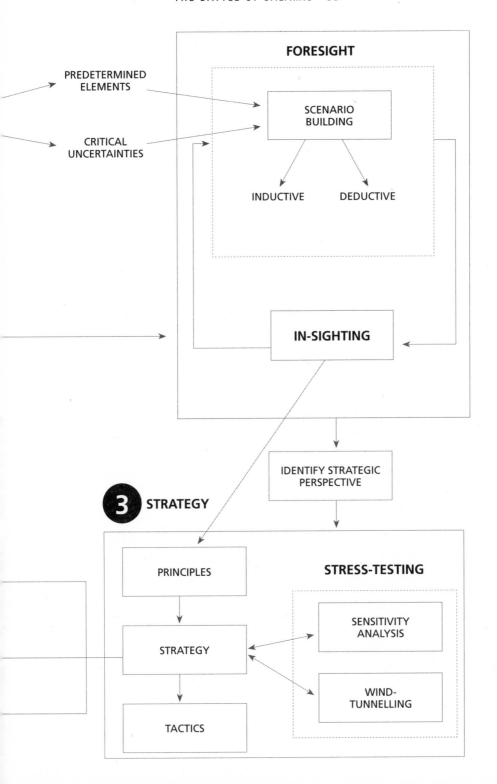

SECTION 2
FORESIGHT

CHAPTER 4

INTRODUCTION TO FORESIGHT

HOW WE ARE HARD-WIRED TO THINK ABOUT THE FUTURE

The desire in humans to know the future is not new. Since ancient times, rulers actively sought predictions of the future to better guide their decisions and thereby preserve their reign. In Greece for example, no king—including the famed Alexander the Great—would dare go to war without first consulting the Delphi Oracle. In Mesopotamia, rulers were guided on strategic decisions by astrologers, who based their advice on the interpretation of planetary movements as clues towards understanding the future. Meanwhile in China, emperors employed diviners who predicted the future using a variety of techniques, one of which included the interpretation of cracks that appeared on animal bones after they were burnt.

Today, the astrologer and oracle no longer influence rulers or decision-makers, yet the age-old desire to know the future has not abated. While we no longer take the divinations of the astrologer or the oracle seriously, a new kind of fortune-teller has emerged to take their place—the professional analyst and forecaster, armed with their toolkit of computer algorithms and mathematical equations. Will the US economy tank in the next year? Will the price of oil continue to drop over the next quarter? Will it be prudent to invest in the Chinese real estate sector? In trying to better plan our course of action in today's complex and increasingly uncertain society, we continue our search for modern-day forecasting.

This very ability to conceive of and contemplate the future is an evolutionary feature that has allowed the human species to adapt and survive till the present-day. While animals possess the ability to deal with recurring problems such as seasonal food shortages, they do this through memory capacity. They neither actively envision the future, nor do they explicitly plan for it.

Human beings, on the other hand, are unique in their cognitive ability to *conceive* of events within a temporal space beyond the present: they are able to mentally time-travel in both directions on the temporal continuum. Our memories of the past thus provide us with the raw materials to construct multiple versions of the future.[1]

In his 1985 seminal article on the temporal organisation of conscious awareness, Swedish neuroscientist David Ingvar poetically refers to this as "memories of the future".[2] This ability to think about the future allows us to make preparations ahead of time: by anticipating events, we can take pre-emptive steps to better secure our future needs.

The evolutionary advantages of conceiving the future and anticipating events can be illustrated in the use of primitive trapping devices dating back thousands of years. Archaeologists have found fish weirs and traps preserved in low-oxygen, still-water environments.[3] The discovery of such primitive traps suggest that our ancestors were able to conceive of a time beyond the present and to predict, effectively, how their current actions, i.e., the use of such fishing traps, could reap consequences in the future, i.e., the capturing of larger amounts of fish with higher nutritional value.

These gadgets and contraptions were conceived of in remote time and space, with the intention for use at a future time. It took imagination— mental time-travelling to an imagined future—and experience to do that. As our ancestors anticipated the reward that would be waiting for them inside the fish weirs, they travelled mentally into the past to generate reasonable expectations from previous experiences.

THE FAILURE OF FORECASTING: FUTURE(S) PLANNING, AND NOT FUTURE PLANNING

The ability to think about the future has been vital for the survival of the human race. We are evolutionarily hard-wired with the cognitive ability to make concrete decisions in the present to secure our future needs based on our judgement of what the future holds.

Yet our prognoses have rarely been on target. Individuals who are supposedly experts in their fields of knowledge have frequently and grossly miscalculated the future of their industry.

Take for instance, Thomas Watson, Chairman of the International Business Machines Corporation, or what is more commonly known as IBM. IBM started off as a manufacturer of computing equipment used primarily for simple tabulation purposes, before it morphed into the computer hardware and software powerhouse of today. Back in 1943, however, Watson was of the opinion that "there's a world market for maybe five computers". For a man who made his living selling computing devices, his prediction could not have been more wrong. Today, the world runs on computing power, and the computer has since come to pervade nearly every aspect of our everyday life.

Darryl Zanuck, a movie producer at the film studio 20th century Fox, got it wrong as well. He argued in 1946 that "[t]elevision won't last because people will soon get tired of staring at a plywood box every night". Of course, that future failed to materialise as televisions became a mainstay in living rooms. By 1960, 90% of American households owned at least one television set.[4]

But perhaps one of the most ironic blunders in judgement in recent history belongs to Robert Metcalfe, the co-founder of the now-defunct digital electronics manufacturer 3Com Corporation. Metcalfe was the co-inventor of the Ethernet technology, a technology that enabled the networking of computers. Yet in 1995, Metcalfe made the prediction that the Internet "will soon go spectacularly supernova and in 1996 catastrophically collapse".

That prediction turned out to be completely wrong. Today, 77% of the developed world and 31% of the developing world are inter-connected via the Internet, and these numbers are only set to grow further.[5]

When the stakes are high, a mis-prognosis of the future can be fatal.

THE BORDERS STORY

At the height of its success, Borders was a company that had over 500 stores and 19,500 employees spread across America.[6] Its shares hit an all-time high of $41.75 on the stock market,[7] with customers raving about the bookstore's bright and cheery expanse of space that allowed them to leisurely browse through the wide selection of books offered. Yet in 2011, Borders went bust. It filed for bankruptcy, closed its remaining 400 stores and laid off all 10,700 of its workers.

What happened?

Borders failed to correctly anticipate the future. It failed to foresee that the Internet and digitalisation would overtake the industry in a way that would ultimately change the rules of the game. It fell behind its competitors, and eventually dropped off the playing field for good.

Borders' failure can be traced back to the 1990s, when the Internet was making its first mainstream appearance to the general public. Amazon, the world's leading web-based retailer today, seized this opportunity to ride on an emergent technology. It rolled out its online bookstore, hedging its bets that the Internet would become a ubiquitous technology with a limitless consumer base.

At the time, Borders' biggest competitor was Barnes & Noble. Recognising the changing tides of the times, Barnes & Noble quickly jumped onto the bandwagon, and in 1997, launched its online store. Borders, on the other hand, waited another year before it established a presence online. In 2001, Borders made the fatal mistake of outsourcing its online operations to Amazon. Its management thought that it was making a smart choice by focusing its energies on its physical stores. In reality, Borders completely missed the boat. It turned its attention to a declining sector, while ignoring the golden opportunity that was the Internet. Tragically, Borders clung on to this short-sighted strategy until 2008.[8]

Borders' misreading of the future shaped other major decisions taken by the chain store. In the early 2000s, Borders made the decision to invest heavily in the music and movie sector. In a time when more and more consumers were increasingly getting their entertainment fix through digital means, Borders was busy stocking its stores with shelves of CDs and DVDs. By then, Tower Records and HMV—heavyweights in the entertainment retailing industry—had already been forced to shut their doors.

The final nail was hammered into its coffin when Borders slipped up on its introduction of an e-book reader. While Amazon rolled out its e-reading device—the Kindle—in 2007, and Barnes & Noble followed up two years later with its Nook device, Borders only did so in 2010 with the Kobo. This lag in timing was disastrous for the company. Today, Kindle and Nook command the largest market share among e-reading devices. The Kobo barely registers in the mind of consumers.

Borders' failure to anticipate the future led to a series of bad strategic decisions. The choices it made had fatal consequences for its future. Borders was eventually eliminated from the competitive game.

WHY ANTICIPATING THE FUTURE IS SO DIFFICULT
Why is it so difficult to anticipate the future accurately?

The future is not linear
First, we are cognitively wired to think of the future as a linear path flowing from the present. Even as our minds travel through the time continuum from the past to the present, we tend to retrospectively represent the present in terms of a linear path originating from past events. This relates to our innate desire for predictability—we intuitively dislike disorder and uncertainty.

The future is not predetermined

Second, the future is not a given. Thinking about the future in linear terms makes us liable to fall into the cognitive trap of thinking that events are either predetermined or that they will always continue as per usual. This is evident in our propensity for hindsight bias.

Human beings tend to treat historical events, in retrospect, as inevitable. Sean Lusk, former head of the UK National School of Government's Strategy Team puts it so eloquently when he writes that "history, in its raw and naked form, tells us that change happens in unpredictable ways. [Yet...] too often what we understand as 'History' has been stripped of its inherent uncertainty and presented to us as a settled panorama of events."[9]

In an experiment based on an actual legal case, Kim Kamin and Jeffrey Rachlinski asked two groups to estimate the probability of flood damage caused by the blockage of a city-owned drawbridge.[10] The control group was only provided with the information known to the city council at the time in which it made the decision not to hire a bridge watcher. The experimental group on the other hand, was given this same set of information, along with the fact that a flood had actually occurred. If the probability of flooding was deemed to be greater than 10%, the city council would be found to have been negligent. Seventy-six percent of the control group concluded that the flood was so unlikely that no precautions were necessary. However, 57% of the experimental group concluded that the flood was so likely that the city's failure to take precautions made it legally negligent. As movie director Billy Wilder says, "Hindsight is always twenty-twenty."

We are also susceptible to the belief that with the accumulation of information and knowledge, we can somehow predict the future. This is called "expert bias".

We tend to give too much credit to the experts when it comes to making judgements about the future. Such confidence is often misplaced. In a 20-year experiment conducted by American psychologist Philip Tetlock, over 28,000 forecasts from 284 experts in various fields, ranging from government officials, university academics to journalists, were collated and studied. In his study, Tetlock asked these experts to make assessments regarding future probabilities. He asked them questions such as, "What are the chances of inflation in the UK rising, staying the same or falling in the next 12 months?" or "Will casualties in the Israel-Palestine conflict fall, rise, or stay the same in the next year?"

The results discredited the judgement of these so-called experts. As Tetlock puts it, a dart-throwing chimp would have been as much help as the paid experts in predicting the future.[11] Despite the illusion of predictability, the future is not a pre-determined given.

We live in an uncertain world

The third and final reason why anticipating the future is so difficult is intimately related to the second point: we live in a complex world where there is no certainty of outcomes. Variables influencing outcomes cannot be easily discerned, and cause-and-effect relationships can seldom be pin-pointed with any great accuracy. In our interconnected, inter-contingent and intense world of today, identification of causal relationships, much less variables, become a question of judgment.

The 2000 Wall Street stock market crash is a sobering example of the sheer complexity of the world we live in today. It is nearly impossible to disentangle the individual factors that led up to the stock market's staggering loss of US$8 trillion. A combination of intertwined factors, including corporate corruption, the overvaluation of stocks, the burst of the dot-com bubble, as well as the rise in Internet trading, all bled into one another, with real-life effects rippling across sectors and borders to impact national economies.[12] Whereas events in the past could be compartmentalised or fully integrated into one overarching system, it is getting more and more difficult to anticipate how different factors can affect and influence one another.

Foresight plays an invaluable role in the art of decision-making. The reason why we make bad decisions has nothing to do with the act of foresight itself; rather, it is intimately tied up with the way we think about the future. The future is not linear, and neither is it predetermined. Embrace uncertainty, and don't promote the illusion of stability and predictability.

OUTLINE OF THIS SECTION

This section aims to equip you with a better way of thinking about the future. This is called future(s)-planning. Instead of using the word "future" in the singular, the FUSE approach accepts that uncertainty is unavoidable, and incorporates it into the analysis.

We do this by leveraging on an exploratory tool known as Scenario Planning. Scenario Planning explores the external universe by identifying and scrutinising the core influences that shape the future(s). Importantly, it reframes your perspectives about the external world, with the goal of getting as accurate a mental picture of reality as possible. This is what will make a difference in the way you make decisions against the backdrop of the future. The more accurate this backdrop is, the better the decisions you will make.

This section begins by first locating the focal question around which your scenarios will be structured. The focal question is concerned with the highest-order concern of your organisation and anchors your scenarios by keeping them focused on what is relevant.

Using the focal question as a starting point, map out the conventional view of the future. We are often not conscious of our own perspectives. When this happens, we act as if we are on auto-pilot, without consideration for the mental map of the future that we are being guided by. By making your view of the future plain and visible, it becomes easier to tease out the underlying assumptions that you are operating on.

Assumptions are extremely important because they form the bedrock of your perspectives. Because they are taken for granted, they are frequently ignored and often slip by unnoticed. If your assumptions are accurate, your mental roadmap will be true to reality. But if your assumptions are incorrect, you may end up in trouble when you discover that your mental bedrock is ultimately unstable. An examination of the assumptions you hold is thus vital to ensure that you are not barking up the wrong tree in thinking about the future(s).

The process of questioning assumptions should have unearthed the key driving forces and predetermined elements governing your future(s). These form the building blocks for the construction of scenarios. Different plausible scenarios emerge when different interpretations of the critical uncertainties are identified.

However, scenario-building need not only take place in an inductive manner. Scenarios can also be deductive. This entails beginning from a desired future and working backwards to understand what needs to happen before that future can occur.

A set of robust, plausible and coherent scenarios will provide you with a better idea of the future(s) you are heading towards. Together with the insights derived from the Understanding process, these will form the strategic perspective against which more effective strategies can be developed.

In summary, there are four key steps involved in the Foresight process (see Fig. 2):

- Locate a focal question
- Map the conventional view
- Identify assumptions
- Build scenarios

In the next chapter, I will begin by illustrating the importance of identifying the right focal question and demonstrating how this is done.

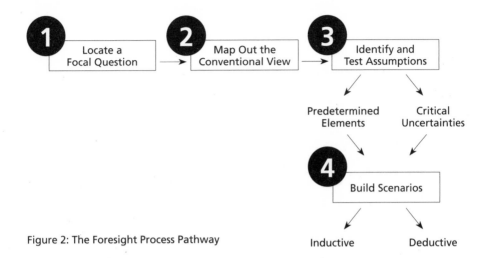

Figure 2: The Foresight Process Pathway

CHAPTER 5
LOCATING A FOCAL QUESTION

THE FOCAL QUESTION DETERMINES WHERE YOU MAKE YOUR DECISION

The focal question clarifies the highest-order concern of your organisation. It should be related to decision-making in a critical area of your organisation's future.

There is no one-size-fits-all focal question. The focal question needs to be determined according to the organisation's specific characteristics and context. The importance of identifying the appropriate focal question cannot be overemphasised. Asking different questions will generate different answers.

In 1999, cognitive psychologists Daniel Simons and Christopher Chabris performed an experiment that highlighted the problem of inattentional blindness. Participants were tasked to watch a video where two groups of people—one group dressed in white and the other group dressed in black—were passing basketballs around. The participants were asked to count the number of passes made between the people wearing white.

This task was not as easy as it sounds; the players constantly moved around, demanding immense concentration from the participants.

Midway through the video, a person wearing a gorilla suit walks in and out of the scene. At the end of the video, participants were asked if they saw the gorilla. Surprisingly, nearly half of the participants missed the gorilla completely.

The "invisible gorilla" test highlights how your choice of focus can blind you to other things that are not related to the focal point. We look out for what we choose to see, and ignore everything else that may be going on in the periphery, even if they are of significance.

This failure to be situationally aware extends to even experts themselves. In a follow-up experiment conducted by psychologist Trafton Drew, radiologists were asked to examine CT chest scans for abnormalities called nodules. These indicators of cancer were tiny, and it took a practiced eye to pick them out quickly and accurately—something that radiologists were trained to do.

Unbeknown to them, Drew had inserted an image of a gorilla that was 48 times the size of the average nodule. At the end of the experiment, only 17% of the 24 radiologists tested spotted this glaring abnormality. What was more confounding was that most of the radiologists who did not notice the gorilla had in fact looked directly at it.[1]

Psychologist Jeremy Wolfe explained, "The radiologists missed the gorillas not because they could not see them, but because the way their brains had framed what they were doing. They were looking for cancer nodules, not gorillas."[2]

The choice of focal question is important because it acts like a pair of blinders that steers your attention in a certain direction. The focal question shapes what you notice, and eventually, the answer or scenario that you come up with.

Returning to the example of Blockbuster brought up in the very first chapter of the book, the video rental firm could have arrived at completely different outcomes if different focal questions were asked. The question "How can Blockbuster successfully disrupt itself in the face of changing technology and consumer behaviour over the next five years?" would have yielded a different set of answers compared with the question "How can Blockbuster best maximise its profits over the next two years?"

The focal question thus reflects strategic priority. This need not be limited to profit maximisation. In fact, as a later chapter will show, profits are more often than not a by-product of higher order goals and priorities. Strategic priorities distinguish the essential from the important.

Netflix is another example that illustrates how different questions reflect different priorities. The question "How can Netflix diversify from its streaming services?" indicates that the leadership has made diversification a priority. On the other hand, a question such as "How can Netflix grow the on-demand streaming pie?" would make it clear that Netflix had decided that its on-demand streaming services would remain at the core of its business.

THE FOCAL QUESTION DECIDES THE SCOPE OF YOUR SCENARIOS

It is important to ensure that your focal question is appropriately scoped. If the scope is too broad, the scenario-building process could combust with the infinite permutations of variables involved. This compromises direction and relevancy. But if the scope is too narrow, important variables that are not immediately obvious may be neglected.

While the scope should allow exploratory space to encourage comprehensibility and out-of-the-box thinking, it should not be so broad that anything goes.

Besides strategic priorities, the scope of the focal question should also delineate temporal and spatial dimensions. How far into the future should the focal question be concerned with? Which locality will you be operating in? Such considerations help to keep the scenarios focused on what is truly relevant. The focal question should thus be concise, boiling down to the core fundamentals.

It may be helpful to view the scoping function of the focal question as a series of concentric circles with decreasing levels of strategic importance as we move further outwards (see Fig. 3).

At its core, the focal question is about decision-making. Beyond this core lie the organisation's strategic priorities. Finally, the outermost layer

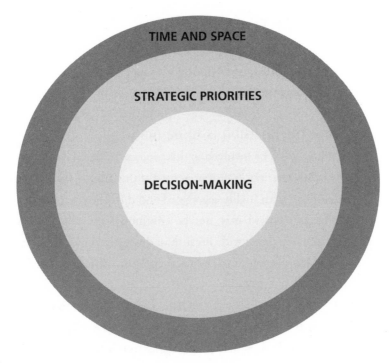

Figure 3: The Scoping Function of the Focal Question

represents the temporal and spatial constraints that bound an organisation's strategy.

Such a model ensures a systematic way of thinking through your choice of focal question.

The focal question should be reviewed periodically

The focal question also needs to be reviewed periodically. Emerging developments could have altered the operating parameters, or new information may now shed greater clarity on previous unknowns. The focal question may no longer be relevant or appropriate.

Regularly return to the focal question to ensure that you are still within the boundaries of your self-defined scope. By making it a point to consistently return to the focal question, you can ensure that your scenarios remain on track.

IDENTIFYING THE FOCAL QUESTION

Because the choice of focal question has lasting implications for the rest of the Foresighting process, it is important to identify an appropriate focal question for your organisation.

Locate where the decision is to be made

First, decide who should be involved in this process. It is vital that a diversity of perspectives and experiences be represented at this stage. This is especially true in organisations with highly segregated and differentiated roles—what one department is privy to may not be common knowledge in another department. To ensure that a wide breadth of divergent understandings and experiences are incorporated into the focal question, different stakeholders should be consulted.

Second, identify a focal area of concern, such as a decision or question that is critical to the future of your organisation. One way would be to identify the major challenges that your organisation is facing today.

Alternatively, questions such as, "What would you ask a real psychic?" could help to kick-start the identification process.

Set goals

Another pathway to identifying the focal question is to start with organisational goals. The focal question could relate to the attainment of these goals, or it could also serve to clarify the goals themselves.

Goals should be descriptive and specific. This compels realism, and increases accountability towards these goals.

As mentioned earlier, goals need not be limited to the pursuit of profits. In fact, the writer John Kay makes a case in his book *Obliquity*, that the most profitable companies are rarely the most profit-oriented.[3] He argues that compared to goals that are direct and straight-forward, indirect goals often lead to more effective outcomes.

Oblique goal-setting is focused on higher-level objectives and purpose. Kay cites the example of Merck and Pfizer, two pharmaceutical companies that adopted contrasting approaches to goal-setting from the 1950s through to the 1990s.

At Merck, President George Merck II made it clear that his corporation's purpose could not lie solely in the business of making money. Rather, profits came about when the corporation was able to demonstrate value to society. He explained, "If we have remembered [that medicine is for the people], the profits have never failed to appear."

Contrast Merck's goal of benefiting humanity with Pfizer's goal of profit maximisation: In 1962, President John McKeen announced, "so far as humanely possible, we aim to get profit out of everything we do".

The end result was immediately apparent. Compared to Pfizer, Merck performed better financially. In fact, it was repeatedly named America's most admired company in *Fortune* surveys. Unlike Pfizer, Merck did not make profit maximisation its core purpose. Yet in their commitment to helping people, profits became a natural by-product of these activities. I will return with an interesting twist to the case of these two companies later in the book when considering the importance of a principles-driven strategic approach.

When considering organisational goals, it may be more effective to begin from higher-level objectives than to go straight to profit maximisation. After all, goals are often complex, made up of many different components that are frequently incompatible and incommensurable. A direct and straightforward path towards the achievement of such goals could end up short-circuiting the ultimate objective.

Determining the focal question lays the important groundwork for the rest of the Foresight process. In identifying this question, locate where the critical decisions are to be taken, and consider your strategic priorities and goals.

The next chapter illustrates how to map out the current perspective in relation to the focal question. This helps to identify the assumptions supporting such a view, eventually allowing them to be tested in order to produce a more robust and accurate view of the world.

CHAPTER 6
MAPPING THE CONVENTIONAL VIEW

MENTAL MAPS AS BLUEPRINTS FOR ACTION

We often make decisions unconsciously without thinking through the decision-making process. This saves us time, but there is the very real danger of missing out on logical fallacies and mistaken assumptions that manifest themselves in the consequences of our decisions. These cognitive flaws are often located in perceptions of reality, and guide the way we make decisions and take action.

In order to uncover defects in your thinking process, map out your existing image of the surrounding world in detail. This needs to be deliberate, because your mental filter can only be adjusted to reflect a more accurate assumption of reality when you recognise your own views for what they are.

The mental map should also be focused. Return to the focal question identified earlier, and use it as a way to frame your worldview.

In this section, I will provide a framework for mapping out your current outlook as it relates to the focal question determined previously (see Fig. 4).

INSTITUTIONS VS. AGENTS

Social phenomena and changes in the environment arise from the interaction and tension between two key determinants—institutions and agents.

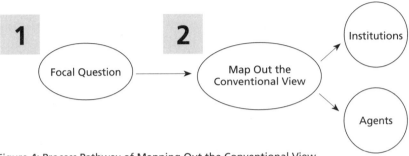

Figure 4: Process Pathway of Mapping Out the Conventional View

While institutions refer to the structural patterns that influence and constrain the choices and opportunities available, agents are the individuals or organisations that act independently to exert an influence on you or your organisation.

For example, a business corporation is looking to expand its operations overseas. Where it chooses to locate its business however, is dependent on the institutions, or structural forces at work—does the host country have a free-trade agreement with the country where the corporation is domiciled? Is the social, political and economic context favourable to the expansion of operations in this new country?

It is also important to look at the actors involved. Is there a sizeable consumer base in the country? What are the other businesses that may be in competition with your organisation?

By locating the nexus at which institutions and agency intersect, it is possible to plot out a map of reality.

Institutions

First, identify the institutions that influence the answers you are seeking. One way of doing this is to systematically work your way through the PEST framework—what are the Political, Economic, Social and Technological institutions that will play a role in your decision-making process? How will these evolve over time?

The following questions may serve as a starting guide for the mapping process:

Political: What kind of political system is there? What kind of policies are the ruling regime likely to pursue that would favour or hinder your organisation? How well-integrated will the country be within the larger global order? What kind of foreign policy will it pursue and how would this affect the running of your organisation?

Economic: How will the international and domestic economy fare? Is there going to be a recession soon? Are certain sectors of the economy over-heated? Is inflation going to be a problem?

Social: How will the demography change? Will there be cultural shifts that would change the face of your consumer base? Will your consumers' habits evolve in ways that affect your goals?

Technological: What are the up-and-coming technologies on the market? Will these become an augmenter to existing technologies, a substitute, or a disruptor? What are the implications for the running of your organisation as well as the achievement of your goals?

Agents

After identifying the institutions and structural forces shaping your world, identify the agents that shape your future. These differ from organisation to organisation, depending on the nature of the sector and industry.

It is possible, however, to think about this in terms of a set of horizontal and vertical axes (see Fig. 5). The vertical axis represents a hierarchical relationship with patrons on one end and constituents on the other end. The horizontal axis represents a flat relationship, with peers at one end and disruptors at the other end.

At the top of the vertical axis are your patrons. These are the organisations/individuals that you rely on. How would your relationship with them change over time? Would the bargaining relationship shift?

In the corporate world, this could refer to a supplier. Or in the case of a government bureaucracy, this could refer to a political master on whom you are reliant for instruction.

At the opposite end of the vertical spectrum are your constituents. These refer to the organisations/individuals that you are accountable to. Again, this varies from consumer base to shareholders, or even to the political constituency. Will their behaviour change as their composition in size, preference and bargaining power evolve?

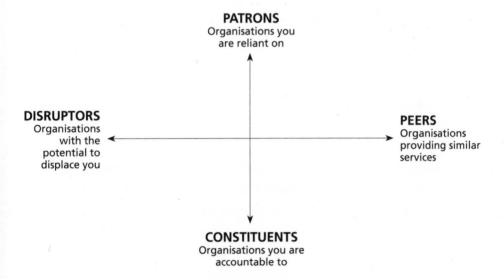

Figure 5: Framework of Agents

Unlike the vertical axis where the relationship is hierarchical, the horizontal axis represents organisations or individuals operating at the same level as your organisation. On one end of the axis are your peers—these are organisations that provide similar services. This need not necessarily mean competition; rather, it acknowledges that there are organisations that fulfil similar functions as your organisation. How do such organisations affect your industry?

Again, it is important to note that this does not always imply negative competition. One need only think about the electric car company Tesla and its strategy of encouraging the growth of the electric vehicle industry. In a nascent industry, such a strategy is aimed at increasing the critical mass of the electric car market.

On the other end of the horizontal axis are the disruptors. Compared to your peers, these agents have the ability to eliminate the role that your company currently plays within the market. They may even rewrite the rules of the game by creating new markets that previously did not exist, or by eliminating existing markets that are flourishing. While such agents may be initially difficult to spot, it is crucial that they are not dismissed easily.

THE INSTITUTION-AGENT MATRIX

To ensure that the map of your worldview is robust, the tension between institutions and agents can be examined by using the following matrix (see Fig. 6):

How would your patrons be affected by political institutions? How could technological advancements create disruptors in your industry or sector? Agents are not always influenced by institutions; in some cases, they possess the ability to shape institutions. For instance, how could your constituents influence social change? Or alternatively, how could your peers influence the outlook of the global economy?

The interactions between institutions and agents should hence be examined in order to come up with a comprehensive and precise map of

	Political	Economic	Social	Technological
Patrons				
Constituents				
Peers				
Disruptors				

Figure 6: The Institution-Agent Matrix

the future. This is important because it will consequently serve as the input for the next step – the identification of assumptions. The more detailed and thorough your mental map is, the more robust and rewarding the identification process will be.

CHAPTER 7
IDENTIFYING ASSUMPTIONS

Identifying assumptions is a crucial part of the Foresight process. This chapter will explain what assumptions are and why it is so important to identify and evaluate them.

WHY IDENTIFYING ASSUMPTIONS IS IMPORTANT

Assumptions are statements taken for granted without proof. They may be explicit, where they are consciously stated and shared by the speaker. Or they may also be implicit, where they are not articulated or even noticed by the speaker. While assumptions may be useful in decision-making, especially when there is simply too much uncertainty to locate variables and causality, it is important to continuously assess and challenge them as parameters change. There are three key reasons for doing so.

Assumptions underpin our outlook of the future

First, assumptions often underpin our outlook for the future and hence the decisions made in the present. For example, human beings tend to fall into the cognitive trap of viewing the future as a linear path originating from the present. This is a business-as-usual, or a BAU, assumption. It stems from our natural desire for stability, despite the often-cited maxim that the only constant in life is change. The BAU assumption is highly dangerous, because it deludes you into thinking that you do not need to adapt to ever-changing parameters. This causes you to make unwise decisions that in turn set you up for trouble in the future.

Assumptions reveal biases

Second, assumptions reveal the biases of the organisation. Because biases are shaped by the internal beliefs, values and perceptions of individuals and organisations, they represent a recurring pattern that affects behaviour and thought processes.

Biases however, are also frequently difficult to spot, so entrenched as they are in the psyche. The identification of assumptions thus provides you with a scarce opportunity to uncover biases that were previously unknown, thereby de-cluttering the mental lens and allowing you to see things more clearly and accurately. This is important when trying to make sense of both your external and internal reality.

Assumptions clarify the focal question

Third, assumptions help to test the focal question. This is because assumptions frequently uncover unknowns or uncertainties that affect the desired outcomes. These are the areas that need to be investigated further in order to arrive at a more precise and appropriate focal question.

As highlighted in the earlier chapter, your choice of focal question has reverberant effects on the rest of the Foresight process. Different questions generate different answers, and it is important to consistently return to the focal question to ensure that the operating parameters have not changed.

In summary, assumptions are important because they underpin your outlook of the future, reveal recurring patterns in your thought processes, and clarify the focal question that will guide the scenario-building process.

HOW TO IDENTIFY ASSUMPTIONS

Although the significance of assumptions cannot be overstated, getting at them is a much harder job. Assumptions tend to be taken for granted, and are frequently overlooked completely. This section provides you with three simple tools for identifying assumptions.

Asking why

The previous step highlighted the need for a blueprint that maps out your conventional view of the future. In order to locate the assumptions undergirding this blueprint, diligently go through each point, armed with the simple but powerful question: why?

Why will the political regime change? On what premises did you base such a conclusion? Why will the real estate market burst? Why will there be no new entrants into your industry? Keep asking follow-up questions until you have exhausted all possibilities. If the answer cannot be sufficiently substantiated, you have just spotted an assumption.

Putting together a Team B

Look for people in your organisation who have not contributed to the foresight process. These individuals would be able to look at your blueprint with fresh eyes, spotting logical fallacies and leaps in logic more easily.

It may not always be possible to assemble a Team B, however. In this case, some imagination would come in handy. Identify the stakeholders involved in the premise you are trying to establish. Imagine yourself in their shoes. How would they react to your statements?

It is important to distance yourself as far as possible from your own views, so as to obtain greater objectivity and thereby effectiveness.

Developing counter arguments and examples

Finally, another way to identify assumptions is to come up with counter arguments to the claim being made and attempt to justify it. For instance, if you had previously estimated that your consumer base will increase in the future, think of possible reasons as to why it will not expand. If the justifications are reasonable, it is time to investigate the original claim.

Similarly, try to come up with counterexamples to any overarching or general claims made. Counterexamples are a common technique used in logic, especially in mathematics, to locate the parameters of possible theories. For example, if the assertion states that all prime numbers are odd, then the even prime number 2 disproves this statement. When this happens, re-examine your statements.

Counter examples are powerful; a thousand examples may not prove a theory but a single counterexample may be enough to disprove it.

Be relentless, persistent and ruthless

To ensure that the process of identifying assumptions is robust, be relentless, persistent and ruthless.

Be relentless in asking why. Keep questioning your claims until you have boiled them down to their most fundamental premises.

Be persistent in pursuing loose ends. Explore different perspectives and alternative viewpoints.

Finally, be ruthless in interrogating your assumptions.

Assumptions are not easy to spot. The next part of the section will provide a typology of assumptions to help you better identify assumptions.

TYPES OF ASSUMPTIONS

Different kinds of assumptions exist. Assumptions may arise about resources, constraints, priorities and capabilities, as well as causality.

> **Resources**: Resources required will not remain in a state of stasis. How would the availability of key resources change over time? Will resource requirements shift in the future as technology advances?

Constraints: We do not operate in a barrier-free world. What are some of the constraints that may hinder our progress in the future? Alternatively, will there be any developments where constraints may be eliminated?

Priorities: Decision-makers may need to re-examine priorities set previously. A priority previously deemed important may no longer be as relevant in a new world order. Likewise, an item that was low on the priority list may move up in importance as conditions evolve.

Capabilities: Leaders need to review the capabilities of their organisation. This could range from the existing infrastructure, the human resources, as well as the organisational structure. As parameters change, capabilities may vary. Again, it is crucial not to assume capability and capacity stasis.

Causality: Causality refers to cause-and-effect relationships. Claiming that increased market share is due to the improvement of a product design may sound intuitive or even desirable, especially if large expenses of money have been allocated to revamping the product's design. However, it is important to consistently challenge such claims. What is the evidence backing the claim? Are there other factors that could have played a role in increasing market share?

A loose typology of assumptions provides you with a framework for systematically identifying assumptions. The next section explains why people frequently fall prey to assumption-making.

WHY PEOPLE MAKE ASSUMPTIONS

Assumptions do not arise in a vacuum. Often, assumptions are founded on a variety of root causes. This section identifies four main factors: past experiences, ideology, biases and ignorance.

History

People often make assumptions based on past experiences. If something happened before, particularly if it occurs on a repeated basis, we tend to assume that it will happen again. One particular instance occurred during the Yom Kippur War between a coalition of Arab States led by Egypt and Syria against Israel from 6–25 October in 1973.

Between 1948 and 1978, Israel fought four major wars with its Arab neighbours. Israel emerged victorious all four times. The Six-Day War in 1967 against Syria, Egypt and Jordan was particularly significant because Israel managed to successfully capture the Gaza Strip, the Sinai Peninsula, the West Bank, Golan Heights and the Holy site of Jerusalem from the three countries. This led to a sense of superiority among the Israelis.

The trend of victorious outcomes for Israel resulted in its intelligence analysts informing scenarios with a poor view of Arab capability, creating cognitive rigidity in the analytical process. To the A'man (the Israeli intelligence branch) analysts, "An Arab would always be an Arab." The Israeli military, meanwhile, scoffed at the possibility of a successful Arab attack. They believed that the Arab forces were simply too incompetent to succeed. In other words, the Israelis assumed a "business-as-usual" scenario. This took the form of a scenario where Israeli might would continue to be vastly superior to limited Arab capability.

Based on the historical experience wrought in the previous four wars, the Israelis made assumptions about the nature and intention of a possible Arabic attack. For instance, they believed that any war with the Arab states would be a protracted one. A drawn-out war would tip the scales in Israel's favour.

Anwar Sadat, then-President of Egypt, had other plans, however. He sought to attack Israel with the intention of restoring Arab military prowess in a limited conflict. His strategy was to fight a short, sharp war that would be quickly brought to a political solution before the gains from a strategic surprise attack was lost to an Israeli counterattack. Under such a scenario, the terms of war would be different from the conditions necessary to end a protracted fight.

On 6 October 1973, an Arab coalition of Egyptian and Syrian forces sprung a surprise attack on Israel. While the Yom Kippur War was eventually won by Israel, early Arabic successes in the conflict led to a restoration of Arab pride. This was exactly as intended by Sadat.[1]

More crucially, it resulted in the realisation among the Israelis that they could no longer maintain their prior assumption that they would always dominate the Arab states militarily. As a consequence of the Yom Kippur War, the Egyptian-Israeli Peace Treaty was negotiated in 1979, and the previously captured Sinai was returned to Egypt.

During the Yom Kippur War, the Israelis had assumed that they could continue to militarily dominate the Arab states. This was an assumption of capabilities as a result of historical experience. Consequently, Israel failed to take the threat of a military attack by the Arab states seriously and was caught off guard when Egypt and Syria unexpectedly launched their attack. Sinai was returned to Egypt, and importantly, Israel came to the realisation that it could no longer take its military dominance for granted.

Ideology

People can also make assumptions based on ideology. As the following example illustrates, the United States entered the Vietnam War in 1964 because it believed in the domino theory—it bought into the unquestioned assumption that if one country falls to communism, its neighbours will also be overtaken by communism. The Vietnam War became a textbook example of a proxy war fought in the Cold War era, with the Soviet Union, China and other communist allies backing North Vietnam, while the US and other anti-communist allies supported South Vietnam.

By the time the war ended in 1975, more than 2.5 million American soldiers had served in Vietnam. More damningly, however, were the statistics for the war dead and wounded: more than 58,000 American soldiers perished, and another 300,000 were honourably discharged because of war wounds.

The assumption that the fall of South Vietnam would catalyse a communist takeover of neighbouring states was one key reason for the decision taken to enter the war. This belief never materialised. After the reunification of Vietnam under the communist North in 1975, contrary to American fears, communism did not spread throughout Southeast Asia. The assumption of causality—that the establishment of communism in one country would lead to a chain-reaction among surrounding countries—failed to hold true. Yet it tragically led to the decision to send 2.5 million American men to war, prematurely ending the lives of nearly 60,000 soldiers.

Biases

More common than ideology perhaps, is the underpinning of assumptions by biases. While biases may be based on values and beliefs, there are two common cognitive biases that frequently influence the development of assumptions.

The first bias is the "availability bias". Human beings have the tendency to judge the likelihood and causal importance of an event by how easy it is to remember or how readily available information about the event is.

This is especially common in doctors. For example, bacterial meningitis shares similar symptoms with the common flu. A doctor who has recently diagnosed two cases of bacterial meningitis is more likely to see it in his next patient, even if the patient, in reality, only has the flu.[2]

Another example is the 9/11 attacks on the twin towers in downtown Manhattan. The shocking nature of the attacks were etched into the minds of ordinary Americans in the period right after the attacks. American politicians have since successfully lobbied for political causes such as the reshaping of foreign policy in the Middle East or for increased defence spending by positioning them as necessary precautions to ensuring that a terrorist attack like 9/11 would never happen again.[3]

Another bias very similar to the availability bias is the "salience effect". People tend to pay more attention to extraordinary features than they would otherwise deserve to receive. Researchers Daniel Kahneman and Amos Tversky found that people often place unwarranted emphasis on salient information when forecasting.[4] For instance, investors are more perceptive to sensational news than they are to seemingly mundane information. The sacking of a company's CEO garners greater attention than the long-term profits of the company, thereby occupying a higher weightage in the decision-making process. The negligence of important factors that feature less prominently or which are slow to develop, can have adverse consequences.

Ignorance or the lack of imagination

Finally, assumptions can arise simply out of pure ignorance, or through the failure of imagination. Popular author Malcolm Gladwell cites shipping magnate Malcolm McLean as an example of an extraordinary leader who did not allow himself or his success to be hampered by assumptions caused by a lack of imagination.

McLean had his beginnings in the trucking industry, before he decided midway to go into the shipping business. At that time, the shipping industry was constrained by the cost of loading and unloading the cargo. The costs were so prohibitive that many multinational corporations that would have increased their profits through overseas expansion could not be bothered with it. Nonetheless, McLean was not satisfied with this state of affairs. Going against the scepticism of onlookers, he set about trying to make shipping a more efficient activity.

By this time, the idea of using containers to transport goods was no longer novel—in fact, people had experimented with the use of containers for 30 years only to fail utterly. Containers were too heavy, bulky and inconvenient. Everyone in the shipping industry assumed that containers were the problem. McLean, however, went beyond the conventional wisdom that containers had to be adapted for effective use in shipping. Instead of focusing on the individual components, McLean adopted systems thinking. He did not try to design lighter containers: instead, he redesigned the connection between the cargo truck and the containers. To facilitate the process of transporting the cargo, McLean thought of a railway line that could help the cranes to transport the containers.

The people who came before Malcolm McLean were restricted by their own mind-sets, as entrenched as they were in their existing worldview. They were unable to go beyond the assumption of the constraints and capability that they had set for themselves, and were consequently tripped up by their lack of imagination. As Gladwell explains, McLean's success was initiated by his willingness to "[reimagine] their world by reframing the problem in a way no one [else] had framed it before."[5]

The importance of imagination in foresight cannot be overstated.

While it is important to identify assumptions, it serves no purpose if nothing is done about them. The final section of the chapter looks at the evaluation and review of assumptions.

EVALUATING ASSUMPTIONS

After identifying assumptions in your worldview, evaluate them. Test your assumptions (see Fig. 7 overleaf). Are they valid?

If they are, keep them, but return to them in the future when parameters change. As the example of the Yom Kippur war shows, one dangerous tendency is to persist with the assumption that the historical precedent would always hold true.

Parameters change. Operating conditions shift. When this happens, be prepared to discard existing assumptions that may have once been true, but have since been rendered irrelevant by evolving circumstances.

In other words, if your assumptions are invalid, discard them. Instead, head back to the drawing board to look at the underlying patterns and

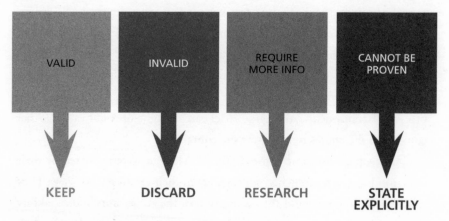

Figure 7: Evaluating Assumptions

forces driving the phenomena you are concerned with. If more information is required, carry out research in the necessary areas.

Sometimes, however, there may be insufficient information to prove or disprove the assumption. When this happens, state explicitly the assumptions being made. Many people are uncomfortable with this notion because it exposes uncertainty. Yet articulating assumptions ensures that people are aware of the mental framework guiding the decisions being made. This makes it easier to adjust the course of action when parameters change or variables become known.

Assumptions form the bedrock of your premises and worldview. If you hope to obtain more accurate constructs about future outcomes, you need to return to the fundamentals to test them and ensure that they are as robust as possible.

CONCLUSION

The identification of assumptions is never easy. Yet it is absolutely crucial to invest both time and energy to identifying the assumptions that underpin your worldview. Foresight is about providing clarity in the way you see the future; the identification of assumptions clarifies your vision. Better-informed decisions can only be made when you are able to accurately see where you are going.

Throughout the FUSE decision-making process, assumptions will continue to surface. Prudent decision-makers will not ignore them, but will diligently clarify and test them.

In the subsequent chapters of this section, the previous three components of the Foresight process are brought together in the development of scenarios.

CHAPTER 8
BUILDING SCENARIOS

THE TRANSFORMATIVE NATURE OF SCENARIOS

The year was 1991. In South Africa, negotiations had begun the year before to dismantle apartheid, a system of enforced racial segregation that had been in place since 1948. These negotiations would last another two years before democratic elections were held in 1994.

The 1994 elections marked the first time universal suffrage was granted to all South Africans. The African National Congress (ANC), a social democratic political party first founded in 1912 in support of increased rights for black South Africans, swept the majority of the seats, forming a Government of National Unity with the Afrikaner nationalist National Party as well as the Inkatha Freedom Party. Over the next two years, the legal apparatus of apartheid would gradually be abolished.

Back in 1991, however, a Shell executive by the name of Adam Kahane arrived in Cape Town, where a very special exercise was being conducted at a conference venue known as Mont Fleur. The initial name of the project was "An Alternative Scenario Planning Exercise of the Left". Later on, it would become known simply as the "Mont Fleur Scenarios".

In a country torn apart by apartheid, the Mont Fleur Scenarios was remarkable in the way it brought together a group of individuals with extremely diverse life experiences. Participants included a former official of the socialist National Union of Mineworkers, his adversary from the white

Afrikaner executive committee of the oppressive Chamber of Mines, and a party head from the ANC. Former enemies, captives and subjugators were all in the same room with one another. It was extraordinary.

Beyond the sheer incredibleness of it all, the diverse nature of the team produced alternative perspectives of the situation facing South Africa. This gifted the developed scenarios with legitimacy.

The Mont Fleur Scenarios also transformed the mental frameworks of individuals by promoting a shared language every one of them could understand. The scenarios did not ask participants to predict what they think would happen, nor did they ask the participants what they believed should happen. Rather, the scenarios focused solely on what participants thought *could* happen.

Because the scenarios were neither prescriptive nor subjective, each of the participants was able to put their personal biases aside.

The participants had fun with this exercise. Some of the more outlandish scenarios included the takeover of the South African government by the opposition's armed forces aided by the Chinese People's Liberation Army. However, implausible scenarios were typically quickly banished when the participants themselves realised the logical flaws in the scenario.

After the scenarios were rigorously tested and evaluated for plausibility and coherency, they were whittled down to four key stories (see Fig. 8 overleaf). The names of the scenarios capture the essence of the story being told:

> **Ostrich**: A free election does not occur. The white segregationists gain in influence. Just like how an ostrich buries its head in the sand, they refuse to negotiate with their political opponents and polarise the country. The various parties are eventually forced to return to the negotiating table under deteriorating social, political and economic conditions.

> **Lame Duck**: There is a prolonged transition period where a weak transitional coalition government runs the country.

Immense uncertainty results, leading to slow growth and development. Incapacity of the country occurs. South Africa in effect becomes a lame duck.

Icarus: A black government comes into power and tries to fulfil the promises it made during its political campaign. Public spending goes through the roof. Increasing expenditure is unsustainable, and eventually causes the economy to crash. This scenario takes reference from the legend of Icarus who flew too close to the sun and melted his wax wings. Icarus subsequently plunged to his death.

Flamingos: A coalition government comes to power and participatory decision-making occurs. This is similar to flamingos, which fly together in groups.

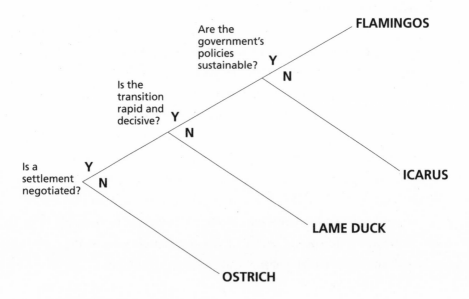

Figure 8: The Mont Fleur Scenarios Map

These scenarios were extremely useful because they challenged the premises of the participants. They exposed logical fallacies, assumptions and leaps in logic in the mental models of individuals, and gave a common focus to a shared future. Having had perspectives reframed, action steps could then be postulated to achieve the common goal.

For example, the "Icarus" scenario highlighted the possibility of a leftist government trying to do too much. This was important because it compelled left-wing economists to consider seriously the implications of socialist policies. Similarly, participants realised that the most optimistic of all the scenarios—the "Flamingos" scenario—was not impossible to achieve, and they were able to map out the steps needed to achieve this particular future.

In the aftermath of the 1994 elections, the scenarios developed at Mont Fleur were to have a transformative effect on the country. Many of the participants at the exercise were prominent individuals in South African society. During the scenario-building exercises, they were able to cultivate trust and develop a shared language with one another. This had a lasting impact on their relationships with each other, consequently changing the course of history in South Africa.

Of the four scenarios developed, "Icarus" was especially useful because it directly challenged the economic orthodoxy of the ANC government. The ANC coalition government was under tremendous pressure from its constituents to borrow and spend money to address the inequalities of apartheid. The "Icarus" scenario, however, made the ANC realise that the threat of overspending, even if for the good intention of promoting social justice, was real. Fiscal imbalance could end up jeopardising the country's future.

Eventually, the South African government took a stance of fiscal discipline, enabling its annual real rate of growth to increase from 1% between 1984 and 1994 to 3% between 1994 and 2004. In the wake of the 2009 global recession, Clem Sunter, Chair of the Anglo American Chairman's Fund, attributed the success of South Africa's post-apartheid transformation to the Scenario Planning exercises: "So take a bow, all you who were involved in the Mont Fleur initiative. You may have changed our history at a critical juncture."[1]

SCENARIO PLANNING IN SINGAPORE

The above example is just but one example of how scenarios have been used successfully to affect a positive outcome by thinking about the future before the future arrives. Other countries that have adopted scenarios in their strategic planning exercises include Singapore, Britain as well as Finland.

In Singapore, the government recognised the utility of Scenario Planning by creating the Scenario Planning Office (SPO) under the auspices of the Prime Minister's Office (PMO) in 1995. Under the SPO, national scenarios were constructed and continuously reviewed through the years.

The inaugural set of scenarios in 1997 underscored the importance and usefulness of such an approach. The 1997 iteration posited two plausible futures for Singapore spread over a 20-year timeline: the first scenario was called "Hotel Singapore", and depicted a country that had prioritised economic imperative at the expense of social cohesiveness and a sense of belonging. The second scenario meanwhile was called "A Home Divided", and painted an image of a country where there was no longer any cohesive national narrative. Rather, society was divided by multiple contrasting and irreconcilable narratives that challenged the national story.[2]

In the two decades after these scenarios were constructed, various social, economic and political developments have taken place. Components of the scenarios developed 20 years ago are now reverberating in present-day Singapore. The prescience of the scenarios, however, is less important than the process of generating the scenarios.

As one participant commented: "In the course of working on these scenarios, we discovered that while geopolitical and economic issues were well on the decision-makers' radar screens, softer 'social' issues like national identity, rootedness to Singapore and community ties received less attention."[3]

Scenarios thus disturbed the traditional way of thinking about Singapore's future. Policymakers realised they could no longer persist in using the singular lens of geopolitical and economic issues to look at the future. The assumption that this state of affairs would continue as per usual was squashed. At the same time, scenarios introduced an alternative way of thinking about the key factors shaping the future of Singapore. Rather than looking purely at geopolitical and economic issues, the role of social experiences among the local population was now highlighted.

Effective scenarios are those that disturb, disrupt or dislocate existing worldviews.

Scenarios disturb

The illustration of the Mont Fleur Scenarios perfectly highlights the transformative nature of scenarios. Scenarios should disturb. They must reframe mind-sets and promote alternative ways of viewing the surrounding world. As futurist Peter Schwartz writes, "scenarios deal with two worlds —the world of facts and the world of perceptions".[4] While scenarios provide direction for further research, they are really aimed at transforming the inner world of decision-makers, as seen in the South African case.

Scenarios disrupt

Scenarios should also disrupt. Kees Van Der Heijden calls scenarios "outside-in thinking", where individuals and organisations are able to stand outside the conventionally defined cognitive space to think outside the box. He contrast this to "inside-out thinking", where we are trapped within our mental frameworks, unable or unwilling to anticipate the unexpected.[5] In the case of the Mount Fleur initiative, scenarios encouraged individuals to question their worldview in a way they would not have ordinarily done.

Scenarios dislocate

Finally, scenarios should dislocate. They should help to surface and clarify assumptions. For instance, the "Icarus scenario" exposed a glaring assumption that left-leaning economists had previously ignored: that sustained social spending would be able to continue unabated without any fiscal consequences. The internally incoherent scenario showed that the premise underpinning such a belief was problematic.

SCENARIO BUILDING

There are two main ways to engage with the scenario-building process. The first makes use of the inductive process, while the second adopts a deductive approach.

Inductive scenario building begins by identifying the building blocks that make up the plausible futures. By assembling the key driving forces, predetermined elements and critical uncertainties, inductive scenario building works to project these trends and patterns forward in order to generate future scenarios.

Deductive scenario building, on the other hand, begins by locating a desired future, and then working backwards to understand what needs to happen in order to get there.

The decision to use the inductive or deductive approach is dependent on the specific needs and requirements of your organisation. Deductive scenario building may work better under a tighter time constraint, while inductive scenarios may produce a more robust scenario set to challenge the conventional worldview. Naturally, this would also demand a higher commitment in terms of time and effort.

Regardless of the approach chosen, the deductive and inductive scenario-building processes share key characteristics and features that make them useful in future(s) planning. The next two sections of this chapter will look at scenarios as interpretations of the future, as well as the importance of imagination and narratives in thinking of the future.

SCENARIOS AS MULTIPLE INTERPRETATIONS OF THE FUTURE(S)

One way of thinking about scenarios is to view them as different lenses that produce different views of the future. As author Betty Sue Flowers writes, "In a scenario team, you develop two or three different pairs of glasses to see the world through. You can put them on and off, and by doing that, it gets easier for you to see the fourth and fifth way."[6]

Scenarios are thus an exploratory tool for constructing plausible futures to develop and test strategy.

When thinking about the future, the number of possible futures that can be dreamt up is infinite, limited only by your imagination. Scenarios, however, form part of the strategic backdrop that decision-making is based on. It becomes impossible, not to mention inefficient and ineffective, to map out all the possible scenarios that could happen.

Inductive scenarios should generate plausible futures. Plausible futures are futures that "could" happen in accordance with present knowledge and information, as opposed to future knowledge of how things work.[7] This helps to narrow down the scenario-set, and keep scenarios more tightly focused.

There are two extremes on this spectrum, however: the appearance of "black swans" and the fulfilment of a probable future.

"Wildcard" events, or what writer Nassim Taleb terms as "black swans", are low probability and high impact events that overtly affect society.[8] While they can be extremely disruptive, they do not fall under the control of any particular individual nor organisation, making it futile to try and predict the appearances of black swans.

At the other end of the spectrum is the occurrence of a "probable" future, or the future that is believed to be most likely to happen. The problem with this, however, is that the "probable" future is likely to be premised on the BAU assumption. As the case of Borders makes clear, this is a dangerous fallacy, and serves no purpose other than to provide you with a fleeting sense of comfort.

Deductive scenario building, on the other hand, begins with the desired future in mind. This is otherwise known as the "preferable" scenario. While this is idealised, it allows you to work backwards to uncover what needs to fall in place before such a future can be realised. This compels a rethink of perceptions about the future as well as assumptions underpinning your worldview.

Scenarios may be interpretations of the future, but they are also fundamentally narratives that tap onto the power of imagination. The final section of this chapter will look at why the narrative function of scenarios is so important.

THE POWER OF IMAGINATION AND NARRATIVES

Scenarios are in essence narratives; they require imagination and insist on coherency to be effective. In a study on the evolution of foresight in humans done by psychologists Thomas Suddendorf and Michael Corballis, they concluded that imagination is a crucial ingredient in the conceptualisation of the future.[9] In fact, it is thought that the evolution of human language arose as a need to convey past and planned future events in order to enhance fitness in social settings.

In a 2013 studio project named "Foresight in Hindsight: A History of Predictions", Dutch architect Reinier de Graaf created a database of predictions to look at what patterns of past predictions could tell us about the future.[10] In particular, he found out that predictions were often most accurate when they were made in the most unexpected domains.

Prophets were most fluent in predicting changes to the economy, those in the arts were most accurate in anticipating technological shifts, businessmen had a surprising knack for discerning the direction of the planet and humanity, and scientists were most adept at envisioning the evolution of culture. What was most striking was how individuals were most accurate when they made predictions in a domain diametrically opposite to their field of expertise.

Why might this happen? The answer lies in imagination. Unconstrained by the cognitive frameworks and mental mind-sets that govern conventional thinking, individuals could give free rein to their imagination, without suppressing the instinct for curtailing surprises and reducing novelty.

Jules Vernes' *From the Earth to the Moon*, first published in 1865, posited a world where man could travel to the moon. A century later in 1969, Neil Armstrong became the first man to walk on the moon.

Aldous Huxley, in his dystopian novel *Brave New World*, published in 1932, dreamt up a future world where babies were made in test-tubes and drugs could psychologically alter the emotional state of individuals. In 1978, the world's first test-tube baby, Louise Brown, was born. Today, there is a whole range of hallucinogens readily available on the market that we can buy to manipulate our thoughts, emotions and consciousness.

As the great scientist and innovator Albert Einstein once said, "Imagination is more important than knowledge. For knowledge is limited, whereas imagination embraces the entire world, stimulating progress, giving birth to evolution."

The use of narratives in scenarios is also important for its ability to account for uncertainty. In today's world where computers have catalysed our move towards a more quantitative society, it is easy to get seduced by the mechanistic and straightforward nature of equations. Yet, numbers thrive on certainty and predictability. There is no scope or flexibility to accommodate the various nuances that make up human life.

Stories, on the other hand, possess the flexibility and depth to take uncertainty into account. They allow for the compression of complexity while providing structure to an often bewildering reality. Stories can be transformative—as the Mont Fleur Scenarios demonstrated, they can be persuasive in providing meaning to events, mitigating the dangers of cognitive dissonance. Crucially, stories are an effective jump-off point for questions and reflections.

CONCLUSION

Scenarios are, in essence, constructs of the future. They represent multiple interpretations of the future, and serve as a handy tool for organisations in the construction of their strategic perspective.

Scenarios are an important aspect of the FUSE process because they are able to transform mind-sets by reframing perspectives and illuminating hidden assumptions and previously unconsidered positions.

This is possible because scenarios are ultimately narratives. They fulfil the human desire for stories, and possess the unique ability to encompass the depth and complexity that define human life.

The next chapter will turn to focus on inductive scenario building, and explore the ways in which this can be done.

CHAPTER 9
INDUCTIVE SCENARIO BUILDING

This chapter maps out a systematic way of developing scenarios inductively. Using the focal question as a guide, map out the conventional worldview. Locate the assumptions driving that view. Then, test and evaluate assumptions to clarify the key driving forces shaping the future. When these have been identified, it becomes easier to identify predetermined elements and critical uncertainties. These come together in different combinations to generate a range of plausible scenarios. Fig. 9 overleaf provides an illustration of how this process would work.

SCOPING YOUR TIMEFRAME

The first step begins with the identification of a focal question. The focal question provides a focal point to scope your scenarios. How limited should your exploratory boundaries be? Alternatively, how far should you extend your gaze outwards to include less apparent elements that could potentially influence your organisation? Based on this focal question, decide on a suitable timeframe in which the scenarios will take place.

There are four broad categories used to classify the passage of time. First, there is the "here and now", which involves itself in immediate concerns.

Then there is what I call the "near world", a future time period of one to five years.

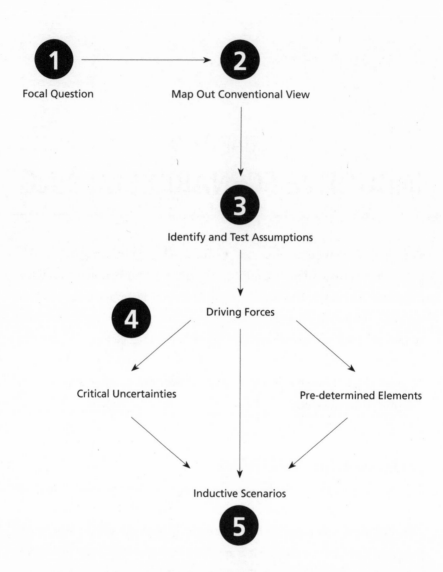

Figure 9: Process Pathway of Inductive Scenario Building

This is followed by the "future world", comprising a six- to 15-year timeframe.

Finally, there is the "far world", which stretches from 16 years to beyond.

There is a judgement call to be made as to which timeframe to work within. Events seldom occur in a sudden fashion; they are frequently an accumulation of small, incremental changes. Depending on the focal question, it might be prudent to situate your scenarios within a longer timeframe. Adopting a longer-term timeframe also provides the temporal distance that can serve to disturb the conventions governing the present.

However, decision-makers may find that thinking too far ahead leads to abstraction and a lack of actionable recommendations. Thus, the option of developing scenarios for the near and future worlds allows for more tangibility.

Once a suitable timeframe for decision-making and Scenario Planning have been determined, identify the key driving forces underpinning the futures. These driving forces will reveal the predetermined elements and critical uncertainties that will shape the futures.

IDENTIFY KEY DRIVING FORCES

The identification of assumptions inherent in your worldview would have shone a spotlight on some of the key driving forces shaping the world that you operate in today.

Key driving forces do not merely posit what may happen; rather, key driving forces explain why certain things will happen. Another way of thinking about them is to think of them as "cues for causality".[1]

Kees Van Der Heijden provides a framework for locating key driving forces using what he calls the "Iceberg Model of Knowledge".

Knowledge is viewed in terms of three distinct layers of an iceberg: at the top are the visible events. Beyond the surface of the water, however, are underlying patterns that cut across these events.[2] At the deepest level is the fundamental structure that gives meaning to these patterns. It is at this third and deepest level that key driving forces can be located (see Fig. 10 overleaf).

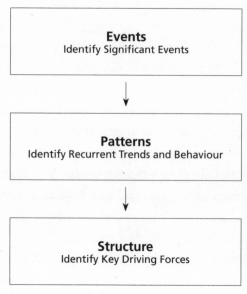

Figure 10: Identifying Key Driving Forces

In a highly complex world where even seemingly random events and occurrences are connected to one another, exercise judgement when deciding on the events that are significant to your organisation. The first order of things is to limit the scope of relevancy: which events within the changing environment possess the greatest potential significance to your focal question?

This is represented as an expanding ring of circles (see Fig. 11). The smallest circle closest to the focal question represents events of clear and immediate concern to the organisation. The succeeding circle meanwhile, refers to events that are not immediately recognisable as having a direct impact on the organisation but which potentially play a role in shaping its future. Finally, the outermost circle consists of events whose future impact are difficult to evaluate. By working outwards, it becomes easier to have a clearer sense of where explorative boundaries should be set.

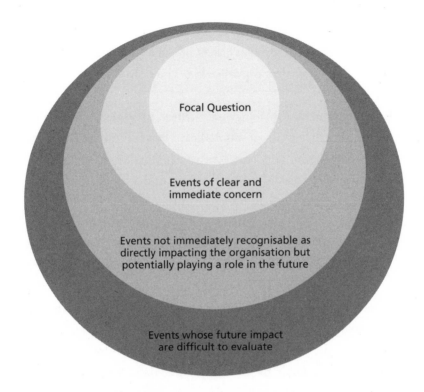

Figure 11: The Scoping Function of the Focal Question

At this point, try to infer causal patterns across these events. Why are these events happening? What is causing these events to occur? Use these causal links to draw up the exact relationship between variables. This will form your underlying structure.

While driving forces may predetermine the direction of movement, specific outcomes may be highly uncertain. By first determining the key driving forces, predetermined elements and critical uncertainties should become more apparent. Multiple interpretations of the future emerge from different combinations of the above two factors. Driving forces are thus the key elements that move the plot of a scenario, determining the story's eventual outcome.

PREDETERMINED ELEMENTS

Even in the midst of uncertainty, it is possible to locate some elements that can be safely classified as predictable. These are called predetermined elements.

Pierre Wack used the following analogy to explain predetermined elements: during the monsoon season, heavy rain falls on the upper part of the Ganges River basin.[3] It is a foregone conclusion that within the next few days, flooding would occur in the lower parts of the river basin.

In the same way, when an undersea earthquake strikes off the eastern coast of Japan, the large amounts of energy released by the subduction of tectonic plates will set in motion an inevitable path for oceanic waves to follow. By tracking the movement of the waves, geologists and scientists are able to sound a tsunami warning to the surrounding islands in the Pacific. By the time the first tsunami waves hit the beaches of Hawaii, the coastal regions would have been evacuated, thereby saving precious human lives. The tsunami is the predetermined event, set in motion by the collision of tectonic plates thousands of miles away. In other words, predetermined elements are simply the foreordained implications of an event that has already occurred.

A frequently cited predetermined element is demography. After all, the babies of today are the labour force of tomorrow. By studying today's birth rate, a picture of the demographics that would exist a decade or two from now can be confidently mapped out. Similarly, while it is impossible to predict the technological inventions of tomorrow, a trajectory of advances based on technology that have already been invented can be mapped out.

Peter Schwartz, who was working at Shell in the 1980s, provides a concrete example of a predetermined element within the American economic sphere: during a 1982 Scenario Planning exercise, several of Shell's strategists were observing the political forces shaping developments in the nation. Based on their observations, they came to the conclusion that the United States government would face a substantial budget deficit throughout the 1980s.

This was due to the confluence of several factors. For one, the two largest components of the government budget—defence spending and social security pay-outs—would increase at a manic pace, supported by the American public. Meanwhile, the US government did not possess any control over the third largest component—interest repayments on the deficit itself.

The strategists at Shell also determined that the US government would not be able to increase its revenue through tax collection as anti-tax sentiments among the American population would continue to strengthen. This was in part due to the expanding middle-classes' feelings of alienation as purchasing power remained stagnant over the previous decade.

America would thus be caught in a conundrum where its citizens petitioned to cut taxes while demanding increased government spending. If this happened, interest on the deficit would become the single biggest element within the budget, compelling the government to borrow from overseas. This would consequently lead to the fall of the dollar value alongside the increase of interest rates and the devaluation of government bonds.

This was what eventually happened.

By carefully observing the interplay of different variables as well as driving forces, Schwartz and his team were able to position the predetermined element of a US budget deficit in all of the 1980s scenarios that they hypothesised, thereby making their analysis robust and effective.[4]

Schwartz offers a framework for identifying predetermined elements.[5]

First, there is what he calls slow-changing phenomena—developments that advance incrementally but steadily. These include the growth of populations, the building of physical infrastructure, and the development of resources.

Then there are also constrained situations, where limitations will compel actors to adopt specific paths of actions. For example, should conventional energy sources run out, countries would be forced to invest in alternative energy sources.

Schwartz also talks about "inevitable collisions", where contradictory factors finally run head-on into each other. The worsening budget deficit in 1980s America is one such example of how gridlock can happen when burgeoning expenditure and declining revenues can no longer be reconciled with one another.

Predetermined elements form the basic building blocks of scenarios. Without them, scenarios become mere fantasies. In the final section of this chapter, the 1970s Shell scenario-building exercise will provide a case study of how inductive scenarios can be constructed using the predetermined elements.

RISKS AND CRITICAL UNCERTAINTIES

Risks refer to events that have a quantifiable probability of occurring. In planning for the future, risk should not be ignored but calculated and factored accurately into the scenarios.

Critical uncertainties, on the other hand, refer to variables that are important but whose outcome is unclear. While you may not know how exactly these figure in the larger scheme of things, you have a firm sense that they nevertheless play a significant role in shaping the future.

It is the action of critical uncertainties that are the most catalytic of variables to consider in scenario development. They allow for variation and range in the scenario set. While predetermined elements are common to all foresight projects attacking a similar focal question, the identification and handling of critical uncertainties will create the differences in the scenarios produced.

Estimating risks and critical uncertainties play a crucial role in developing the value of the scenarios. The capacity to challenge convention, stretch the imagination, and induce disruption—or at least discomfort in decision-makers—is ultimately determined by using these variables effectively.

USING THE BUILDING BLOCKS FOR GENERATING SCENARIOS

The most famous scenario-building exercise took place at Shell in the early 1970s.

At the time, the Shell management team was concerned about how they should be scheduling new facilities in the upcoming decade. Oil discovery and recovery was an extremely resource-intensive activity, and any decision to install a new oil rig was not taken lightly. In order to make a prudent decision, Shell needed to know how oil demand and supply was going to look like over the next few years.

First of all, oil supply is determined by the available resources and behaviour of oil-producing states. While the calculation of oil reserves may be straightforward, the Scenario Planning team had to identify the cues for causality that would guide the behaviour of oil-producing states. By looking at patterns of behaviour, the team was able to pin-point the motivating forces guiding these countries' oil policies.

In addition to the amount of oil reserves available, oil-producing countries tended to decide on oil production rates based on their ability to spend this oil income productively. For instance, in Saudi Arabia in the late 1960s, oil production would have generated more income than the government could meaningfully spend. In such a scenario, it made both political and financial sense to leave the oil underground, instead of converting it into currency, which would depreciate over time.

When Shell scanned the oil-producing countries, they looked at the interaction between oil reserves and the country's need and ability to spend their oil income productively. When they did this, they realised that none of the OPEC countries had both ample reserves and ample absorptive capacity. In other words, oil supply could be expected to decline.

The Shell scenario-planning team turned to look at the behaviour of oil-importing countries. The projected numbers were expected to continue dropping, driven by a lack of alternative energy resources and increasing domestic demands.

Even as oil supply was expected to decline, it was anticipated that oil demand would rise.

Taken together, the trend of increasing oil demand and decreasing oil supply meant that an oil shock was inevitable. This became the key predetermined element as identified by the Shell team. What was uncertain was how the world would respond to this oil crisis. The construction of different scenarios was thus based on the adoption of possible solutions. Fig. 12 below shows a decision-tree that maps out the way scenarios were constructed.

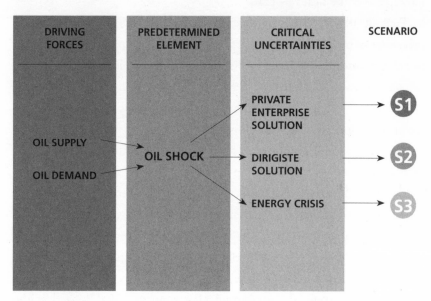

Figure 12: The Shell Inductive Scenario Building Exercise

According to the analysis performed by the Shell team, three different scenarios would occur when the oil shock happen. Because the team could not know which of these outcomes would materialise, they called them "critical uncertainties". Nevertheless, an educated guess was made.

The first scenario saw the private sector coming to the aid of declining oil production by innovating new means of energy production (S1). The second scenario, meanwhile, posited that governments would intervene (S2). The third scenario saw neither the private sector nor governments stepping up to the plate. As a result, an energy crisis ensues (S3).

In 1973, members of the Organization of Arab Petroleum Exporting Countries (OAPEC) declared an oil embargo. Oil prices shot through the roof. However, Shell had made the necessary preparations. Its upstream managers, involved in Exploration & Production, had begun looking for new relationships with producing nations. Its downstream segment, meanwhile, was forced to be more prudent in their investments. As a whole, the organisation worked to decentralise the decision-making and strategic process. From its scenario-building process, Shell realised that different motivations and circumstances would govern the behaviour of oil-producing countries differently, and there was a greater need to respond independently.

Before the oil shock of 1973, Shell had been called the "ugly sister" of the seven major oil companies by *Forbes*. When the oil crisis hit, however, Shell's foresight placed it at a significant advantage vis-à-vis the other oil companies. Shell eventually emerged from the crisis stronger, catapulting to the top of the heap.

CONCLUSION

Inductive scenario building is a useful tool for clarifying the future. It does this by projecting trends and patterns forward through the identification of predetermined elements and critical uncertainties.

The next and final chapter of this section turns to look at deductive scenario building. Unlike inductive scenario building, the deductive approach works backwards by starting from a desired future.

CHAPTER 10
DEDUCTIVE SCENARIO BUILDING

In Indonesia today, the 12th century King Jayabaya remains widely revered among the Javanese population. His prophecies, made nearly a millennium ago, continue to persist within the popular imagination, making prominent appearances in political speeches and the mass media.

During the 19th century Dutch colonial period, one particular prophesy of Jayabaya gained much traction among the local population: Java would be liberated from its European oppressors with the coming of a "Just King", or *Ratu Adil*. This "Just King", like Jayabaya, would be an emissary of Allah. (In the Hindu version both the *Ratu Adil* and Jayabaya are described as the incarnations of the Hindu deity Vishnu.)

This prophecy formed a focal point for the locals to rally around, eventually mobilising large resistance movements against the Dutch.[1] The most famous rebellion was led by a man named Diponegoro, who was widely believed to be the *Ratu Adil* in question.

We will never know if Jayabaya was truly a psychic. Jayabaya's prophecy, however, came to represent for the Javanese people a scenario of an ideal future where the people no longer lived under Dutch oppression.

The prophecy served as a desired end-point, and motivated the people to action. With a clear picture of their ideal future, the Javanese were able to map out the steps that they had to take in order to move closer to achieving such a future.

Deductive scenario building is similar. By mapping out the ideal future, external enablers and derailers can be identified by working backwards. This helps to assess the plausibility of such a scenario.

CONSTRUCTING YOUR IDEAL FUTURE

Constructing a preferable scenario of the future is the most straightforward element of the entire Foresight process. Often, without even deliberately setting out to do so, we usually already have an idea of how our ideal world would look like.

The key then, is to map out this ideal scenario in detail. What kind of scenario would place you in the best position to achieve your goals?

As it was with the inductive scenario-building process, the first thing to do is to determine the timeframe that you wish to operate in.

Following this, identify the desired outcomes. Where do you want your organisation to be after a predetermined period of time? Be specific and be precise. Ask yourself which political, economic, social and technological conditions would best achieve these desired outcomes? Weave together a narrative of this preferred future.

IDENTIFYING ENABLERS AND DERAILERS

Having constructed the ideal scenario, work backwards to identify external enablers and derailers. Enablers are essentially factors that facilitate the pursuit of the desired future, while derailers are factors that hinder the attainment of this same future.

What would be needed to attain this preferred future? Conversely, what would deter this future from being realised?

Recall the PEST framework used earlier (see Fig. 13 overleaf). By systematically using the PEST framework to identify enablers and derailers in the external environment, the future can be better clarified.

Using the ideal scenario as the starting point, deductive scenario building compels you to seriously consider factors previously overlooked or overstated.

By working backwards to figure out how such an ideal future could occur, logic gaps, misplaced optimism and invalidated assumptions should begin to surface. A scenario previously thought of as feasible may turn out to be based on some very questionable premises. On the other hand, certain scenarios may be found to have been too quickly dismissed.

Political	**Economic**
What are the global, regional, and national political developments that will affect the achievement of the desired future?	How would changes in the global, regional and national economy affect the desired future?
Social	**Technological**
Which social factors and developments would influence the future of your organisation?	How can current advances in technology be applied in a way that affects your organisation's future?

Figure 13: PEST Framework

CONCLUSION

There are three key takeaways from the FUSE Foresight process.

First, assumptions are powerful. They form the bedrock of mental models, and ultimately affect the way you see the world. The problem, however, is that they are often invisible.

A more effective scenario-building process requires you to be conscious of your assumptions and deliberate in your attempts to test and evaluate them. It is only by clarifying assumptions that you are able to obtain a more objective perspective of what is going on around you.

Second, even after assumptions have been clarified, it is often difficult to uproot or transform entrenched mind-sets. This is where scenarios come in. The use of coherent narratives helps the human mind to make that cognitive leap to accept alternative perspectives when facts and figures fail.

This concludes with the third and final point: imagination is more important than knowledge. As Einstein once stated, "[...] knowledge is limited to all we now know and understand, while imagination embraces the whole world, and all there ever will be to know and understand." Without imagination, we will be stuck in the same old rut, simply accepting the status quo, unable to envision a better future. Without imagination, it is difficult to embrace the uncertainty of the world—you remain trapped in a mental prison of your own making.

Simply clarifying your understanding of the external world, however, is insufficient. The next section on Understanding turns inwards to examine the internal world. Using the insights derived from both the external and internal environment, a strategic perspective can be developed. It is against this backdrop that strategy is formed.

THE FORESIGHTING PROCESS

1. **Locate the focal question**
   - The focal question keeps the Foresighting process focused and relevant.
   - The focal question should be reviewed periodically.
   - The focal question clarifies the highest-order concern of your organisation.
   - To identify the focal question:
     - Decide who should be involved
     - Identify a focal area of concern
     - Consider higher-level organisational goals

2. **Map out the conventional view of the future in relation to the focal question**
   - A map of your existing view of the future helps to uncover assumptions.
   - This process can be facilitated using the Institution-Agent Matrix (see page 77), where interactions between institutions and agents are studied.
   - Institutions are structural patterns that influence and constrain the opportunities available. They may be found in the realm of:
     - Politics
     - Economy
     - Society
     - Technology
   - Agents are individuals or organisations that are able to act independently to exert an influence on the opportunities available. They include:
     - Patrons
     - Constituents
     - Peers
     - Disruptors

3. **Identify and evaluate assumptions**
   - Assumptions are important because they:
     - Underpin our outlook of the future
     - Reveal biases
     - Clarify the focal question
   - To identify assumptions:
     - Ask why
     - Put together a Team B
     - Develop counterarguments and counterexamples
   - Assumptions may be about:
     - Resources
     - Constraints
     - Priorities
     - Capabilities
     - Causality
   - We make assumptions because of:
     - Past experiences
     - Ideology
     - Biases
     - Ignorance
   - Assumptions need to be evaluated:
     - If they are valid, keep them
     - If they are invalid, discard them
     - If more information is required, conduct further research
     - If they cannot be proven, state them explicitly

4. **Build scenarios**
   - Scenarios are constructs of the future.
   - Effective scenarios are able to transform mind-sets by reframing perspectives.
   - The use of narrative in scenarios also allows complexity and uncertainty to be incorporated into the story.

○ Scenarios can be deductive or inductive:
- Inductive scenario building projects trends and patterns forward through the identification of predetermined elements and critical uncertainties.
- Deductive scenario building begins from the desired future. It works backwards to identify the enablers and derailers that would either facilitate or hinder the attainment of such a future.

SECTION 3
UNDERSTANDING

CHAPTER 11
INTRODUCTION TO UNDERSTANDING

GNOTHI SEAUTON – "KNOW THYSELF"

In ancient Greece, anyone who wanted to consult the Delphi Oracle had to first pass through the forecourt of the Temple of Apollo, where, if legend is to be believed, the god Apollo himself ordained the inscription of the Greek precept *Gnothi Seauton*, or "Know Thyself."

Croesus, King of Lydia, was one of the many pilgrims who sought advice from the oracle. His question was simple: "Sons were born to me, and therein Apollo's word was not false: but nought did these sons profit me. For one was dumb, and the other was cut off by death in the prime of manhood. Whereupon I sent again to ask the oracle what I should do to enable me to pass the remnant of my days most happily."[1]

To this, Apollo replied through the oracle: "Know thyself, Croesus; then happy wilt thou live and die."

Croesus was overjoyed upon receiving this counsel: after all, "other men, indeed, one might or might not know: but each must know himself."

Yet, as Croesus tragically discovered, his joy was but fleeting. Unable to accurately assess his own capabilities, he made the ill-advised decision to take on the Persian army. The Persian army turned out to be far stronger than his own military force, and Croesus consequently died a defeated man in captivity, a kingdom wrecked and an entire royal lineage destroyed.

We learn two things from this story. First, self-knowledge is essential. Second, self-knowledge is difficult to attain.

THE IMPORTANCE OF SELF-KNOWLEDGE

The great military general and strategist Sun Tzu once said, "If you know the enemy and know yourself, you need not fear the result of a hundred battles. If you know yourself but not the enemy, for every victory gained you will suffer a defeat. If you know *neither* the enemy nor yourself, you will succumb in every battle."

The previous section highlighted the importance of foresight by exploring how the mental lenses used to perceive the future ultimately affect your understanding of the world. Yet as the story of Croesus demonstrates, foresight alone is not enough.

Without genuine insights into yourself, you will not be able to effectively evaluate how you should interact with the external environment to generate the best possible outcomes.

Strategy, then, is not so much a response to the external environment than it is a response to your external environment *according* to the conditions of your internal world.

The great philosopher Socrates was acutely aware of the importance of self-knowledge. In a conversation with Euthydemus, an ambitious young man with knowledge but no practical experience, Socrates extolled the benefits of self-knowledge while warning Euthydemus of the dangers of self-delusion. It is worth quoting Socrates at length:

> "Isn't [it] obvious that people derive most of their benefits from knowing themselves, and most of their misfortunes from being self-deceived? Those who know themselves know what is appropriate for them and can distinguish what they can and cannot do; and, by doing what they understand, they both supply their needs and enjoy success, while, by refraining from

doing things that they don't understand, they avoid making mistakes and escape misfortune." [2]

Self-knowledge permits you to accurately assess your options based on the knowledge of what you are able and unable to do. You will not walk off a cliff because you know that you cannot fly. Similarly, a general would not choose to go to war if he or she knows that the troops are ill-equipped to fight a strong enemy.

The maxim holds true in business as well. Take the multinational conglomerate Procter & Gamble (P&G), for example. P&G is one of the world's largest companies selling packaged goods, counting more than 80 brands under its belt. Braun, Downy, Gillette, Olay, Pampers, Oral-B and Tide are just among a small sampling of its brands that rake in more than US$1 billion in net sales annually.

Driving the development of these products is a keen focus on innovation. Like many other product companies, P&G traditionally relied on a strong internal Research and Development (R&D) department in its efforts to continuously innovate. Yet in the early 2000s, the management team was forced to come to a realisation about their internal capabilities in the midst of a changing external environment.

The P&G R&D team had hit a plateau in terms of productivity, and the innovation success rate laid stagnant at around 35%.[3] The market sent a strong signal about its declining growth when P&G's stock plummeted by more than half, from $118 to $52 a share.

Then-Vice President of Innovation, Larry Huston, was tasked with coming up with a solution to this problem of innovating. Huston understood a few things: he understood that R&D budgets were rising faster than sales growth; he understood that the rise of technology was unprecedented; he understood that P&G was now a $70 billion company with very different capacities and capabilities than when it was a $25 billion company. Finally, Huston also understood that P&G, with its wide range of products, would not be able to build all of the scientific capabilities it needed by itself.[4]

In a break away from conventional business strategy, Huston introduced a new innovation model known today as "Connect + Develop". Under this model of innovation, P&G no longer depended on an internal team of scientists and researchers. Rather, it decided to "view the outside world as the other half of [its] R&D lab".[5] By 2006, more than 35% of its new products on the market were developed in part outside of the company, compared with 15% in 2000. Another 45% of the initiatives in P&G's product development portfolio had key elements that were discovered outside the company. More significantly, R&D productivity increased by 60% as the innovation success rate doubled alongside a drop in innovation costs.[6]

Understanding its own limitations had allowed P&G to take appropriate action. P&G first recognised that its nature and characteristics as a large company had changed. What it could and could not do was no longer the same as when it was a much smaller company with a lower shareholder value.

Second, P&G was cognizant of its *inability* to expand innovation further by depending exclusively on an internal team of researchers. This self-knowledge spurred the company to take action, eventually producing concrete and visible benefits in the form of increased growth and falling costs.

SELF-KNOWLEDGE IS NOT EASY

As Croesus discovered, however, the second thing about self-knowledge is that it is not easy to acquire. In fact, it can be downright difficult.

The Greek philosopher Thales, when asked about the most difficult thing to know, replied, "Thyself." Yet we are often deceived into thinking that the converse is true.

The Foresight process talked about the mental filter used to view the external environment. Assumptions can cloud this vision, resulting in perceptions that are warped and inaccurate. We encounter a similar phenomenon when trying to understand our inner world. This phenomenon is otherwise known as "biases".

A bias is a tendency or inclination that shapes the way you perceive things. Because it is often implicit, it becomes a blind spot in your judgement and evaluation of information, including the way you evaluate yourself.

One common bias that frequently muddles self-perception is the "overconfidence effect". Researchers have shown how time and time again, people consistently overestimate their own abilities regardless of actual performance.

In a study conducted by psychologist Ola Svenson in 1980, he interviewed two groups of drivers—one group included students from the University of Oregon, while the other consisted of students from the University of Stockholm.[7] In each group, Svenson discovered that people tended to regard themselves as being more skillful and less dangerous than the average driver: 88% of students in the US regarded themselves as being safer than the median driver while 77% of the Swedish students thought themselves so.

In another survey done on the self-perception of drivers, Caroline Preston and Stanley Harris compared 50 drivers whose driving had resulted in serious accidents with another 50 drivers who never had a driving accident. When asked how they would rate themselves as "safe" drivers, both groups had almost identical proportions of people who deemed their driving skills better than average. This was despite the fact that out of the 50 drivers involved in accidents, 34 of them were judged to be at fault.[8]

The tendency to overestimate our own abilities hinders us from obtaining an accurate assessment of ourselves.

But why do we tend towards overconfidence when assessing our own abilities?

Scholars have identified three key reasons. The first is that overconfidence provides psychological benefits. As writer Aldous Huxley notes, "If most of us remain ignorant of ourselves, it is because self-knowledge is painful and we prefer the pleasures of illusion."[9] Human beings tend to cling on to a better image of ourselves because to do so otherwise would be damaging to our self-esteem,[10] to our mental health and even to the way we are motivated on certain tasks.

A second reason lies in our cognitive processes. Man is not the rational creature that economists frequently posit him to be. Instead, there are numerous logical fallacies in the way we process information that results in a distorted view of ourselves. For example, people are more likely to recall their successes as compared to their failures, making it difficult to obtain an objective assessment of their true abilities.[11]

A third reason is related to the association of overconfidence with social benefits. Researchers from the University of California, Berkeley, found that people frequently overestimated their performance or abilities because of the incentive to achieve higher social status.[12]

In other words, the overconfidence effect derives from three distinct factors: our psychological desires, our cognitive process, and the incentive factor. These are the same forces that underpin many of the other biases encountered on a day-to-day basis.

A later chapter will highlight some of the common biases encountered in our ordinary lives. A typology of these biases will help to identify some practical and useful solutions to mitigating such biases. It may not be possible to eliminate biases completely, but their effects should hopefully be reduced to a minimum.

OUTLINE OF THE SECTION

The second chapter of this section focuses on confronting biases. One of the keys to acquiring a better and more accurate understanding of yourself is to remove the biases clouding your vision. The first step to self-knowledge, then, is to become aware of your biases, and work towards mitigating them as best as you can.

Having accomplished that, return to the scenario-set previously developed in the earlier section on Foresight. In light of the different plausible future(s), what is the desired vision for yourself and your organisation? Where do you want to see yourself and your organisation in the future?

Self-knowledge goes beyond the mere identification of your strengths and weaknesses; it demands a conscious articulation of what you desire for your future. Visualising the desired end-point does two things for you: one, it highlights clearly the action steps needed to take to get there; and two, it serves as a motivating force that spurs you into action. In an organisation where there may be multiple layers of hierarchies and separate departments, the development of a shared, desired vision for the future serves as a focal point that everyone can work towards.

The third step in the Understanding process is "In-sighting". Against the backdrop of the scenario-set and the desired vision, map out the internal enablers and derailers affecting your pathway to your desired future. While enablers aid movement towards the desired future, derailers are obstacles that prevent you from reaching your vision of the future.

While a set of enablers and derailers were identified in a previous chapter on deductive scenario building, these were related to the external environment. In-sighting turns your focus inwards to uncover the internal factors that will either advance your cause or hamper your drive towards your desired vision.

The sequencing of steps here is deliberate. The desired vision plotted out earlier serves as a focal point of concentration: rather than simply listing strengths and weaknesses, the identification of enablers and derailers compels the anticipation of possibility in relation to a given vision.

At the same time, evaluate yourself in light of external conditions by returning to the use of the scenario-set. This differs from the conventional SWOT (Strengths, Weaknesses, Opportunities and Threats) approach because the internal aspects are now examined with the external environment in mind. Both the internal and external environment are aligned to an appropriate degree.

Finally, establish the strategic perspective. This step connects the outputs from the Foresight and Understanding processes with the Strategy process. The strategic perspective forms the backdrop for strategy formulation. It is a statement that articulates how you want to get to your desired vision based on an identification of enablers and derailers. If the strategic perspective is clear, your strategy will be clear.

The entire process pathway for Understanding is mapped out in Fig. 14.

The next chapter begins by understanding why biases, particularly those that are not immediately obvious, are so dangerous. A few particularly salient biases that affect decision-making will be identified, and mitigating solutions presented.

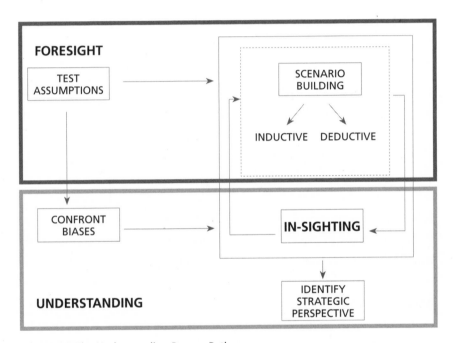

Figure 14: The Understanding Process Pathway

CHAPTER 12
CONFRONTING BIASES

Biases affect decision-making behaviour. They are often implicit. It is important to spend time interrogating your subconscious to identify your biases. If the inner workings are not appropriately tweaked and adjusted, changes to the exterior will be merely superficial.

IDENTIFYING BIASES: A TYPOLOGY OF BIASES

Biases are rooted in psychological and cognitive processes. However, they may arise for a number of reasons, including that of ideology, historical experience, operational experience, institutionalisation, heuristics and bounded rationality.

Biases can only be recognised when you are aware that such biases exist. In order to facilitate this process, a typology of biases is provided (see Fig. 15).

Biases are grouped into four key categories: motivational biases, organisational biases, reductionist biases, as well as framing biases.

While motivational biases are primarily a product of psychological factors, organisational biases derive from the structural characteristics of institutions. Reductionist and framing biases, meanwhile, are a result of faulty reasoning in our cognitive processing.

Motivational Biases	Organisational Biases	Reductionist Biases	Framing Biases
1. Egocentrism 2. Confirmation Bias 3. Cognitive Dissonance 4. Positive Illusion	1. Integration 2. Decentralisation of Incentives 3. Groupthink	1. Single-Cause Fallacy 2. Correlation-Causality Fallacy 3. *Deformation Professionnelle*	1. Salience Effect 2. Sunk-Cost Fallacy 3. Hyperbolic Discounting

Figure 15: Typology of Biases

MOTIVATIONAL BIASES

Motivational biases are related to the human ego. It is a form of bias that places the individual at the centre of his or her world, without regard for other individuals or considerations.

Egocentrism

The most obvious motivational bias is egocentrism. Egocentrism is rooted in self-interest. This is problematic, especially when organisational well-being is not aligned with individual well-being. People become biased towards making choices that protect their personal positions. This could threaten the overall welfare of the organisation.

Confirmation bias

A common by-product of egocentrism is confirmation bias. Individuals tend to gravitate towards information that confirms their own beliefs and hypotheses. Consequently, this may lead to satisficing outcomes when individuals become trapped inside their own mental framework and are unable to consider alternative perspectives.

In a study done by researchers at the University of Texas at Austin, South Korean investors who frequented Internet message boards were found to seek out opinions corresponding to their own. These investors were not interested in alternative views; instead, they actively sought similar views so as to validate their own opinions, falling prey to confirmation bias.

The problem was, confirmation bias blocked out different views that could have helped to procure greater accuracy and objectivity. This created a false sense of infallibility, and led to misplaced overconfidence among investors.

A bias towards one's own opinions placed these investors at a disadvantage. In the same study, investors who exhibited overconfident behaviour as a result of confirmation bias were more likely to obtain lower realised returns. Not only was their information more likely to be inaccurate, their misplaced sense of confidence also spurred them to trade more frequently.[1]

Cognitive dissonance

The centrality of the self in the decision-making process makes it easy for cognitive dissonance to occur. When contradictory information emerges to disrupt the existing values, beliefs and attitudes held by individuals, individuals may attempt to rationalise the contradicting piece of information away, or try to avoid the new piece of information entirely.

Leon Festinger, a social psychologist who first studied cognitive dissonance in 1957, conducted an experiment in which participants were asked to complete a boring task. Afterwards, they had to tell another person that the task was exciting. Half of the participants were paid $1 to do this, while the other half was paid $20.

Participants were asked to evaluate the experiment. Those who were paid $1 were more likely to indicate that the tedious task was fun and enjoyable compared to the participants who were paid $20 to lie.

This result differed from the projected outcome posited by behaviourist theory, which predicted that those who were paid $20 would enjoy the task more since they would associate it with a higher payment.

Cognitive dissonance theory, on the other hand, believes that those who were paid a mere $1 would feel the greatest dissonance between their action and their reward. As a result, they try to rationalise their behaviour by convincing themselves that the act was not that boring after all.[2]

In a different participant observation study, Festinger looked at a cult group that believed that the earth was going to be destroyed by a flood. When this did not happen, core members of the group tried to rationalise the inconsistency by arguing that the earth was spared from destruction because of their faithfulness.[3]

Humans often commit cognitive dissonance because they find it difficult to accept that they may have been wrong. As the historian Avi Shlaim writes, "Once a preconception or a theory about the enemy behaviour becomes settled, it is very hard to shake it until it is too late because of the human attachment to old beliefs and the equally stubborn resistance to new material that will upset them." This is a dangerous situation to be in, especially when the stakes are high.

Positive illusion bias

A final motivational bias I will touch on here is known as the positive illusion bias. Again, self-evaluation can become horribly skewed when people believe that they can control the uncontrollable.

In a series of experiments done in 1975, Ellen Langer illustrated how people often overestimated the amount of control they possessed, even when the situation was governed purely by chance.[4]

In one of her experiments, she divided her respondents into two groups. The first group was allowed to pick their own lottery tickets, but the second group had another person pick it for them. When the participants were given the option of exchanging their ticket for one with a higher probability of winning, the individuals who had selected their own lottery ticket were less likely to choose to take part in this exchange. This was in spite of the higher probability of winning offered by the new lottery ticket. People seemed to believe that the act of choosing their own ticket increased their chances of winning. In other words, they believed that they wielded greater control over the outcome of the lottery by being personally involved in the selection of the lottery ticket.

The belief in one's ability to influence chance is misleading, and may lead to unpleasant consequences when caution is thrown to the wind.

ORGANISATIONAL BIASES

Compared to motivational biases, organisational biases are more apparent because they can be found in the structural inadequacies of organisations. There are three key organisational biases that frequently occur. They are listed below.

Integration

The first organisational bias is the failure of integration.

This is unsurprising. In the business climate of today, complex organisations face heterogeneous environments where the pace and rate of change in different sectors may be at variance to each other. In order to promote greater flexibility, complex organisations often differentiate themselves into smaller subsystems that operate in separate silos.

Nonetheless, there remains a need for integration. Organisations need to have a unified flow of information and knowledge to maintain efficiency and effectiveness in their operations. The contradiction lies in the way differentiation and integration are inherently antagonistic to one another. As Paul Lawrence and Jay Lorsch show in a comparative study of six organisations, there is an inverse relationship between the degree of differentiation and the degree of integration of behaviour and orientation obtained between these subsystems.[5]

The lack of integration in complex organisations leads to severe ramifications when important pieces of the puzzle are left unconnected. The September 11, 2001 attacks are a sober reminder of the grim consequences when intelligence is not adequately integrated among the relevant agencies.

The final 9/11 commission report released in 2004 highlighted the inadequacy of coordination between national intelligence agencies.[6] Sadly, it was not for lack of information that the 9/11 attacks happened; rather, the lack of information integration across agencies permitted one of the worst terrorist attacks in recent history to take place on American soil.

In the year and a half leading up to the 9/11 attacks, the FBI had the opportunity to monitor two of the 9/11 hijackers—Nawaf al-Hazmi and Khalid al-Mihdhar—via an informant. The problem was that the FBI had no idea who the two men were. The CIA, which had identified the two men as potential terrorists, did not pass on pertinent information to the FBI. This created information gaps, and forsook windows of opportunities that could have diverted the course of history.

Since 9/11, American intelligence agencies have been working towards a better integration of information and coordination efforts. This includes the establishment of interagency centres, such as the National Counterterrorism Center (NCTC) and the National Counterproliferation Center (NCPC). In addition, there has been greater emphasis placed on information sharing by means of the Information Sharing Environment (ISE), a partnership that aims to bridge the gap between foreign and domestic intelligence responsibilities. Collaborative Technology Tools have also been developed to further foster a culture of collaboration and improved information sharing.

Decentralisation of incentives

Related to the problem of integrative biases is the misalignment or decentralisation of incentives. When organisational and individual incentives are not aligned, two things may happen.

The first is that people with the relevant insight may not act to implement positive change because they lack a personal incentive to do so.

The second is that people may have a personal incentive to harm the organisation. This in particular, often happens when organisations become too highly differentiated. A collective action problem may arise in which leaders of subsystems are rewarded for pursuing narrow interests that are unaligned with the greater good of the organisation.

Groupthink

Finally, organisational biases can be found in the phenomenon of groupthink. One of the most embarrassing foreign policy gaffes committed by a US president was the failed Bay of Pigs invasion of Cuba in 1961. Why did a group of highly-trained and intelligent men believe that a small group of 1,400 soldiers would be able to defeat and overthrow Fidel Castro's regime?

As Irving Janis wrote in his 1972 book, aptly titled *Victims of Groupthink*, the desire for consensus suppressed any realistic appraisal of alternative paths of action.[7] John F. Kennedy's advisers were pressured by an atmosphere of docility based on a set of social norms that discouraged dissenting opinions. Consequently, the Bay of Pigs invasion was a brutal failure, with more than 1,200 of the soldiers captured and another 100 slaughtered.

Just as overconfidence may arise from the desire for greater social status, the converse is also true. People may try to fit in or conform to the prevailing order of the day to ensure that their social status is not threatened. However, social factors are not the only reason why biases occur. The next section will look at a few common cognitive biases.

REDUCTIONIST BIASES

Biases may occur as a result of our cognitive processes. One group of cognitive biases that commonly occur is known as reductionist biases. These biases operate like a filter, sieving out portions of information that may be relevant and significant.

While reductionist biases may not always be detrimental—for example, the use of heuristics based on operational experience helps cut down on the time spent on decision-making—they may restrict your understanding of the world, thereby affecting the way you make decisions.

Single-cause fallacy

The single-cause fallacy is one such example. This refers to the tendency for people to reduce complex problems to a single causal factor.

For instance, a politician might claim that the introduction of the death penalty has led to lower crime rates. Yet such a statement is necessarily reductive in the way it leaves out a host of other plausible explanations.

For instance, security measures may have resulted in better surveillance and hence crime prevention. The decline in poverty rates could also be another factor in accounting for the fall in the crime rate as people become secure in their basic needs. Even demographic change, in the form of an ageing society, could be another plausible explanation for the drop in crime.

To reduce a complex phenomenon to a singular cause is dangerous because it neglects other causal factors involved. This has repercussions in the way decisions are made: in this case, it could lead to a stricter enforcement of the death penalty. It is thus important to examine all the possible factors involved before jumping to a hasty conclusion.

Correlation-causality fallacy

Another common but dangerous reductionist bias is the correlation-causality fallacy. This refers to the tendency for people to assume that if two events consistently occur together, then one has to be the cause of the other.

To return to the previous example, if crime rates drop after the death penalty is introduced, it might be tempting to conclude that a causal relationship exists between the two: introducing the death penalty promotes lower crime rates. However, this is a rash conclusion to jump to. Even though the timing of the two events appear to be almost simultaneous, other factors need to be considered. Correlation does not equate to causality.

To use another example, it was discovered that homes with pools use 49% more electricity per year compared with homes that did not have a pool.[8] While it is easy to leap to the conclusion that pools use up more energy, a closer examination of the comparison between homes with pools and those without highlights the presence of other factors as well. Pool owners may exhibit behavioural differences from those without a pool, thereby resulting in the former's higher consumption of electricity.

For one, homes with pools tend to have more occupants. They typically have on average 9% more children than non-pool homes. More occupants means increased energy use. At the same time, homes with pools typically enjoyed a higher income. Higher incomes may in turn support more expensive consumption habits, such as the possession of energy-guzzling devices such as a jacuzzi or air-conditioning.

While it is easy to assume that correlation equals causation, it would be wiser to refrain from making such leaps in logic. Just because the rooster crows before the sun comes up does not mean that the rooster's crow actually causes the sun to rise.

Deformation professionnelle

Deformation professionnelle is French for "professional deformation", or what is loosely translated as "job conditioning". As its name implies, it refers to the way your professional training distorts your view of the world. As psychologist Abraham Maslow puts it, "If you only have a hammer, you tend to see every problem as a nail."

In the previous section, I cited the example of Malcolm McLean, who arrived at a solution for the transportation of heavy containers. McLean was not the first person in the shipping industry to try and figure it out. But he was the only one who was not hampered by his or her professional training—when McLean decided to enter the shipping industry, he did so by leaving behind a successful career as a trucker.

As an industry outsider, McLean was able to approach the problem from a different perspective, unrestrained by any entrenched mind-sets reinforced by years of on-the-job training. As a result, the world now has McLean to thank for the global trade we enjoy today.

Even as reductionist biases narrow your field of vision, framing biases skew perspectives. The final part of the chapter looks at framing biases and how they affect the way you look at the world.

FRAMING BIASES

For a long time, the key theoretical framework underlining the study of economics and politics was the idea that man is ultimately rational. According to this belief, individuals based their decisions on calculating the lowest cost that was required to obtain the highest amount of utility according to their own self-interest.

In 1979, psychologists Daniel Kahneman and Amos Tversky released a seminal paper on Prospect Theory that effectively challenged this view.[9] Rather than objectively assessing the value of expected outcomes, individuals tended to weigh problems in terms of prospects and losses. The decision-making process becomes contingent on the value the individual attaches to the perceived prospects and losses involved. Losses are deemed as being less acceptable compared to gains, even if the gains were to massively outweigh the losses involved.

In 1981, Kahneman and Tversky followed up on their Prospect Theory paper with another article that focused on the importance of framing in decision-making.[10] They showed how the same problem framed differently could lead to differences in decision-making, based on people's emotional responses.

In an experiment conducted by the researchers, participants were asked to choose between two options of treatment for 600 people stricken with a deadly disease. Treatment A was said to be able to save 200 lives, while treatment B had a one-third probability that 600 people would be saved, but a two-third probability that no one would be saved. Although both treatments were essentially referring to the same thing, an overwhelming 72% of respondents picked treatment A. The positive framing in the first instance, where the emphasis is on the number of people saved, caused a logical skip in people's brains, leading them to believe that treatment A was actually better than treatment B. In reality they both represented the same thing.

The inability to logically execute a cost-benefit analysis is hampered by your mental framing. This is demonstrated in the following biases.

Salience effect

The salience effect is the inclination to remember characteristics or events that are prominent and outstanding, at the expense of other pertinent or relevant information. For example, airplane crashes are huge, dramatic events that fill up columns of newspaper space. Car crashes, on the other hand, do not receive the same amount of attention. Unsurprisingly, more people are afraid of flying than they are of driving.

Yet the odds of dying in a plane crash is staggeringly low. David Ropeik, a Risk Communication instructor at Harvard University, found that the chances of someone dying in a plane crash is one in 11 million. Contrast this to the odds of dying in a car crash: according to Ropeik, the chances of dying in a car accident is one in 5,000.[11]

The salience effect influences the decision-making process when more emphasis or attention is given to events or individuals than they truly deserve. In a study done by Olivier Dessaint and Adrien Matray, company managers were found to increase the amount of corporate cash holdings after a hurricane, despite the absence of any real liquidity risk.

Because hurricanes are a particularly salient event, they are easily imprinted in people's consciousness, thereby affecting decision-making. Over time, as memories of the hurricane fades, the salience effect also disappears. Nonetheless, the damage is done. For shareholders, managers' decisions to increase cash holdings lead to higher retained earnings, thereby negatively affecting the firm's value.[12]

Be careful to guard against the salience effect. Even in the face of remarkable events, take care to assess the situation objectively.

Sunk-cost fallacy

Another cognitive bias that occurs more frequently than we like to think is the fallacy of sunk costs. While the rational man may be expected to reverse decisions or modify behaviour that will lead to negative consequences, in reality this is often not the case. The more we invest in something, the more unwilling we are to abandon it, regardless of the additional cost incurred.

George Ball, the former American Undersecretary of State, made the following observation about US involvement during the Vietnam War: "Once large numbers of US troops are committed to direct combat, they will begin to take heavy casualties in a war they are ill-equipped to fight in a non-cooperative if not downright hostile countryside. Once we suffer large casualties, we will have started a well-nigh irreversible process. Our involvement will be so great that we cannot—without national humiliation—stop short of achieving our complete objectives. Of the two possibilities, I think humiliation would be more likely than the achievements of our objectives – even after we have paid terrible costs."[13]

The US involvement in the Vietnam War can be read as a classic example of the sunk-cost fallacy. Although the US was losing a large number of soldiers on a daily basis, it had pumped in too many men and resources for it to even conceive of pulling out. The US leadership could not look past the "sunk costs" of dead soldiers and retreat from the war. This only forced it further into the ethnical black hole it had climbed into.

The sunk-cost fallacy makes an appearance within the National Basketball Association (NBA) as well. Researchers Barry Staw and Ha Hoang found that teams that spent more on individual players were more likely to give them greater playing time and a longer tenure with the NBA franchise. Rather than playing and keeping the most productive players, teams were likely to be affected by significant sunk-cost effects on important personnel decisions.[14]

The implications of the sunk-cost fallacy on decision-making is obvious: instead of cutting losses right there and then, there is a tendency to persist in a losing strategy in the desperate hope that the losses can be recouped.

Hyperbolic discounting

A final common cognitive bias relates to hyperbolic discounting, where individuals maintain myopic perspectives about the future. Research has shown that when given two similar rewards, respondents are likely to pick the reward that is more immediate, even if it is of a lower value.

Hyperbolic discounting thus hinders consideration of long-term benefits and consequences, especially when these are compared to benefits in the near-future. Such myopic thinking is dangerous. Anticipation of the future is key if one wants to survive and flourish in a competitive environment.

CONCLUSION

Recognising the various kinds of psychological, social and cognitive biases is just the beginning of the Understanding process. In order to effectively reduce the negative effects of biases, you need to equip yourself with the right tools and techniques to confront them. The next chapter will present a number of methods for mitigating biases.

CHAPTER 13
MITIGATING BIASES

Biases are difficult to completely eliminate or avoid. However, steps can be taken to mitigate the adverse effects of biases. Mitigating biases can be an immensely uncomfortable experience. To be successful, leadership must be committed and invested in the process.

There are four key steps that organisations can take to mitigate biases: the first is to increase self-awareness of implicit biases; the second is to redesign organisational structures; the third is to conduct systematic decision analysis; and the fourth is to engage in scenario building.

INCREASE SELF-AWARENESS OF IMPLICIT BIASES

Studies done by researchers at Princeton University show that people tend to see themselves as being less susceptible to bias than others.[1] While they are able to spot psychological, cognitive and motivational bias in others, their own biases become a blind spot that they are unaware of. This is problematic because you cannot act to rectify a problem that you are not conscious of.

One reason why this happens is because people tend to assign greater value to introspective information rather than the action taken when assessing themselves for bias. This is in contrast to how they assess other people for biases: a greater emphasis is placed on others' behaviour without regard for introspective thought processes or intrinsic motivations.[2]

Because biases tend to operate unconsciously, their influence is often hidden from introspection.[3]

The first step is to adopt a more detached view of one's own behaviour or proposals. Having a trusted friend critique behaviour or an external consultant review plans are some ways to get perspective on your own biases and assumptions.

It helps as well to be aware of some of the common biases that people often fall prey to. This provides guidance as to what you should be looking out for.[4] For example, a business may have recently invested several thousands of dollars into developing a new product. However, the product may fail spectacularly upon its release into the market. The company is now faced with the choice of pulling the plug, or to continue marketing efforts in a bid to increase product sales. The business product manager decides that the product is "too big to fail", given the huge resources invested in it, and is determined to "earn back" the cost of developing the product.

If the manager understands the sunk-cost fallacy, she would have taken a step back to reassess her choice of decision. However, if she is not aware of this cognitive trap, regardless of how long and hard she pours over her decision, she will not be able to reconcile herself to the fact that the development cost is not recoverable regardless of the outcome. As a result, this sunk cost should not play a part in the decision-making process.

The second step is to ensure that everybody in your organisation is adequately equipped to recognise biases. This can be accomplished through basic training, and an overall conscientious effort to raise the team's awareness of common biases.

When biases are recognised and correctly identified, measures can be appropriately mapped out to address for these biases.

REDESIGN ORGANISATIONAL STRUCTURES

Earlier on I identified three types of organisational biases, namely, integration failure, decentralisation of incentives, and groupthink.

These are all intimately related to the way the organisation is structured, and relies heavily on design. This is a deliberate process that begins with the diagnosing of the problem. Only when this is done, can the correct remedy be applied to the problem.

Integration failure

No organisation can be perfectly integrated without losing some of the benefits that come with differentiation. The key is to figure out where the optimal level of trade-off lies. While it is possible to maintain deep pools of specialised knowledge, there should be an overarching mechanism to integrate different pools of knowledge in a timely and accurate fashion. This can take the form of cross-functional teams that oversee diverse departments, or it can take the form of a shared platform where members are able to access information from other sources within the team.

Decentralisation of incentives

Another common bias faced by organisations occurs when there is a misalignment between organisational and individual incentives. As mentioned in the previous chapter, two things can occur when this happens. The first is that individuals lack incentive to pursue activities beneficial to the organisation; and second, that individuals may have their own competing personal incentive contrary to the intent of the organisation.

It is important to ensure that all the different units within the organisation participate in a common vision or goal. Everyone needs to be on board with the articulated organisational goal, and care should be taken to ensure that there is no conflict between the activities of the different components. Differentiation should not come at the expense of disunity. For example, unit A's success should not negatively affect unit B's outcomes.

Effort should also be made to closely couple desired organisational outcomes with individual compensation. This need not be limited to monetary reimbursements, but can and should extend to other less tangible items, such as recognition and promotions.

Appropriate checks and balances can be established to ensure that individuals are not subverting the organisation's welfare in favour of their own well-being. This may entail setting up an independent advisory board with oversight functions, or it may involve removing discretionary powers from a single unit. Again, this needs to be balanced against the need for flexibility and agility in responding to time-sensitive and unanticipated issues.

Monitoring mechanisms can also be reinforced by the institutionalisation of harsh penalties for self-serving behaviour. Penalties reduce the appeal of such incentives by making it even costlier to partake in such actions.

Groupthink

Groupthink happens when the desire for group consensus and conformity suppresses critical opinions. There are three methods for overcoming groupthink.

The first is to encourage an environment where people are unafraid of airing dissenting views. This requires a high degree of trust, and a safe space where people know that they will not be penalised for stating contrarian opinions. This is highly contingent on the leadership style adopted. If team members feel that directives come from the top-down with no space for critical opinions, they are less likely to raise them in a shared environment. Even as a culture of dissent is encouraged, however, care should be taken to ensure that critical opinions are substantiated. If everyone disagreed on the basis of personal preferences or emotions, then opposing views lose their utility.

The second way of mitigating groupthink is to adopt an adapted version of the Delphi method. A list of questions is prepared and disseminated among participants. However, answers are entirely anonymous. These answers are then shared with the participants and participants are invited to modify their previous answers accordingly. After a predetermined criteria is achieved (for example, the number of rounds, or the degree of consensus between answers), a shared opinion is achieved. The anonymity eliminates the desire to conform to the prevailing sentiment while offering the chance for the majority to listen to alternative views.

A third method of reducing groupthink is to be deliberate about demanding alternative views. There is more than one way of achieving this. For example, the group could designate a devil's advocate to play a contrarian role. Or the team may engage in role-playing whereby different members take on different positions to analyse the issue. Of course, another way would be to engage external perspectives entirely.

From organisational biases, the final two sections in this chapter will move on to dealing with the negative effect of cognitive biases.

BEING SYSTEMATIC

With reductionist and framing biases, the problem arises when information is not processed in its entirety or holistically. To avoid this, ensure that there is a systematic way of processing information.

A decision-tree is one such tool that can help to achieve this. By mapping out all the alternatives, it opens up the possibility of other factors and options.

Once this is done, a thorough cost-benefit analysis can be performed. The cost-benefit of different options should be quantified to allow assumptions and biases to come to the fore. This allows other people to assess and evaluate the justifications behind the different options, leading to a more robust reasoning process.

SCENARIO BUILDING

While a decision-tree provides a systematic framework for considering information in a holistic manner, scenario building utilises the power of narrative to achieve a similar effect.

Because scenarios are in essence narratives, they need to be internally consistent and coherent in order to be convincing. As such, the construction of scenarios should facilitate the discovery of logical inconsistencies or fallacies. As scenarios are built up, elements that do not make logical sense will be discarded. Simultaneously, plotlines have to be substantiated with a plausible backstory, thereby further clarifying and eliminating any assumptions and biases.

Biases are internal blind spots that hinder your objective assessment of the external and internal environment. While biases may not be eliminated completely, their harmful effects can certainly be mitigated. This chapter has provided four key ways of targeting biases:

First, be aware of biases.

Second, redesign organisational structures.

Third, adopt systematic decision analysis.

Fourth, construct scenarios.

The next chapter will continue to examine the internal environment by illustrating how one can develop a desired vision of the future.

CHAPTER 14
DEVELOPING A DESIRED VISION OF THE FUTURE

An earlier chapter on Foresight offered an explanation of how deductive scenario building works. This requires envisioning the ideal external environment where you would be best placed to achieve your desired outcomes.

Unlike deductive scenario building, however, where attention is concentrated on the external environment, the desired vision of the future is concerned with your internal environment.

SIGNIFICANCE OF THE DESIRED VISION

The development of a desired vision should accomplish two main things:

First, it should motivate people into action. It should be feasible yet inspirational. It should also be tangible. If the entire organisation is unable to take part in this visioning exercise, the desired future should be communicated throughout the organisation to ensure that everyone is on the same page.

Second, the desired future should produce a set of guidelines for decision-making. By mapping out the ideal end-point, the action-steps involved should become clearer.

As it was with the scenario-building process, the first thing to do is to determine both the timeframe for the future, as well as your timeframe for action. This would typically follow the focal question previously identified.

Once the timeframe is scoped out, define the desired future. The matrix below helps to serve as a starting point (see Fig. 16).

Achievements

First, recognise the baseline from which you are starting. What has your organisation done thus far? What are some of the outcomes that have been achieved?

Achievements can be further broken down into three smaller sub-sections. What were the goals attained? Which values worked for you as an organisation? How have the organisational structure, status and role been successful?

Articulating your organisation's achievements will enable you to take stock of what has already been accomplished, as well as what you had hoped to do, but have not been able to. This is important, because it gives you a sense of the distance that you will have to cover to get from where you are today, to where you want to be.

Goals

Next, articulate your goals. Like the focal question, goals should be descriptive and specific. This makes it easier to visualise the abstract.

Goals should also be written down to increase accountability. In an experiment conducted among 149 participants coming from a range of different backgrounds and nationalities, researchers found that participants who wrote down their goals accomplished on average 6.44 of their goals.[1] Participants who did not write their goals down, on the other hand, achieved only an average of 4.28 goals.

In addition, when participants were asked to formulate action commitments and send their goals, action commitments, and weekly progress reports to a supportive friend, the average mean goal achievement increased further to 7.6. The very act of committing your goals to paper forces you to be more accountable.

Achievements	Goals
• Goals • People • Organisation	• First Principles • Purpose
People	**Organisation**
• Values • Organisational Culture	• Organisational Structure • Status • Role

Figure 16: Matrix of Desired Vision

Goals should also incorporate first principles about your organisation —these are the basic, fundamental truths that cannot be negotiated. They need not be limited to desired outcomes; first principles should also serve as a compass for determining the means to the end.

Finally, goals should be infused with purpose. As highlighted with the case of the two pharmaceutical companies Merck and Pfizer, profits often come about as a second-order consequence of focusing on higher-level purposes. When people start to see the value that your organisation adds to their lives, profits will naturally follow.

In thinking about your goals, remember: the more precise and specific you are, the easier time you will have mapping out the action steps required to get to your goals. At the same time, goals should go beyond mere profit maximisation. Instead, take care to incorporate first principles and a higher order purpose into your goals.

People

Your desired future should also contain a description of the values and organisational culture that you wish to develop. While this may appear to be "soft" components compared to "harder" targets such as the quality of products or services, they cannot be overlooked.

As Steve Jobs once said, "[…] most companies have completely forgotten 'Management by Value.' You want to hire people with the same values as you and even though you might argue a lot, you know you're trying to get to the same place."

While outcomes are important, how you choose to get there is important as well. More often than not, values and culture end up influencing the very choice of your desired outcome.

Organisation

Finally, organisation refers to the structures, status and role that you hope to see your organisation achieve. Just as values and culture shape the desired future, organisation will also affect desired outcomes.

For example, an overly hierarchical organisational structure may be too inflexible when it comes to the execution of strategy. An independent finance department may spur greater accountability within the organisation. A decentralised management structure may promote greater agility in responding to particular circumstances. The choice of organisational structure, status and role will shape the way your future unfolds.

Achievements, Goals, People and Organisation are a framework to ensure that your desired vision is comprehensive.

After mapping out the desired vision for the future, I will illustrate in the next chapter how internal enablers and derailers can be identified.

CHAPTER 15

IN-SIGHTING

Charting out a desired vision of the future makes introspective inquiry more focused and purposeful. The In-sighting process is done against the context of the desired vision and scenario-set.

Rather than using the terms "strengths" and "weaknesses", the terms "enablers" and "derailers" are deliberately used. Enablers are factors that facilitate the pursuit of your desired vision, while derailers are factors that hinder the attainment of the desired future.

Fig. 17 is a basic matrix identifying enablers and derailers.

Leadership	Resources	Organisation	People
What are the desired leadership and management styles? What will derail your organisation?	What are the desired human and financial capital? What will derail your organisation?	What is the desired organisational structure? What will derail your organisation?	What are the desired culture and values? What will derail your organisation?

Figure 17: Matrix of Enablers and Derailers

APPROACHES TO IN-SIGHTING

Below are three avenues that can be used to identify the various internal enablers and derailers that will either steer you towards, or pull you away from, your desired vision.

Evaluating past experiences

The first method requires the evaluation of past performances. This is where the "achievement" portion of the earlier chapter comes in handy. By going over past achievements, ask yourself: why did you attain a certain outcome? What did you do right? What did not work as well? Would these factors be helpful in promoting your desired vision of the future?

Tapping into industry norms

In the same way, industry norms can also be used to trigger ideas. What is distinctive about your organisation? Which areas can you specialise in so as to create a distinct and differentiated value proposition?

Benchmarking

Finally, you may also want to benchmark yourself against industry best practices. Which are the areas where you have scope for improvement?

MITIGATING BIASES

Even as you undertake the In-sighting process, remember to guard against implicit biases.

Encourage a culture where people can express diverse views freely. There should not be any repercussions or condemnation when people speak up with critical viewpoints. However, dissenters need to substantiate their points with facts and well-reasoned arguments. Such a culture should bolster a habit of corroboration and justification.

There should also be a concerted effort to actively seek out alternate views. This can take the guise of various techniques, including seeking out the perspectives of outsiders, role-playing and designating a devil's advocate. These will be particularly useful when attempting to counter the difficulties of introspection.

Once the different internal enablers and derailers affecting the future have been identified, they should be utilised in a meaningful way. The next section will demonstrate how such insights should be employed.

REFRAMING THE PROBLEM

In the battle of Salamis, the Athenians utilised their self-knowledge to achieve their desired future of fighting off the Persian invaders.

Athenian commander Themistocles knew two things about the Athenian military forces: it had a strong navy, but its army was weak and stood no chance against the larger and more formidable Persian land forces. Instead of choosing to fight on the Persians' terms, Themistocles reframed the problem: he leveraged on the Athenians' strengths.

By forcing the Persian military to go to battle at sea, Themistocles was able to tap into the traditional strengths of the Athenians. He did this while bypassing a weak point that he knew could not be overcome in that short period of time. The Athenians may not have been able to overpower the Persians on land, but when the battle was forced out to sea, their naval power was so mighty that the Athenians eventually won the war.

Even as you consider internal enablers and derailers, do not limit your thinking or framework for action. Ask yourself: is there any way to re-frame the scenarios so that a traditional strength could now be utilised for the benefit of the organisation? Can derailers be avoided? Otherwise, what should be done to mitigate such weaknesses?

The Chinese table tennis team provides another example of leveraging strengths. The Chinese have a long-standing tradition of winning the Olympic Gold medal in table tennis. At the 1984 Olympics, a reporter asked the Chinese coach the secret of their success.

The coach replied, "Here is our philosophy: if you develop your strengths to the maximum, the strength becomes so great it overwhelms the weakness. Our winning player, you see, plays only his forehand. Even though he cannot play backhand and his competition knows he cannot play backhand, his forehand is so invincible that it cannot be beaten."[1]

In the business world, Proctor & Gamble (P&G) adopts this same approach in its strategy. According to A.G. Lafley, P&G's former CEO, the company takes time to identify what is working. It then goes one step further to understand why certain processes or attributes are succeeding. Once they have located the source of this success, P&G implements this practice in its offices around the world with great speed.[2] The strength of P&G's competitive edge then, can be credited to the way in which it focuses on what it does best.

Jay Barney gives another example of the watch manufacturers Rolex and Timex as companies that have chosen to emphasise different areas of strengths.[3] Although both companies are in the same industry, they make use of very different resources and attributes. Rolex focuses on its quality manufacturing, commitment to excellence and its brand presence. Timex, on the other hand, focuses on its high-volume, low-cost manufacturing skills and abilities. Both firms continue to be successful in their respective market segments.

Depending on the desired vision and the scenario-set, different organisations will arrive at a different set of enablers and derailers based on their own unique circumstances. In the final section of this chapter, I use an actual example from FMG's consulting business that illustrates how deductive scenario building, vision casting, and In-sighting work hand-in-hand to yield real outcomes.

BACKCASTING

At FMG, we have conducted foresight workshops for clients to cope with uncertainty and to shape purposeful plans for the longer term.

Developing a shared desired vision, especially at the incipient stage of the client's development, is immensely fruitful. Ideally, participants selected for this exercise should come from diverse backgrounds and possess different work experiences. By bringing them altogether in an honest and open setting, it is possible to build on one another's differences and similarities to arrive at a shared desired vision for the future. Because this is a process that includes everyone's inputs, participants will be more likely to view the derived vision as legitimate, and not merely as a corporate relations exercise imposed by the top management.

Typically we divide the participants into four small teams, with each one assigned to work on a desired aspect for the future: Achievements, Goals, People and Organisation. The teams are then rotated around the room, with two individuals from the original group staying behind to present their conclusions to the incoming group. This allows the different teams to interrogate each other's answers and develop a 360 degree picture of the dimensions of their future plans.

At the end of the rotations, conclusions are mapped onto post-it stickers and classified neatly on a big wall. This is an important step because it allows everyone involved in the exercise to see for the first time a visual map of the future they want to achieve.

Next, participants vote on the vision that resonates the most with them. In this way, the desired vision of the future transforms into a shared future—one that has been personally considered and agreed upon by the organisation. The importance of articulating one's desired vision for the future cannot be understated. By mapping the future, our participants are able to visualise their desired future, creating a palpable sense of excitement and expectation within the organisation.

From here, it becomes easier to work backwards to identify the enablers and derailers that would either facilitate or hinder the desired future.

During the exercise, two sets of enablers and derailers are located. The first set deals with the external factors, and requires participants to visualise both positive and negative elements in the outer environment that could affect their future.

The second set, meanwhile, looks at internal enablers and derailers—internal elements within the organisation itself that would either contribute towards or hamper the realisation of the desired future.

This deductive exercise is very useful. By participating in this back-casting exercise, our clients are able to map out the concrete steps that they need to take to move towards their desired future. For example, clients are able to identify internal enablers and derailers of which they were previously unaware. During one such workshop, one of our clients came up with a whole new organisational structure that would better position them to achieve their goals.

By also thinking about external factors, our clients have the opportunity to consider several "what-if" scenarios. "What-if" stress-testing challenges organisational thinking and forces consideration of what is needed both internally and externally to move with confidence towards a desired future.

CONSTRUCTING A STRATEGIC PERSPECTIVE

In-sighting goes beyond simply listing strengths and weaknesses. It goes one step further by plotting these out against the desired future, giving the entire exercise purpose and direction. Enablers and derailers are located, allowing a clearer and more meaningful roadmap to be constructed.

By this time, you should be familiar with both your external and internal environment. The integration of insights from both the Foresight and Understanding process forms the strategic perspective. It is against the backdrop of this strategic perspective that strategy should be formulated.

The strategic perspective can be summed up into a key statement that articulates what you want to achieve and how you are going to attain it: we want to get to X by doing Y by the time Z.

Having a strategic perspective is important because it forms the foundation for generating good strategies. Whereas X represents the highest level of change you wish to achieve, Y answers how you intend to move towards such an outcome. X is thus based on the shared, desired vision established earlier in the Understanding process. Y, on the other hand, depends on the outputs derived from the In-sighting process. What are the enablers and the derailers that you need to focus on in order to achieve the highest order outcome that you desire?

There are a few things to look out for when deciding on the strategic perspective.

Aligned purposes and values

First, be careful to ensure that the strategic perspective is aligned with the organisation's basic purpose and values. Regardless of how impressive the strategic perspective sounds, if it does not go straight to the heart of your core purpose and values, it is ultimately irrelevant.

Measurable

Second, the strategic perspective should be measurable, and hence expressed in concrete terms, to be achieved over a specified period of time. This allows you to review your progress at suitable intervals, and provides an accurate and tangible way of assessing whether you have to adapt your strategy appropriately.

Feasible

Third, the strategic perspective needs to be realistic. It has to be feasible. Otherwise, there is no point in articulating it since the outcome would not be achievable anyway.

Legitimate

Fourth, the strategic perspective should be acceptable to the people in the organisation. If the strategic perspective is unable to garner legitimacy among the very people who are supposed to be executing the strategy, it would not work. The strategic perspective needs to motivate people and spur them onwards. By ensuring that diverse perspectives from within the organisation have been represented in the process thus far, a credible and empowering strategic perspective can be arrived at.

CONCLUSION

The Foresight and Understanding processes are meant to make the strategic perspective as robust and accurate as possible. This will help to formulate strategies that are effective in deriving the desired outcomes.

The next section will look at the Strategy process of FUSE. This can be broken down into two key components.

First, strategy formulation is discussed. I will argue that this requires two core elements: strong leadership and defined principles. One chapter is devoted to each aspect.

Second, I will highlight the need to stress-test the strategies developed. This is to ensure that formulated strategies are robust and are able to withstand unexpected surprises in the environment.

THE UNDERSTANDING PROCESS

1. **Confront biases**
   - Biases affect our behaviour, the way we process information and the way we make decisions.
   - They are often implicit.
   - Biases can be grouped into four categories:
     - Motivational biases
     - Organisational biases
     - Reductionist biases
     - Framing biases

2. **Mitigate biases**
   - To acquire a more accurate understanding of yourself, you need to mitigate the negative effects of biases.
   - This can be done in four ways:
     - Increase self-awareness of biases
     - Redesign organisational structure
     - Conduct systematic analysis
     - Engage in scenario planning

3. **Develop a desired vision of the future**
   - The desired vision of the future is concerned with the future state of our internal environment.
   - It should motivate people into action and produce a set of guidelines for decision-making.
   - The desired vision of the future can be organised according to four categories:
     - Achievements
     - Goals
     - People
     - Organisation

4. **Conduct In-sighting**
   ○ In-sighting is conducted to identify the internal enablers and derailers that would either steer you towards or pull you away from your desired vision.
   ○ There are three ways to conduct In-sighting:
   - Evaluate past experiences
   - Tap into industry norms
   - Benchmark against best practices

SECTION 4
STRATEGY

CHAPTER 16
INTRODUCTION TO STRATEGY

In 2007, Reed Hastings, founder and CEO of the online streaming company Netflix, made a painful decision to abandon long-anticipated plans to push out its own streaming hardware. The team had been hard at work for months on the project, and everyone was excited about its release.

On the same day that the team was in the studio preparing for the initial advertising efforts, Hastings pulled the plug on the entire project. Entering the hardware market would have placed Netflix in direct competition with other established players such as Sony and Apple. This would compromise its core business in streaming software and diminish Netflix's ability to expand its software uptake among hardware providers. Hastings thus had a strategic choice: to diversify into the hardware industry or to stick to the production of streaming software. He chose the latter. Today, Netflix leads the global on-demand streaming industry.

Netflix had a clear and defined strategy. It concentrated exclusively on a pre-defined core business instead of diversifying into other products.

WHAT IS STRATEGY?
What kind of strategy should organisations adopt? Going by the vast array of strategy books lining the shelves at the bookstore, everyone seems to have an opinion on what the best strategy *should be*. But what exactly is strategy?

Nancy Huston, former senior vice president of the multinational pharmaceutical corporation Pfizer, Inc., strips the word down to its bare essence: "Strategy is very simple. It's about *what* and *why*, not *how* and *when*."[1]

Contention over definitions of strategy arises when attempts are made to prescribe the *what* and the *why*.

Prominent business historian Alfred Chandler in 1962 called strategy "the determination of the long-run goals and objectives of an enterprise, and the adoption of courses of action and the allocation of resources necessary for carrying out these goals."[2]

Nearly a decade later, Kenneth Andrews, one of the founding fathers in the field of business strategy, labelled strategy as "the pattern of objectives, purposes, or goals and the major policies and plans for achieving these goals, stated in such a way as to define what business the company is in or is to be in and the kind of company it is or is to be."[3]

In the 1980s, management authority Michael Porter contended that competitive strategy required "positioning a business to maximise the value of the capabilities that distinguish it from its competitors."[4]

Each of these definitions vary, but they are all prescriptive. Chandler focused on the allocation of resources to achieve pre-determined long-term goals, while Andrew emphasised the need to determine the core business of the firm. Porter, meanwhile, identified comparative advantage as key to getting ahead in business.

At FMG, we adopt a principles-based approach. Principles serve as a guide to strategy formulation, allowing for greater flexibility in an uncertain world, as opposed to rigid and mechanistic rules. This is a more useful approach since prescriptions, by their very nature, will eventually fail once everyone adopts them, since they would have become predictable and ultimately duplicable.

To better understand the significance of a principles-based approach, I will first trace the evolution of strategy through history. The popular conception of what strategy *should* be has changed throughout time;

needless to say, the FUSE approach to strategy formulation differs from previous understandings of strategy.

Following this, I will situate the FUSE approach to strategy formulation within a typology of strategy, where various conceptions of strategy are classified according to their underlying philosophies. This will set up a theoretical foundation for the rest of the section.

THE HISTORY OF STRATEGY

The first mention of strategy in the annals of history can be traced back to its use in military warfare. *The Art of War*, written by the Chinese general Sun Tzu in the sixth century BCE, lists the principles, strategies and tactics that govern success in warfare.

However, the word "strategy" is itself thought to derive from the Greek word *strategos*, which was used during the Classical and Byzantine period to refer to the role of a military general. The modern-day meaning of the word "strategy" finds a closer fit with the Greek words, "*strategike episteme*" (general's knowledge) or "*strategon sophia*" (general's wisdom).[5]

Strategy was thus thought of in terms of the role of a general leading an army. The general issues orders to direct and guide the actions of the troops under him or her, with the ultimate objective of winning the war.

This understanding of strategy remained exclusively within the realm of military warfare until the late 1800s, as advances in industrialisation accelerated the expansion of market capitalisation. As consumer bases swelled to include the working class, businesses also begun to grow at an exponential rate.

The end of the 19th century marked more than a century since the Industrial Revolution catalysed dramatic economic and social transformation. The economic powerhouses of the US and Western Europe witnessed the emergence of several large, vertically integrated and multidivisional corporations, which sought to wield influence over market forces by acquiring greater market share and value.

This demanded a new way of thinking about doing business. The business world shifted from one that was by-and-large benign, to an environment that was becoming increasingly competitive and cut-throat. The vocabulary of warfare was thus transposed onto the business world, and strategy became the new buzzword as the role of the manager increasingly mirrored that of the military general.

It would not be until the 1950s, however, that the study of strategy in business began to crystallise into distinct schools of thought. The first wave of studies came close on the heels of a popular trend in military warfare in the wake of World War II. Operations Research, with its promotion of scientific management, became all the rage in America and Great Britain, where it had been used to great success on the Pacific and European battlefields.

Elite business schools on the east coast of America quickly appropriated the language and philosophy behind Operations Research. Alfred Sloan of General Motors and academic Alfred Chandler both championed the importance of managing and coordinating formal processes driven by rational analyses. Business could be planned right down to the minute detail to improve efficiency. The role of strategy, as it was understood then, was to ensure that nothing was left to chance. In other words, structure followed strategy.

Under such a conception of strategy, the business environment was first analysed. The organisation's competencies and weaknesses were then assessed. The results of these analyses were finally channelled into an action plan that culminated in profit maximisation. Models such as the SWOT and PEST frameworks facilitated such analyses, and quickly won over business managers because of their user-friendly nature.

In the 1970s and early 1980s, the focus on rational analyses expanded to include decisions about diversification and portfolio planning. Managers begun asking themselves what business(es) the company should be in.

Igor Ansoff, another founding father of corporate strategy, argued that the choice of industry, as well as the company's position within it, should be the centrepiece of strategy formulation.[6] It was at this time that portfolio analysis models, such as the Boston Consulting Group's (BCG) Growth-Share Matrix and McKinsey's Business Strength Matrix, also began to emerge.

Take BCG's Growth-Share Matrix,[7] for example. This model mapped the relative market performance of a business unit into four distinct categorisations that warranted different actions.

In a similar way, McKinsey's Business Strength Matrix laid out a framework that aids managers in deciding which business units they should be allocating resources to. This understanding of strategy as portfolio analysis retained popularity through the 1980s.

In the 1990s, however, it became increasingly clear that such an understanding of strategy was no longer sufficient. Markets were becoming saturated, and the business environment was only becoming more and more competitive.

Under these changing conditions, BCG's founder Bruce Henderson wrote an article entitled "The Origins of Strategy".[8] Henderson pointed out that markets could not grow infinitely—there will come a tipping point at which available resources would no longer be able to support the ever-increasing number of companies around. At this point, business competition would ape that of nature: natural selection would ensure that only the fittest would survive.

There was one important distinction, however: while individual organisms in nature cannot preselect for a biological trait, businesses, on the other hand, "can use their imagination and ability to reason logically [...] to make strategy possible." Strategy became a "deliberate search for a plan of action that will develop a business' competitive advantage and compound it."

Henderson's article marked a clear shift towards a focus on competitive advantage. Models such as Michael Porter's five forces of competition as well as C.K. Prahalad and Gary Hamel's idea of core competence took hold of the business world's imagination.[9]

As the 2000s arrived, however, large strides in technology meant that the rules of the game had changed once again. Having a competitive advantage was no longer sufficient: innovation was now the new name of the game. In particular, it was not enough to be innovative; businesses had to practise disruptive innovation. Popularised by writer Clayton Christensen, the term "disruptive innovation" came to describe innovation that created new markets by appealing to a different set of values from the current norm.[10]

Seen through the lenses of history, the post-war period saw the emergence of four key trends within the business world: the 1960s was marked by objectives-based planning, while the 1970s and 1980s heralded a shift towards strategies of diversification and portfolio analysis. As competition increased, it appeared more and more imperative that companies developed their competitive advantage. In the last two decades or so, however, the focus has shifted to the idea of disruptive innovation.

TYPOLOGIES OF STRATEGY

Business historians have attempted to make sense of evolving understandings of strategy by drawing up a typology of the philosophies underlying different prescriptions of strategy.

Henry Mintzberg was the first to attempt to do so. As early as 1978, he introduced a simple typology that characterised the strategy process into two main schools of thought (see Fig. 18 overleaf): the first posited that strategy could be developed in a deliberate manner. According to this belief, strategy can be carefully calibrated according to anticipated future developments. The second school of thought, meanwhile, believed that strategy is emergent. It cannot be pre-planned in any intentional manner; instead, strategy emerges as a response to unfolding developments that cannot be adequately anticipated before time.

Richard Whittington later built on this dualistic typology by including an additional axis he termed as "outcomes" (see Fig. 19 overleaf).[11] At one end, outcomes are thought of solely in terms of profit maximising. At the other end of the spectrum, outcomes have a more pluralistic character. The intersection of the two axes (processes and outcomes) thus gives rise to four different quadrants of strategy: classical, evolutionary, systemic and processual.

Figure 18: Henry Mintzberg's Typology of Strategy

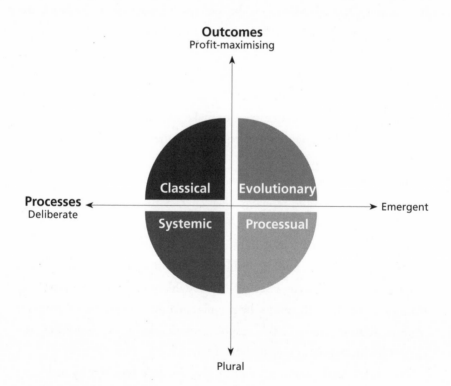

Figure 19: Richard Whittington's Typology of Strategy

Classical perspectives of strategy rely on the ability of the manager to accurately and effectively analyse and plan business operations in order to achieve maximum profits. This assumes steady state conditions.

The evolutionary perspective, however, views the market as being too complex and unpredictable for any kind of deliberate planning to be adopted. The key to profit maximising is to ensure maximum flexibility in reacting appropriately to changes in market conditions.

Systemic and processual perspectives of strategy depart from the classical and evolutionary perspectives in that outcomes may not only be limited to profit maximisation. On the contrary, the desired outcomes are often pluralistic, going beyond mere securement of increased profits.

Systemic and processual perspectives of strategy differ from one another in the way they view the strategy process. In an environment where outcomes are not limited to the accumulation of profits, systemic approaches insist on the need for local accommodation. Processual approaches, on the other hand, take a reactive view of strategy: it is only by being close to the ground that organisations are able to adapt and survive the tumultuous climate of the free market.

FMG'S APPROACH

Knowing the history and typology of strategy provides the context for situating FMG's philosophy of strategy within historical and current understandings of strategy.

FMG's philosophy of strategy formulation

FMG's philosophy is shaped by three core principles:

First, we believe that people possess the ability to make deliberate choices in the present to affect outcomes in the future. We may not have control over the key driving forces shaping our external environment, but we do have control over the way we choose to react to these forces.

Second, these choices are guided by enduring principles that are both conscious and purposeful. This is in contrast to a mechanistic view of strategy, where every step is dictated and predetermined. Unlike preceding conceptions of strategy such as the BCG's growth matrix, we do not provide a prescriptive model with rules governing behaviour.

Rather, the FUSE model places processes at the heart of our philosophy. There can be no differentiation if everyone followed the same strategy. As such, no single normative model can be universally applied. Instead, strategy needs to be based on a set of principles and strategic perspectives tailored to the individual organisation.

Third, commitment to this set of enduring principles as well as the belief in deliberate action needs to be balanced with the flexibility to adapt to changing conditions. While principles set the parameters around which decisions are framed, agility when setting the course within these given boundaries is important. In a complex and uncertain world, such flexibility cannot be understated.

Situating our philosophy of strategy within Whittington's typology of strategy, the FUSE approach to strategy formulation lies at the intersection of the plural end of the outcome axis and the middle portion of the processes axis (see Fig. 20).

What strategy is

The FUSE approach to strategy views strategy as a deliberate and conscious choice leading to a coherent, directional and purposeful set of actions that affect the future.

First, strategy has a clear intent. It should unify the organisation by providing a sense of purpose to the different activities taking place. This purpose needs to be deliberately and consciously derived. There is no room for muddling through at this stage.

Second, strategy is about commitments. Strategy should demand the investment of significant resources and efforts that are not easily reversible. This means that there will be risk. But as Reed Hastings puts it, "If you are not genuinely pained by the risk involved in your strategic choices, it's not

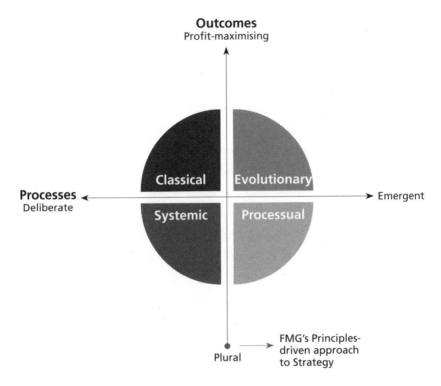

Figure 20: The FUSE Process of Strategy as situated within Richard Whittington's Typology

much of a strategy." A manager plans, but a leader strategises.

Third, strategy is about direction of effort and resources. This requires that the strategic perspective be accurate—both the scenario building and In-sighting processes have to be robust and rigorous in order to guide organisational direction.

Key ingredients for strategy formulation

Three key ingredients are needed for the FUSE Strategy process.

The first is leadership. The leadership needs to have vision, imagination, boldness and commitment. Without these essential components, it will be difficult for strategy to be clear, committed and directed.

The second are principles. As mentioned repeatedly, principles guide the formulation process. While they drive the definition of your desired outcomes, they also delineate how goals are achieved. This provides a clear direction for strategy formulation while maintaining the flexibility to adjust to changing conditions.

The third is stress-testing. Even with strong leadership and a clearly defined set of principles, strategies need to undergo rigorous testing to ensure that they remain effective under real-life conditions and changing parameters. By employing the techniques of sensitivity analysis and wind-tunnelling, strategies that are even more robust and resilient can be promoted.

The process of strategy formulation is summed up in the flowcharts below and opposite (see Figs. 21 and 22).

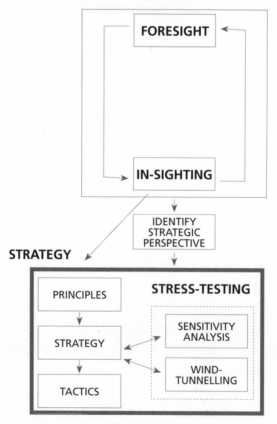

Figure 21: The Strategy Process Pathway

APPROACH TO STRATEGY FORMULATION

INGREDIENTS FOR EFFECTIVE STRATEGY FORMULATION

Figure 22: FMG's Approach to and Ingredients for Effective Strategy Formulation

The next three chapters will each look at one key ingredient of effective strategy formulation. Chapter 17 explores the importance of leadership in the Strategy process by highlighting the need for bold, visionary, imaginative and committed leadership.

Chapter 18 meanwhile, breaks down the strategy formulation process into three different layers. It begins by determining principles used in the generation of strategy. From the strategy produced, tactics can be arrived at.

The final chapter in this section looks at the process of stress-testing. How can strategy be robust and resilient? Techniques of sensitivity analysis and wind-tunnelling will be introduced here.

The next chapter begins with a man named Elon Musk.

CHAPTER 17
LEADERSHIP MATTERS

Elon Musk is a man of many hats. He co-founded the online payment service PayPal and electric automobile company Tesla. If that wasn't enough, he also founded space shuttle manufacturer SpaceX. Musk is currently the chairman of solar panel manufacturer SolarCity, and runs Tesla and SpaceX full time.

History has yet to pass its final verdict on Musk's legacy—we don't know if SpaceX will meet its stated goal of setting up the first human colony on Mars, and we cannot know right now if Tesla would catalyse an automobile revolution where electric cars become the new mainstream. But strategy is about making difficult choices in an uncertain world, and Musk has had his share of tough decisions to make.

This chapter offers an account of how Musk has visibly demonstrated real leadership skills in navigating the choppy waters of an uncertain world.

ELON MUSK

When Elon Musk was growing up in Pretoria, South Africa, his mother thought he was deaf. His concerned parents took him to the doctor, who certified that Musk's hearing was perfectly functional. The boy was just in his own world. He had an exceptional ability to concentrate with a focus so singular that he would tune everything out.

Musk also possessed a voracious appetite for knowledge alongside an insatiable sense of curiosity. According to his mother, Musk always had his nose in a book, with a sponge of a mind that relentlessly soaked up information. This thirst for knowledge forged in him a strong conviction that there was no problem that could not be fixed, just solutions that had yet to be found.[1]

By the time he was 12, Musk had successfully sold his first software programme for $500—a game he called Blaster. He went on to complete his undergraduate studies in economics and physics at the University of Pennsylvania and subsequently enrolled in a PhD programme in energy physics at Stanford University. Two days after class started, however, he dropped out. In the midst of the dot-com boom of the early 1990s, Musk founded his first company, an online city guide called Zip2 Corporation. In 1999, the computer company Compaq bought over Zip2, netting Musk a cool $22 million dollars.

Musk subsequently followed up with X.com, an online financial services/payment company, which later evolved into PayPal. In 2002, eBay acquired PayPal for $1.5 billion, making Musk, for the second time, a multimillionaire many times over.

In 2002, Musk founded his third company, Space Exploration Technologies Corporation, or SpaceX. SpaceX became the first privately-owned company to manufacture spacecraft for commercial space travel. In 2008, SpaceX successfully sent the first privately owned rocket up into space. This was followed by sending a spacecraft to the International Space Station in 2012.

One year after the founding of SpaceX, Musk co-founded Tesla Motors, an automobile company that specialises in electrical automobiles. In 2008, the Tesla roadster was introduced as the world's first all-electric car. Despite its lack of reliance on traditional fossil fuels, the model does everything that the conventional gasoline car does, but better. It is able to travel for 300 miles (480 km) on a single charge, and achieves an acceleration rate from 0–60 in an impressive 5.5 seconds.

Musk's penchant for sustainable energies surfaces again in his involvement with the solar energy company SolarCity. Musk helped to kick-start the company with his cousins in 2006, and is the current chairman of the firm. By 2014, SolarCity was the largest installer of solar panels in the US.[2] To encourage increased uptake of solar power, SolarCity has also adopted a solar lease option where homeowners pay lower utility fees per month compared with conventional electricity.

How does Musk run his companies? Musk's leadership is one that symbolises imagination, vision, boldness and commitment.

ELON MUSK'S LEADERSHIP PRINCIPLES

Musk has a clear set of principles that run through all three of his companies, the chief of which is the ultimate goal of improving the future of humanity. This demands a commitment to sustainability and the ability to take seriously what other people deem as "ridiculous".

Take, for instance, Musk's belief in a world where nuclear fusion, a self-sustainable human colony on Mars and airplanes that take off in a vertical position are all possible. One might be forgiven for thinking that these are the ramblings of a madman, but Musk is serious: his desire is to fundamentally transform "the way human beings travel, the energy we consume, and our legacy as earthbound beings."[3]

What seems ridiculous to other people is within the realm of possibility for him. Musk is not afraid to imagine beyond what is normal, and to dream big. J.B. Straubel, Musk's co-founder at Tesla, described the entrepreneur as someone who drives a "think-bigger mentality". According to him, Musk is "always imagining something so large it's terrifying."[4]

But Musk's ability to imagine, and to think big, drives a forward-looking vision. As his counterparts are focused on short-term profit, Musk is envisioning the future. Musk is not interested in incremental improvements, but in momentous advances. As Musk explained, "You can run a company where you're really under the gun to make a lot of short-term optimisations.

But that makes it difficult to make big technology advancements."[5]

The result of Musk's imagination and vision has been a willingness to invest in space and electric vehicles, even when it was not commercially viable to do so. For 11 years SpaceX did not have a single customer. Its first customer came in 2013, when the Dragon spacecraft was selected by NASA as a replacement for its older space shuttles. This marked the first time a US private company had delivered supplies to the International Space Station.[6]

Musk's ability to think big and think long-term contributes as well to his commitment to systems thinking. He recognises that in order for Tesla and SpaceX to attain their goals, they have to ultimately create the critical mass and infrastructure necessary to propel an entirely new paradigm shift.

Tesla's goal as mentioned earlier is to wean the world off an unsustainable diet of fossil fuel to one that relies on a more sustainable solution of solar electricity. In order to make this a reality, Musk's strategy has been to enter Tesla car models at the high end of the market, where customers are willing to pay a premium to cover the initial costs of technology development, and then drive down the price as much as possible to achieve a higher unit volume.[7]

In a bid to create this greater critical mass, Musk made an unexpected move in June 2014. He released the intellectual property rights to the technology Tesla had developed. Investors and competitors alike were stunned. For firms that rely heavily on technological innovation for profits, patents are the lifeblood of the company. Yet here was Musk, open-sourcing all of Tesla Motors' intellectual property.

The simple explanation was that Musk recognised that if Tesla wanted to change the fundamental way people consumed fuel, they could not inhibit other people from advancing this type of technology. By sharing knowledge, expertise from outside of Tesla could help push technological innovation, accelerating the rate at which people converted to electric cars. After all, as Musk wrote, "[Tesla's] true competition is not the small trickle of non-Tesla electric cars being produced, but rather the enormous flood of gasoline cars pouring out of the world's factories every day."[8]

Musk is thus clear about his highest-order intent. This allows him to eliminate options that do not contribute to these desired outcomes. It also permits him to have the boldness to deliberately lose a battle or two in order to win the war.

STAY THE COURSE

On 2 August 2008, SpaceX launched its rocket, the Falcon 1, into space. This was their third try, and it failed. When Musk emerged from the control room where he had been watching the launch, he walked past the waiting press and addressed his team directly. Musk made it clear that he was in for the long haul. He acknowledged that the goal of launching a rocket into outer space was never going to be easy, and announced that he had made significant investments to provide SpaceX with the financial security to attempt two more rocket launches.

Musk also told his staff that they would "need to pick [themselves] up, and dust [themselves] off, because [there was] a lot of work to do." He vowed that SpaceX would press forward with plans for Falcon 1's fourth flight, saying "For my part, I will never give up, and I mean never."[9]

Musk's fierce commitment turned the atmosphere around. As one staff member described it: "Within moments the energy of the building went from despair and defeat to a massive buzz of determination as people began to focus on moving forward instead of looking back."[10]

In the days and weeks following the third launch attempt, the SpaceX team got together and figured out the cause of the failure. By the seventh week, they had another rocket "fully manufactured, integrated and on location ready to fly again."

On 28 September 2008, less than two months after the failure of the third launch occurred, SpaceX successfully launched the Falcon 1 vehicle in the Pacific, sending it into orbit around the earth. SpaceX became the first private company to send a rocket into space.

CONCLUSION

When Musk started SpaceX, no other private company had ventured into the space manufacturing business. It was seen as too expensive and too risky for the profit-driven private sector to invest in. Furthermore, space travel for the ordinary man still seemed like a pipe dream.

But Musk had the imagination and the vision to go beyond conventional wisdom. Guided by a drive to better the lives of humanity, Musk poured immense amounts of time, effort and resources into SpaceX. He was clear about his intent, and committed in his purpose.

Musk was not impulsive, however; he had the foresight to cater for the possibility that it might take a while for SpaceX to successfully send a rocket into space. Musk prepared for this contingency by making the financial arrangements necessary to absorb several rounds of failure. This is also known as stress-testing.

In the next chapter, I will demonstrate how strategy can be formulated using a principles-driven approach.

CHAPTER 18

FORMULATING STRATEGY

The formulation of strategy can be thought of in terms of a three-level hierarchy: principles guide strategy, which in turn determine the tactics adopted. The chapter is thus divided into two main parts: the first part explores the importance of principles, while the second discusses the formulation of strategy and tactics.

PRINCIPLES VS. STRATEGY

In thinking about strategy formulation, always begin with your principles firmly in mind. Principles are the core guiding precepts of any organisation that are usually non-negotiable. Once decided upon, they should not be altered as a result of inadvertency.

In contrast to principles, strategy is malleable and tactics completely flexible.

John Young, former CEO of Hewlett-Packard, identifies the temporal difference between principles and strategy, although he uses the word "practices" instead of "strategy": "Our basic principles have endured intact since our founders conceived them. We distinguish between core values and practices; the core values don't change, but the practices might."[1]

Principles guide decision-making

Principles constitute the fundamental beliefs, attitudes and values that add up to "the way we do things around here". They serve as a standard upon which important decisions are to be made. They do not only determine the end goals in mind, but they often concern the preferred means to achieving such goals.

In an interview, Elon Musk spoke about the importance of first principles, asserting that "it's important to reason from first principles rather than by analogy. The normal way we conduct our lives is we reason by analogy. [With analogy] we are doing this because it's like something else that was done, or it is like what other people are doing. [With first principles] you boil things down to the most fundamental truths... and then reason up from there."[2]

Musk was speaking about first principles in the context of problem solving. He used the example of SpaceX. Before establishing the company, Musk and his team were concerned about the costs involved in building a rocket. They set about trying to obtain an estimate, but instead of using an analogy-based solution of comparing products that were already on the market, they returned to the first principle rule: SpaceX figured out what were the necessary components of a rocket and calculated the cost of obtaining these raw materials.

Their findings were momentous. At that time, the cheapest US rocket would have cost around $65 million. However, by breaking down the rocket into its component parts, SpaceX realised it could build a rocket for about 2% of the typical price. Consequently, it built its first rocket with a selling price of just $7 million.[3]

Just as SpaceX returned to the most basic components in its search for an accurate cost estimate, principles revisit the core essentials. They strip away the unnecessary portions and retain the bare fundamentals that form the bedrock of your organisation's strategy and tactics.

As a result, principles are able to unify and guide organisations in their decisions, regardless of how complex the external environment may be or how big the organisation may be.

The ancient Greek poet Archilochus had a saying: "The fox knows many things, but the hedgehog knows one big thing." The philosopher Isaiah Berlin later appropriated this saying in an essay entitled "The Hedgehog and the Fox." He used this categorisation to divide writers and thinkers into two groups: the hedgehog, who viewed the world through the lens of a singular definitive idea that unifies and organises everything; and the fox, for whom the vast and complex experiences of the world prevented the formation of any unifying idea.

What does this mean for businesses? In his book *Good to Great*, management author Jim Collins extrapolates from Berlin's categories to explain what he calls the hedgehog concept. To Collins, hedgehogs are the ones who understand that "the essence of profound insight is simplicity." They are the ones who possess the acute ability to discern underlying patterns from the overwhelming complexity that characterises our world; and they are the ones who are able to differentiate the essential from the important, filtering out whatever is simply unnecessary.

In his research, Collins found that comparison companies (vis-à-vis the good-to-great companies) frequently sunk when crises struck. In the words of Collins himself: "They would try to run, making bad decisions at forks in the road, and then have to reverse course later. Or they would veer off the trail entirely, banging into trees and tumbling down ravines."[4]

The good-to-great companies, however, had clear principles that guided their decisions. This enabled them to make quick decisions from the onset, thereby setting a coherent course.

Principles thus act like a compass: they help point you in the direction you want to be heading in.

Principles help to discriminate between options

Principles also serve to discriminate between options by dealing with the whys and the hows.

During the late 1960s America underwent a demographic shift. The projected birth rate was expected to level off and decline. At that time,

Johnson's Baby was a leading American brand of baby skincare products, while Gerber Products led the baby food market. The two brands took a look at this key trend, and came up with contrasting strategies based on their respective principles.

For Gerber, it decided to expand its product and service lines. It ceased to limit its activities to the sales of baby food, and bought an insurance company, a nursery school chain and a nursery accessories company to boost sales.

Johnson's Baby, on the other hand, took a different approach. Instead of diversifying its products and services for infants, it decided to market its products to the adult population.[5]

These strategies worked well for both companies. Johnson's Baby experienced growth across its range of baby products. Its Baby Shampoo went beyond the infant and toddler market to subsequently become America's top-selling shampoo. Gerber Products, meanwhile, rapidly conquered new markets in its bid to diversify its products. Less than three years after it pushed out a line of vinyl pants that went over cloth diapers, it was able to claim more than 50% of market share.[6] After entering the juvenile furniture market, Gerber quickly moved to the top of the pack, securing 20% of the entire business.

Johnson's Baby and Gerber Products were both successful in countering the discouraging trend of a declining birth-rate. However, their choice of strategy was ultimately guided by a set of principles that governed the distinct decision-pathway available to them.

Gerber Products' slogan at that time was, "Babies are our business". This core commitment guided its strategy; rather than diversifying its targeted audience, Gerber would diversify the range of products and services offered to its intended audience.

Johnson's Baby, on the other hand, adopted a differing set of principles. Its tagline was, "Best for the baby—best for you", with a commitment to the family, especially the relationship between mother and baby. In the 1970s, it began marketing its baby products to families with the underlying message that "baby products are milder than others."

Gerber Products and Johnson's Baby both had strategic choices to make as the birth rate plummeted in the 1970s. They could have made similar choices, but they didn't. This was because their predetermined principles dictated the range of options that were available of them. Gerber Products' core value laid in providing products and services to babies, while Johnson's Baby, on the other hand, was focused on the family.

In a world where the range of options may be frequently endless, principles discriminate effectively between options. Because principles are driven by a set of values that are not easily replicated by other organisations, they help to differentiate organisations from each other.

Principles are not solely about profits

Henry Ford once said, "A business that makes nothing but money is a poor business."[7]

For businesses to survive, profit-making is necessary. But profit maximisation cannot be one of the core principles underscoring strategies. An obsession with numbers will ironically distract you from the very mechanism of making money, that is, your value proposition to the public. As John Kay argues in his book *Obliquity*, in order to have the best chance at solving problems, approach them indirectly.

In today's world where uncertainty reigns, the challenges faced are often complex. Approaching them head-on often gets us nowhere. Rather, goals are usually achieved by pursuing intermediate objectives, or by working towards a higher-level goal with the by-product of profits-making.

In their book *Built to Last*, Jim Collins and Jerry Porras write, "Visionary companies pursue a cluster of objectives, of which making money is only one—and not necessarily the primary one. Yes, they seek profits, but they're equally guided by a core ideology—core values and a sense of purpose beyond just making money. Yet paradoxically, the visionary companies make more money than the purely profit driven companies."[8]

In his book, Collins praised the pharmaceutical giant Merck. Merck's principles went beyond mere profit-making, as espoused in the words of its president in 1950, George Merck II: "We try never to forget that medicine is for the people. It is not for the profits. The profits follow, and if we have remembered that, they have never failed to appear."[9]

In 1987, Merck developed a new drug called Mectizan that could cure river blindness, a common illness that plagued remote communities in Africa, Latin America and the Middle East. However, those who needed the drug most could not afford it. In October that year, the Merck leadership decided to establish the "Mectizan Donation Program" where it literally gave away the drug. Today, after more than one billion treatments in over 117,000 communities, there has not been any new cases of river blindness in four of the six affected countries in Latin America and nine regions in five African countries.[10]

John McKeen, Merck's contemporary at rival company Pfizer, took a different tack, stating bluntly that "So far as is humanly possible, we aim to get profit out of everything we do."

In the early 1990s, as Collins was writing his book, Merck was repeatedly named as America's most admired company in surveys conducted by *Fortune* magazine.[11]

In the time after the book was published however, Merck lost sight of its founding principles. Instead, it became obsessed with profit maximisation at the expense of people. In 2000, in a letter to shareholders, then-CEO Ray Gilmartin wrote: "As a company, Merck is totally focused on growth."

Around the same time that the letter came up, Merck was pushing out a new arthritis drug called Vioxx, which had become wildly successful, with more than 2.5 billion in sales by 2002. By 2004 however, Merck was forced to pull the drug from stores as reports of increased incidents of heart attacks and strokes begun to emerge. By early 2005, the US Food and Drug Administration (FDA) had officially attributed up to 139,000 deaths to Vioxx.[12]

In 2008, an article from the Journal of the American Medical Association revealed that Merck had ghost-written clinic trial manuscripts on Vioxx prior to its release. These manuscripts were subsequently endorsed by academically affiliated investigators who barely understood the research.[13] The credibility and ethics of Merck were called into question.

In the wake of the 2004 Vioxx saga, Merck's stock price plummeted from $45.07 a share on 30 September to $33 the next day. It was also subsequently hit by lawsuits, and in 2007 Merck agreed to set aside $4.85 billion to settle lawsuits from family members.[14] A year later, Merck had to settle for another $58 million with 30 states alleging that Merck engaged in deceptive marketing tactics in the promotion of Vioxx.[15]

In contrast, we have the case of Johnson & Johnson. In 1982, seven people died in the Chicago area after consuming cyanide-laced Tylenol, the best-selling product at Johnson & Johnson at that time. This was a case of deliberate drug tampering, and was not related to any kind of quality control issues on Johnson & Johnson's part. The company moved quickly to pull all 31 million bottles of Tylenol capsules from shelves and offered a replacement product free of charge. This came with a hefty price tag of more than $100 million, in addition to the millions of dollars needed to re-launch the product into the market at a later date.[16]

Johnson & Johnson's stocks suffered briefly in the aftermath of the drug-tampering case. However, just two months after the crisis struck, it was back up to its pre-crisis levels of sales. Its quick and determined actions to put the consumer first above all else, even at the expense of making money, restored consumer confidence in the brand.

By consistently sticking to its core values above and beyond profit maximisation, Johnson & Johnson has remained one of the leading pharmaceutical companies in the world today. Merck on the other hand, deviated from its founding principles of focusing on people. In its bid to focus exclusively on the pursuit of profits, it has ironically reached a new low in its financial history.

In summary, there are three key components to principles:

One, principles form the essential foundation as to how and why your organisation does things.

Two, principles differentiate between the options available to your organisation.

Three, principles should not be solely about profit maximising.

As John Kay pointed out, oblique approaches to strategy have benefits over the longer term.

FORMULATING STRATEGY

Most of the hard work should have been completed by the strategy-formulation stage. Because so much of Strategy is shaped by the strategic perspective, it is crucial that the Foresight and Understanding phases are completed as throughly as possible. Strategy formulation can be broken down into four key steps (see Fig. 23 overleaf):

First, identify the focal question.

Second, know the principal considerations facing your organisation.

Third, map out the options available.

Finally, evaluate these options according to the principal considerations identified earlier. From this evaluation, decide on the most optimal strategy that answers your core question.

Identify the focal question

The first step in strategy formulation is to identify where and what decisions are to be taken. These decisions should be framed within the context relevant to the organisation, and their importance weighed accordingly. For Netflix, its focal question concentrated on its ability to entrench and further its dominance in the online-streaming industry. The significance of this question was in turn intimately related to Netflix's survival as a company.

Focal questions should not be trivial. Answers to these questions need to have real consequences.

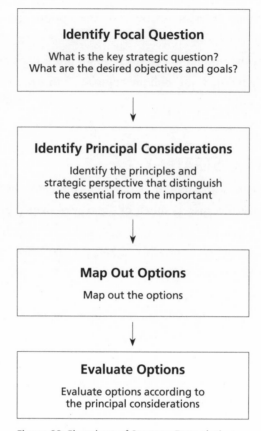

Figure 23: Flowchart of Strategy Formulation

Identify principal considerations

The second step involves identifying the principal considerations. Principal considerations form the boundaries of your options. They comprise of two key components: principles and the strategic perspective identified earlier. These should help to separate the essential from the important.

Map out options

From here, proceed to map out the options available. Imagination is crucial. The greater the range of options, the more robust your eventual strategy will be.

Evaluate options

Finally, based on the options generated, evaluate them according to the principal considerations arrived at earlier. The strategic perspective derived from the Foresight and Understanding process should have highlighted what needs to be done against the context of the desired vision and scenario-set. Your principles further filter your options by identifying the pathway that your organisation has previously committed to. This will ensure that your strategy formulation process pathway is sufficiently resilient.

In the final section of this chapter, I will use an actual case study of a company to illustrate how strategy formulation works.

THE RISE OF AIRBNB: CREATING AN EXPERIENCE OF BELONGING

Airbnb is a start-up that has achieved phenomenal success within a very short span of time.

Within eight years of its founding, the online-based home rental company already has a valuation of $13 billion, with a total of $884 million raised in venture funds. Its stable of employees has expanded rapidly from its initial pair of co-founders to 1,600 people. As of end-2014, it counted 20 million guests and 800,000 property listings across 34,000 cities spread across 190 countries.[17] In fact, its number of listings has surpassed established hotel chains such as the Hilton Worldwide or InterContinental Hotels Group.

Airbnb, however, was born out of a pragmatic need for rent money. In 2007, designers Brian Chesky and Joe Gebbia were having trouble paying the rent for their San Francisco apartment. To finance their rent, they decided to try and rent out lodging space. The opportunity presented itself when a design conference came to town. Participants were left scrabbling around for accommodation when hotel rooms were quickly snapped up.

At that time, Craigslist, the barebones online classified site, had been thriving for more than a decade, and offered one viable option to their problem. Chesky and Gebbia, however, felt that such an approach was too impersonal.[18] They built their own website instead and added a couple of pictures of their loft. The initial response wasn't encouraging—Chesky and Gebbia only managed to attract three people to stay in their place at $80 a night. Nonetheless, the initial spark for a great business was ignited.

Not only did the first three renters have an affordable place to stay, they also received an experience a hotel stay would never be able to provide. In the words of Chesky, the three renters "learned [their] favorite places to grab coffee, ate the best tacos in the city, and had friends to hang out with whenever they wanted."[19]

The desire to create a sense of belonging

The desire to create a sense of belonging and home would become a central principle that would guide Airbnb's strategy in developing its brand.

Today, if you log onto Airbnb's website, you will see the words "Welcome Home" placed prominently across its homepage. This language of belonging and home is replicated strongly in their marketing materials across different platforms.

"We imagine a world where you can belong anywhere." "Hospitality is both who we are and what we do."

These are just two of the other Airbnb slogans representing their value proposition. While this may sound like clever advertising, the convictions underlying such slogans undergird the whys and the hows of what Airbnb does.

In an interview with the online magazine Inc.com in 2014, Chesky espoused the values of his company, stating, "Airbnb is about so much more than just renting space. It's about people and experiences. At the end of the day, what we're trying to do is bring the world together. You're not getting a room, you're getting a sense of belonging."[20]

Principles give purpose and direction to strategy

For Airbnb, the underlying principle of why the company does what it does, and how it chooses to do it, is traced back to this core value of belonging.

Airbnb seeks to create a sense of belonging and foster a belonging of home. This belief comes out very strongly in the story that Airbnb has created for itself, and ultimately drives the strategies that they have adopted to guide their future steps.

Steered by the principles of creating a sense of belonging and home, Airbnb's strategy has been to focus on becoming a full-blown hospitality brand that offers an end-to-end experience based on a culture of sharing by local communities.

The principle of creating an experience of belonging thus shapes the way Airbnb goes about doing things. As Chesky himself says, Airbnb starts "with the perfect experience and [works] backwards."[21]

For instance, workflow is organised around the goal of providing a seamless Airbnb experience. A Pixar animator was hired to create illustrations of each stage of the trip from both the host's and the guest's perspectives. These included a total of 30 identified stages, such as "browsing for the right place", "checking out", and "feeling prepared and ready for guests". Different teams are assigned to look after the various steps, so as to achieve the ideal experience for both the host and the guest.[22] As Chesky puts it himself, "[Airbnb's] business isn't [about renting] the house. [It] is the entire trip."[23]

A good strategy commits action in a clear and coherent manner. It also unifies the organisation by providing purpose to the way things are done.

Principles justify commitments

The commitment to providing the most hospitable experience for the guest extends throughout Airbnb's tactics. It demands, but justifies, the amount of resources that go into such tactics.

For example, the company acquires significant costs by sending out an army of professional photographers to capture shots of Airbnb listings.[24]

While the typical community-based rental classified website relies on amateur photographs, usually captured on phone cameras, Airbnb wanted to elevate the experience of the guest, beginning from the browsing stage. This entailed significant investment. However, because it was an investment that was ultimately aligned with the larger strategy, the founders were willing to make that commitment.

Other tactics include rolling out a set of hospitality standards to improve the Airbnb guest experience. A "hospitality lab" was also set up in Dublin, where hosts could get free training on hospitality standards and where Airbnb could also learn from studying the interactions between hosts and guests.

Principles help to discriminate among options

Principles also whittle down the strategic options available to your organisation.

Airbnb has no lack of options. They could have focused on keeping costs down, or expand horizontally into other sharing sectors. But the emphasis on experience, and one which promotes a sense of belonging, eliminated these options as growth paths for the company.

Using the Airbnb story as an illustration, it is easy to see how the FUSE approach to strategy formulation works. Principles matter. They are non-negotiable and are non-malleable, providing meaning and consistency to Strategy. In the case of Airbnb, the founders believed fundamentally in the importance of experience and belonging.

These principles guide the strategy adopted by Airbnb, which in turn mapped out the future options that the company could take. Airbnb chose to focus on creating an integrated experience of a home away from home, driven by a strong emphasis on hospitality.

From these broad strokes, the finer details of tactics were hammered out. The entire strategy process thus provides clarity and coherency. It also provides flexibility; Airbnb is not tied down to a permanent strategy, but is free to evolve according to the changing environment.

CONCLUSION

This chapter began by emphasising the importance of principles in strategy formulation. Principles guide decision-making, discriminate between options and go beyond the profit motive. In fact, principles steer the strategy formulation process because they determine the hows and the whys.

Once the core principles are established, it becomes easier to formulate an effective strategy that is organisation specific. The core question is first identified, before locating the principal considerations found in the principles and strategic perspective. From here, the options available are mapped out and evaluated according to these principal considerations.

These are all steps designed to help you arrive at an effective strategy targeted at your organisation's unique conditions and circumstances. However, strategy formulation does not end here. In order to ensure that your strategy is as robust and resilient as possible, you will need to subject it to stress-testing.

The final chapter of this section does exactly that—I will demonstrate the importance of stress-testing while elaborating on two key methods of sensitivity analysis and wind-tunnelling.

CHAPTER 19
STRESS-TESTING STRATEGIES

To ensure confidence in your strategies, you need to stress-test them. Locate the critical threshold at which the particular strategy no longer becomes viable.

WHY STRESS-TESTING IS IMPORTANT

Stress-testing can produce several levels of outcomes: robustness, resilience, and what writer and academic Nassim Taleb terms as "antifragility".

Robustness reflects an attitude where nothing is permitted to fail under conditions of change. This demands a tremendous commitment of resources to create redundancy and to cover all contingencies. As a result of this attitude, inflexibility occurs.

Resilience tries to anticipate possible contingencies that may crop up along the way. Resilience differs from robustness, however, in that it recognises the infinite nature of possibilities that may arise, as well as the futility of trying to prepare for each contingency.

Resilience thus emphasises recoverability. Its end-point is not to cover all contingencies, but to ensure that organisations can be confident of recovering from an unanticipated shock.

Antifragility goes beyond resilience. Antifragile organisations seek to thrive on shocks and disruptions. Taleb uses the mythical Greek monster

Hydra as an example. The Hydra was a ferocious, multi-headed serpent-like monster. Each time one of its heads was cut off, another two heads grew back in its place. In other words, disruption only made the Hydra stronger.

Expect change, and anticipate that there will be volatility in the variables involved. Black swans can and do occur.

While antifragility may represent the end stage on this spectrum of responses, it is not realistic to expect that antifragile strategies can always be achieved. When weighed against the consumption of scarce resources, the scale or nature of the problem may not require the strategy to be antifragile.

There can also be different strategies for different issues. For example, medical and power generation systems should be robust. You want them to be robust because you do not want them to fail in the face of natural or man-made threats. Social systems, on the other hand, should be resilient. Society needs to possess the ability to recover from unanticipated shocks. With economic systems, antifragility is vital. When crises hit, you want the economy to not only bounce back unscathed, but to take advantage of the crisis to become even better.

Stress-testing is crucial for strategy to be even more effective. There are two main ways to do this: the first is to perform a sensitivity analysis, and the second is to execute a technique called wind-tunnelling.

SENSITIVITY ANALYSIS
The Challenger tragedy

On 28 January 1986, thousands of spectators gathered at Cape Canaveral in Florida to watch the launching of American space shuttle Challenger. Just 73 seconds after the Challenger lifted off, the crowd's cheers of excitement turned into cries of horror as the shuttle exploded in a ball of flames, killing all seven people on board. Flaming debris rained down into the Atlantic Ocean for an hour after the explosion.

For the millions of Americans tuning in to the live screening of the Challenger launch that morning, the horrifying images of the shuttle's explosion were to remain etched in their memories for a long time after.

In the aftermath of the explosion, engineers and scientists came together to determine the cause of the tragedy. In June 1986, investigations revealed that the accident had been caused by a failure in the O-rings in the shuttle's right solid rocket booster. O-rings are small rubber rings that seal the joints between sections of the rocket booster; they prevent combustible gases from leaking. Because they are cheap and easy to manufacture, O-rings are widely used in machine design.

The morning of 28 January, however, was exceptionally cold, with temperatures dropping to 18°F (-8°C). Despite the fact that O-rings had only been tested up to temperatures of 40°F (4°C), NASA decided to go ahead with the launch. It was only later that investigators found out that O-rings lose their elasticity and become brittle when the temperature drops below a certain degree. When O-rings are cooled to a certain temperature, they become compressed and take longer than normal to return to their original shape. This had severe implications for the Challenger launch, because the O-rings were meant to prevent gas leaks.

On the morning of the launch, the below-freezing temperatures meant that the O-rings had hardened. This prevented them from fully sealing, and hot gases begun leaking through the joints. The flames passed through the failed seal, burning through the external fuel tank and one of the supports that attached the booster to the tank. Consequently, the booster broke loose and collided with the tank, causing liquid hydrogen and oxygen fuels from the tank and booster to mix together. The mixture of gases ignited, blowing the entire space shuttle to smithereens.[1]

The O-ring was an incredibly simple device compared to the complex machinery that made up the space shuttle. Under ordinary circumstances, the O-rings would have fulfilled their role of preventing leaks in the seal. However, the team did not think about the operating assumption: what if temperatures went below 40°F (4°C)? Would that affect the structure and integrity of the O-ring? What was the critical threshold temperature at which the O-ring loses its functionality? The failure to test for variations in the behaviour of the O-rings eventually led to the tragic loss of seven human lives.

PERFORMING A SENSITIVITY ANALYSIS TEST

A sensitivity analysis can also be thought of as a what-if analysis. How would changes in the variables involved affect the projected outcome?

The first step in sensitivity analysis is to identify the assumptions undergirding the choice of strategy. List both the explicit and implicit assumptions and from there, identify the key variables that will influence the desired outcome.

As mentioned during the Foresight process, assumptions, especially those of an implicit nature, are frequently difficult to spot. To avoid blind spots, a Team B—a group of independent testers—could be set up to provide the strategy team with a fresh perspective and a non-biased viewpoint. They should scrutinise the strategy meticulously to identify assumptions that the strategy team may have overlooked.

You should be looking out for the critical threshold at which order-of-magnitude changes in outcome occur. Ask yourself, if variable X increases by A%, how would that affect your outcome? Or, if variable X increases by A% but variable Y decreases by B%, what effect would that have on your outcome?

This is easier to do when you know the relationship between variables or when variables are quantifiable. Mathematical modelling software can thus be utilised to perform the calculations and computations. However, this is not always possible. The relevant data may not be available, or it may not be possible to determine the relationship between variables and outcomes.

Sometimes this problem can be rectified by further research. In most cases, however, you will need to find a way to quantify these variables.

First, list down the assumptions and variables involved. Then, look for ways in which these variables may vary and estimate their probabilities/

frequencies. Assess as well the consequences of these variations, further classifying them into categories of high impact, intermediate impact and low impact. From there, you will be able to obtain an idea of the kind of critical thresholds you should be expecting.

Sensitivity analysis is not the only way to stress-test strategies. While sensitivity analysis tests the structural integrity of the strategy itself, wind-tunnelling returns the focus to the external environment by testing the strategy against the previously developed scenario-set.

WIND-TUNNELLING

During the Foresight process, a set of scenarios concerning the external environment was developed. These scenarios should have already identified key driving forces and predetermined elements, leaving only the critical uncertainties as a source of differentiation.

The term "wind-tunnelling" comes from the word "wind tunnel". Wind tunnels were first invented towards the end of the 19th century when aeronautical technology was still in its incipient stage. The wind tunnel was a tubular passage that allowed air to move quickly over the aircraft mounted in the middle. The wind tunnel was used to study how an aircraft would fly under real-life conditions in the air.

In the same way, wind-tunnelling is a way of testing strategies against the backdrop of plausible futures to see how they would hold up under each scenario. A strategy that works only under ideal conditions is, in effect, a useless strategy. You want a strategy that can thrive over a range of environmental conditions.

In his book *A Demon of Our Own Design*, Richard Bookstaber argues that the 1987 Wall Street stock market crash was caused by the complex mess that the financial system had evolved into. Given how tightly coupled the entire system had become, the possibility that the unravelling of one segment would lead to multiple chain reactions increased. The solution, according to Bookstaber, is to stop developing evermore complex financial instruments in favour of simpler instruments.

Drawing a parallel with the natural world, Bookstaber gave the example of the cockroach and the T-Rex. Compared to the small and simple cockroach, the T-Rex is huge and terrifying. Yet the T-Rex has long since been extinct, while the cockroach continues to survive and thrive.

Bookstaber labels the cockroach as a survivor that has ridden out "many unforeseeable changes—jungles turning to deserts, flatland giving way to urban habitat and predators of all types coming and going." The cockroach is an example of a "coarse" species that has been able to survive across time because of its simplicity in design. Because it is not complex in its biological make-up, it occupies a less specialised niche, thereby allowing it to survive across a variety of conditions.[2]

The T-Rex, on the other hand, belongs to "a species that is prolific and successful during a short period of time, but then dies out after an unanticipated event." It is "well-designed for the known risks of one environment but not for dealing with unforeseeable changes."

Stress-testing is an indispensable step in the strategy-formulation process. It ensures that your strategy is resilient both internally *and* externally by means of two different processes. The first process of sensitivity analysis questions the assumptions and variables inherent in the strategy itself. The second process of wind-tunnelling shifts the focus outwards to test if and how the strategy would hold up against plausible future scenarios.

CONCLUSION

At the beginning of this section, I spoke briefly about Netflix's strategy of concentrating on its software business. This strategy was one that was driven by principles unique to Netflix: the firm saw its focus on the on-demand streaming industry as key to its very existence. This principle subsequently shaped the strategy employed—a strategy that had a clear intent, and which committed significant resources in a specific and coherent direction towards the desired outcome.

Netflix decided to discard months and months of hard work and preparation to further grow its share of the streaming market. This was not an easy decision to make. Strong leadership was necessary. Netflix's CEO Reed Hastings understood what it took to achieve the desired outcome, and was prepared to take the necessary risk.

Strategy formulation does not stop there, however. In the final chapter of this section I talked about the need for stress-testing. By ensuring that strategies are robust and resilient enough in the face of changing conditions, success can be better ensured.

The next section will conclude by looking at how strategies can be executed effectively and fruitfully.

THE STRATEGY PROCESS

1. **Understanding Strategy**
   - Strategy is a deliberate and conscious choice leading to a coherent directional and purposeful set of actions that affect the future.
   - There are three important ingredients for successful strategy formulation:
     - Leadership
     - Principles
     - Stress-testing

2. **Leadership Matters**
   - Leadership is essential. Good leadership is characterised by:
     - Imagination
     - Vision
     - Boldness
     - Commitment

3. **Strategy Formulation**
   - Principles guide strategy, which in turn determine the tactics adopted.
   - Principles are core guiding precepts which are non-negotiable. They are important because they:
     - Guide decision-making
     - Discriminate between options
     - Are not solely about profit maximisation
   - Strategy serves as a coherent guide to tactics. They are long-lasting commitments, whereas tactics are short-term responses to the current environment.

     ○ Strategy can be formulated in a sequential manner:
- Identify the core question
- Identify principal considerations
- Map out your options
- Evaluate your options according to your principal considerations

4. **Stress-testing Strategy**

     ○ It is important to stress-test your strategy to ensure that it is robust, resilient and anti-fragile enough to withstand unforeseen contingencies.

     ○ There are two ways to do stress-testing:
- Perform a sensitivity analysis by locating the critical thresholds of variables at which changes in outcomes occur.
- Perform wind-tunnelling by testing the strategy against the scenario-set developed during the Foresighting process.

SECTION 5

EXECUTION

CHAPTER 20

INTRODUCTION TO EXECUTION

DISRUPTING ONESELF

At the onset of the 1970s, the semiconductor company Intel became synonymous with the memory chip business. This was unsurprising; Intel helped launch the industry when it released its 1103 device in October 1970.

Intel's 1103 device was the first ever dynamic random-access memory (DRAM) integrated circuit to be produced. It was capable of storing up to 1,024 digits—an amount which sounds ludicrous today, but which represented a technological breakthrough in the 1970s.

As the technology developed and the market matured, new entrants also begun jostling for a share of the pie. With its first-mover advantage, however, Intel was able to enjoy a dominant share of the memory chip market. By 1983, sales had hit the $1 billion mark.[1]

All of this was to change in the 1980s.

Before the early 1980s, Intel's competitors were mainly small American companies competing to outbid each other in technological innovation. But by the mid-1980s, large Japanese memory chip companies accelerated to gain a majority of the market share. Not only did these companies possess a larger capacity for production, they made cheaper and higher quality memory chips than those produced by their American counterparts. By 1985, Japan had overtaken the United States in its share of the global semiconductor market.

In response, Intel worked hard to improve the quality of their products and lower costs. But the Japanese were still able to outdo them. They undercut Intel's selling price and produced semiconductors that were just as good, if not better, than what Intel was offering to its customers. Clearly, something had to change.

In 1985, Intel's then-president Andy Grove sat down with its CEO and chairman Gordon Moore. Grove turned to Moore and asked, "If we got kicked out and the board brought in a new CEO, what do you think he would do?"[2]

Moore replied almost instantaneously, "He would get us out of memories."

Grove was stunned. For years, Intel and memory had come to mean one and the same thing. Memory formed the most basic foundation of all of Intel's manufacturing and sales activities. Who could conceive of Intel without thinking of memory chips? Even as meeting after meeting was called to decide if Intel should abandon the memory business, resistance against change persisted within the team.

Yet, against the harsh changing realities, the management team knew that running the business-as-usual, or what I call BAU, was no longer tenable. Their strategy had to change. More than this, their entire organisation had to change. Intel could no longer stay in the memory business.

By the late 1980s, Intel had moved out of memory and into microprocessors. They disrupted the very same formula and culture that had made Intel so successful in the 1970s.

THE IMPORTANCE OF EXECUTION

In 2014, Intel reported a record revenue of $55.9 billion, an increase of 6% from 2013's figures.[3] This placed it nearly $30 billion in revenue ahead of its closest competition, Qualcomm.[4] Today, Intel's microprocessors are widely used in personal computers and laptops all across the globe, and the tagline "Intel Inside" has become a recognised and trusted stamp of quality.

Compare this to the fates of Intel's counterparts in the 1970s: names such as Unisem, Advanced Memory Systems and Mostek have long disappeared.

Intel has not stood still. It continues to lead technological change and anticipates new waves of technology. Over the last few years, Intel has been looking to the emerging Internet of Things (IoT) market: in December 2014, Intel announced the release of its IoT Platform. It intends to entrench itself in the emerging IoT market by creating the basic infrastructure for solution providers to construct their products and services cheaply and quickly.

The fact that Intel is still a major player in such a competitive industry is the greatest testimony to its ability to disrupt itself not just once but repeatedly. The crisis of the mid-1980s was not its last; in the 1990s, fierce competition in the microprocessor industry once again compelled Intel to change its strategic direction to the PC market. In both cases, Intel managed to successfully disrupt itself to shift its strategic direction.

The story of Intel is the story of effective foresight-led Execution.

Without effective execution, the best-formulated strategy amounts to nothing. As Bali Padda, COO of the Lego Group has it, "Strategy is only as good as the execution behind it."[5]

Lawrence Hrebiniak, emeritus professor at the University of Pennsylvania's Wharton School of Business, agrees, arguing that the "implementation [of strategy] is more important than strategy formulation."

Yet despite its importance, execution is often not given due attention within the decision-making process. A 2013 survey by the Economist Intelligence Unit (EIU) of more than 400 global CEOs found that the number one challenge facing corporate leaders in Asia, Europe and the United States, was executional excellence. In fact, 61% of respondents conceded that their firms found it challenging to close the gap between strategy formulation and the day-to-day implementation.[6]

Former US Secretary of State Collin Powell, in expressing his admiration for the late founding Prime Minister of Singapore Lee Kuan Yew, describes his respect for the latter as going beyond just vision and determination, saying, "Vision and determination are not as important as execution, [which is the act of] making something happen. [Lee Kuan Yew] was a leader who made many great things happen in Singapore."

Strategy is about getting things done.

This chapter will review the existing frameworks and tools popularly used to organise the execution process, and introduce the FUSE approach to effective foresight-led Execution.

THE PROBLEM WITH EXISTING FRAMEWORKS

There are two management frameworks or techniques that are mainstream today.

The first technique is known as Management by Objectives (MBO) and was first outlined by Management guru Peter Drucker in his 1954 book *The Practice of Management*. It was further developed by his student George Odiorne and became popularised through MBA programmes from the 1960s to the present day.

MBO is sold as a systematic and organised approach where both managers and employees work together to achieve predetermined goals. The MBO approach seeks to ensure that individual goals are carefully aligned and coordinated to facilitate the larger organisational goal. Using this approach, organisational goals and planning flow are meticulously broken down into specified steps for individual members of the organisation to execute. Progress towards these objectives are monitored and evaluated at regular intervals, and employees are appropriately rewarded when these goals are achieved.

The Balanced Scorecard (BSC) method is the other management technique widely practiced today. Pioneered by Robert Kaplan and David Norton in the 1990s, the Balanced Scorecard provides a set of measures that afford managers a comprehensive view of the business.[7] Although not directly involved in the implementation process, the Balanced Scorecard is used to monitor and evaluate the performance of the strategy being implemented—an important component of the Execution process.

The Balanced Scorecard approach is centred around four fundamental perspectives: the customer perspective, the internal perspective, the innovation and learning perspective and finally, the financial perspective. By linking goals to distinct measures, the Balanced Scorecard aims to allow managers to know what is working and what is not. It brings together a bird's eye view of the organisation by piecing together different components of the same puzzle.

In the industrial age of the 20th century, both methods may have helped to make the management process more efficient through better planning. In the networked age of the 21st century, however, they are antiquated and ineffectual.

Overly mechanistic and planned

First, the effectiveness of the MBO and Balanced Scorecard frameworks are premised on the assumption that larger organisational objectives can be broken down into individual goals, which can in turn be broken down into smaller action steps. Further, the frameworks *assume* that these action steps are definitive.

In reality, this is rarely the case. It is not possible to cover the myriad of scenarios that can arise each day. The interconnected nature of the networked world makes it difficult to operate in silos, or to predict the ripple effects of any event. Various factors and institutional forces act in unanticipated ways to produce a set of circumstances completely different from the control environment.

Hampering flexibility and agility

Second, the mechanistic nature of the two frameworks constrains latitude and discretion to act autonomously and promptly according to their judgement of the situation at hand. Organisations may become dogmatic in following the prescribed policy—*even* when it does not line up with the organisation's values or strategic direction.

For example, a hotel employee may refuse a disgruntled guest a room upgrade, citing company policy as justification. In the larger scheme of things, however, sticking to the regimen may mean missing the forest for the trees—the guest may go away feeling unvalued, and decide never to visit again.

In a world where dense and extensive networks have shrunk time and space, feedback loops are becoming increasingly shorter and more rapid. Organisations need to have the agility to react promptly to contingencies as they unfold. If the hotel employee had to wait for a response from the manager, who in turn had to seek clearance from his supervising coordinator, a nasty review posted to social media may have gone viral in the intervening time. In a rapidly evolving and complex 21st century, a new approach to Execution needs to be found.

A FALSE DISTINCTION BETWEEN STRATEGY AND EXECUTION?

One increasingly popular school of thought that tries to mitigate the shortfalls of the two frameworks rejects the distinction made between strategy and execution.

Henry Mintzberg first argued in 1978 that strategy is inherently emergent. We cannot plan for it; rather, as external conditions and experience evolve across time, the optimal strategy emerges as the organisation modifies its plans accordingly. Tools such as the MBO and the Balanced Scorecard methods are thus not only ineffective, they may also be counter-productive.

A more recent iteration of this argument is found in academic Roger Martin's 2010 article "The Execution Trap," where he asserts that managers cannot make high-level, abstract choices and assume that these can be easily translated into simple steps for implementation. Rather, employees face numerous choices while carrying out their day-to-day operations. These decisions directly translate into strategic choices, making the line between strategy and execution ultimately pointless.

Martin instead proposes that strategy be thought of as a choice cascade. Senior management make decisions that middle management subsequently base their decisions on. When these decisions trickle down to staff members on the ground, these employees should in turn be empowered to make "thoughtful choices within the context of the decisions made above them."

The problem with such an approach is that it leaves too much to chance. How can a manager take concrete steps to better organise his team? In other words, an emergent approach does not provide a framework for effecting better execution.

THE FUSE APPROACH

The FUSE model adopts a principles-based approach to Execution. FMG's philosophy is consistent and simple: we believe that we have the ability to make deliberate choices in the present to positively affect outcomes. However, we also believe that deliberate planning needs to be balanced with the flexibility to adapt to local and changing conditions.

As explained at length in the previous section on Strategy, strategy formulation needs to be driven by principles that are consistent and immutable. This allows greater flexibility in the crafting of strategy and tactics in accordance with local conditions and an evolving environment. In other words, strategy and tactics are malleable, guided by a set of parameters as determined by an organisation's core principles.

By using a principles-based approach to strategy as the starting point, the process of execution becomes less rigid. It is not so much about actualising a list of action-steps than it is about providing the agility and flexibility to act within pre-established boundaries.

In the networked world today, a principles-based approach provides a framework to cope with the deluge of information coming our way every second of the day, while allowing us the space needed to deal with contingencies and unexpected events.

OUTLINE OF THIS SECTION

The next three chapters lay out the framework for the Execution process. This is divided into three broad segments: implementation, review and adaptation.

The next chapter on implementation begins by returning to the Intel story. Intel had organically created a market for itself by inventing the memory chip. It was tempting to stay in this sector and try to hold ground. To pursue something so antithetical to its established strategic thrust, the company would have had to rouse itself against strong organisational inertia.

Yet Intel was able to successfully implement a strategy that disrupted a core identity of the firm. How was it able to do so?

The next chapter answers this question by looking at how large organisations can effectively create an environment conducive to disruption. Here, disruption refers to a drastic shift in the strategic direction.

There are two ways disruption may occur: the first is called "induced disruption", where circumstances beyond your control forces you to change gears. Avoid this.

The second kind of disruption is termed "auto-disruption". This is a change prompted from within, in anticipation of shifts in the external environment. This is the kind of disruption we want to achieve. Getting there, however, is difficult. This can only be attained when both the leadership and strategy of the organisation are credible.

This is what I call the 5Cs Action. Credibility is required to facilitate a disruptive environment for promoting the effective implementation of a new strategy. But Credibility in turn can only be attained when there is Consultation, Communication, Coordination and Commitment.

Execution does not end when a strategy has been successfully implemented, however. Instead, outcomes need to be continuously evaluated. This allows the progress of the strategy to be monitored, and the results to be judged. If it is a success, make sure that it worked for the right reasons. Conversely, if it is a failure, understand why it failed, and prescribe the appropriate remedy to turn the situation around.

The final chapter of this section closes with a look at the need for adaptation. Even after coming up with a robust framework for implementation and evaluation, things can and *will* change. As British economist John Maynard Keynes famously said, "When the facts change, I change my mind."

In the same way, when the environment changes, adapt your strategy accordingly. We may have had the best strategy at *that point of formulation*, but we certainly cannot expect conditions *at that time* to stay the same forever. Depending on the circumstances, we may have to return to our starting point in the FUSE framework, to re-examine and review a dynamic Foresight process.

The pathway flow of the Execution process is illustrated in Fig. 24.

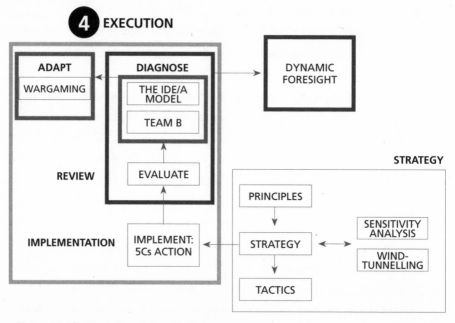

Figure 24: The Execution Process Pathway

CHAPTER 21
DISRUPTIVE IMPLEMENTATION

THE NEED FOR DISRUPTION

Foresight-led Execution begins with the ability to disrupt oneself. This requires transformative commitments and not simply statements of intent.

This approach demands change. First, change needs to be *purposeful*. Rather than changing for the sake of change, change needs to be meaningful. There is a difference between successfully changing and changing for success. Sure, we want to be successful in the changes that we make, but we also want to make sure that these changes are taking place to better secure our organisation's future.

Secondly, change when you can and not when you must. There is an important distinction between what we call "induced disruption", where we are forced by circumstances to change accordingly, and "auto disruption", where we possess the agency to drive change. In the case of the former, conditions outside our control limit the agency we have over our own actions: we do not determine our circumstances; rather, we react *passively* to circumstances.

Borders and Blockbuster are examples of companies that were unwillingly forced to change. They ignored shifts in consumer habits, and failed to keep up with technological advances. The result was that they were left at the mercy of external forces. In the particular cases of Borders and Blockbuster, they were slow to adapt, and were eventually eliminated from the game.

Intel did not wait for circumstances to become dire. It had sufficient lead-time to expand its capacity in dealing with change, and was consequently better equipped to handle the changes that were coming its way.

Disrupt yourselves in a purposeful manner. This disruption should arise from the desire for success, rather than from any compulsion to change for the sake of change.

In a survey completed in 2015, eight in 10 managers reported that their companies failed to exit declining businesses or to kill unsuccessful initiatives quickly enough.[1] The sunk-cost effect, or organisational inertia, is a powerful force that prevents organisations from making transformative changes.

The key to successful disruption is to ensure that leadership and strategy are ultimately credible.

5CS ACTION: CONSULT, COMMUNICATE, COORDINATE, COMMIT, BE CREDIBLE
Consult

In order for the leadership and strategy to be credible, stakeholders need to be consulted. This includes people at the forefront of the organisation—the ones running the day-to-day operations—and people at the peripheries of the organisation. While they may not be close to the organisational centre, they are nevertheless the first ones to feel the direct impact of changes in strategic direction, or changes in the external environment.

Communicate

Even if the strategy is credible, the way it is conveyed needs to be credible as well. This includes being consistent in the choice of language used. If the message is ambiguous, employees lose confidence in the senior management's commitment to the strategy. Furthermore, communication facilitates organisational alignment, further bolstering the credibility of the strategy, as everyone in the organisation—from the highest echelons to the people on the ground—is directly aware of the strategic decisions taken.

Coordinate

Coordination is vital. While vertical alignment occurs during the Communication phase, horizontal alignment occurs during the Coordination phase. Different units and departments within the organisation, especially when there are highly differentiated or competing functions, need to be willing to cooperate with one another to achieve the broader strategic direction of the organisation. When everyone is on the same page, the credibility of the strategy also increases.

Commit

Commitment refers to resource allocation. While resource allocation is often thought of in terms of the disbursement of resources, more resources allocated to one area means less resources allocated to another area. Resources are finite. Commitment may thus require us to make the painful decision to withdraw resources from areas that are no longer strategically important. The presence or absence of resources is the tangible expression of commitment.

Consultation, Communication, Coordination and Concentration culminate in the fifth and most important C: Credibility.

Be credible

Credibility is key to strategy gaining traction.

People need to be able to trust and believe in the leadership and the strategy. First, they need to believe in the leadership. Second, they need to believe that the strategy would actually work. The two operate in a mutually reinforcing fashion with leadership being the primal factor—without credible leadership, there can be no credible strategy.

When there is credibility, it becomes easier to disrupt the status quo. Fig. 25 overleaf is a visual depiction of the 5Cs Action.

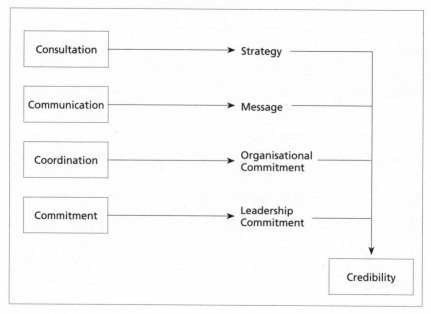

Figure 25: The 5Cs Action

CONSULTATION

In his book *Only the Paranoid Survive*, Andy Grove writes about the need to recognise Cassandras in the company.[2] Cassandra, of course, refers to the Greek princess who possessed the gift of prophecy, only to be cursed by the god Apollo by never having anyone believe in her prophecies.

The Cassandras in your organisation are frequently the people who are the closest to the ground and who are the first to recognise impending signs of danger. However, just as Cassandra's prophecy about the fall of Troy was ignored by the Trojans, bad news is rarely well-received, and these same people are often written off as naysayers.

At Intel, however, Grove took warnings from his ground staff seriously. He cites an example of a sales manager in charge of the Asia-Pacific region, who had sent him an email beseeching him to take a look at a development the manager had found alarming. Grove's first instinct was to dismiss it. After all, California was a long way from Asia, and who knew if the manager's hunch was even right?

Despite its distance from the organisational core, the periphery is often the best place to look for early warning signals. Grove uses the analogy of snow: when spring arrives, snow first melts at the periphery, because this is the area that is the most exposed. In the same way, you need to pay attention to people who are at the periphery: they are often the first ones to feel the effects of change.

At the same time, people working at different levels or in different departments within the same organisation will have varying opinions and perspectives that are not immediately obvious to senior management. It is worthwhile to listen to them, or at the very least, to be open to what they are saying.

Consultation helps to strengthen strategy.

Firstly, it increases the diversity of perspectives. Senior management may know the most, but it does not mean that their perspective is always the best. Even from their vantage point at the top, the leadership's perspective remains limited. Consulting with people from different positions and different functions within the hierarchy will help to ensure that there is more than one perspective being considered.

Secondly, consultation provides a sanity check. The top leadership may be too far removed from ground operations to recognise the operational implications to accurately gauge the real-life feasibility of target outcomes. This is in contrast to people working on the ground, who frequently operationalise many of the more abstract ideas and strategies coming from the top. From their operational experience, they are more likely to be aware of whether a projected outcome is realistic or not. This is important, because "unrealistic plans create the expectation throughout the organisation that plans simply will not be fulfilled."[3] When expectation is realised as experience, the expectation that targets are just a perfunctory number for upper management to feel good about will eventually crystallise into a norm that becomes hard to shake off. Avoid forming such bad habits.

Thirdly, consultation increases the buy-in of stakeholders. Because inputs from the various stakeholders within the organisation are sought out and actively considered, the strategy in question also gains greater legitimacy. Furthermore, strategy is no longer considered exclusively within an abstract or ideational realm; instead, it is tested against operational realities by the same people who will be charged with implementation.

How to go about consulting your organisation

Instead of seeking different people's opinions at random, psychologist Gary Klein suggests a more effective and systematic way of garnering feedback from focus groups within the organisation. He calls this a "pre-mortem".[4]

A pre-mortem is similar to a post-mortem where group members analyse what went wrong. The obvious difference however, is that unlike a post-mortem, which takes place only after the strategy has been implemented, a pre-mortem takes place even before the strategy is rolled out. A pre-mortem is thus akin to a thought experiment where everyone pictures the strategy failing. The task of the group is to figure out what went wrong. To make this a more credible process, encourage a diversity of participants.

The causes of failure can be attributed to three core categories: Assumptions, Operationalisation, and Outcomes (see Fig. 26).

Using this framework to visualise the implementation process, it becomes possible to locate problems that might arise *before* the strategy is even implemented. This closely aligns the strategy with actual operating realities

Assumptions	Operationalisation	Outcomes
What are the operating assumptions underlying the strategy? Do they require revision?	What are the immediate operationalisation problems that will occur? What are the resources needed for implementation to succeed?	Are the goals set realistic, or do they require revision? What are the possible externalities that can arise from the implementation of the strategy?

Figure 26: Causes of Failure

by tapping upon the diverse experiences of the participants. Needless to say, this will help to save time, energy and resources that would otherwise be wasted.

Once consultation is completed, the strategic decision needs to be communicated. In the next section, I turn to look at the communication process.

COMMUNICATION

When Intel decided to shift its strategic focus from memories to microprocessors, it left no room for ambiguity in its senior management's communication to its employees. As Grove puts it, "the time for listening to the Cassandras is over. [...] The time to issue marching orders—exquisitely clear marching orders—to the organisation is here."[5]

At Intel, senior management was acutely aware of the need for a clear strategic intent. In particular, Intel enlisted their middle management as key nodes within the communication chain. While senior management may have made the big decisions, it was middle management and the people on the ground who made the decisions that directly translated into real outcomes.

At Intel, the strategic shift towards microprocessors happened not just because the leadership decided that it should be so. It happened because middle managers were making everyday decisions to make microprocessors Intel's core business.

Communication was not one-way. At each step in the chain of command, questions were encouraged, asked and answered, increasing the legitimacy of the strategy and strengthening strategic understanding.

Communication thus serves two critical functions.

First, it promotes an understanding of the strategy as well as the rationale behind the strategic decision. People cannot implement what they do not understand.

Second, communication ensures organisational alignment. In large, complex organisations, decision-making tends to be decentralised. It is important that staff members see the big picture and understand how their roles contribute towards that larger objective.

What needs to be communicated

Many managers appreciate the importance of communication. What they are less aware of, however, is what exactly *should* be communicated.

In communicating strategy, it is important that managers resist the temptation to feed members with a list of overly detailed steps; no one remembers a long-winded and complicated to-do manual. Members on the ground are also likely to run into unexpected circumstances, in which case a rule book would be of no help.

Communicating principles

Instead, managers need to communicate the principles that underlie the strategies being adopted. Using a principles-based approach, people can be empowered to make on-the-spot decisions when discrepancies between theory and reality occur.

When principles are communicated, employees have the latitude and discretion to act autonomously according to the situation at hand while ensuring that these decisions remain aligned with the broader principles of the organisation. This is because principles form the parameters and guidelines within which action takes place.

One of the most famous examples of execution by principles is the story of the Four Seasons hotel chain. The Four Seasons chain is widely recognised as one of the most luxurious hotel brands anywhere, and remains distinguishable today by its service excellence.

Founded in 1961 by Isadore Sharp, the underlying principle driving operations at the Four Seasons has consistently been "the simple idea that if you treat people well, the way you would like to be treated, they will do the same."[6]

Early on, Sharp realised the importance of having a unified team that consistently provided excellent service to customers. In order to do so, the company had to share a common purpose underlined by a common set of values.

Sharp set out to create a written code of values that would unite his employees and provide a focal point from which people could answer the question: "Does this deal, this decision, this action, square with [Four Season's] values?"[7] With the help of his director of advertising Doug Hall, Sharp made this operating principle of the Golden Rule explicit and clear to his employees: "Do unto others as you would have them do unto you."

Before communicating this Golden Rule to the rank-and-file however, Sharp wanted to make sure that the people at the top were committed to this principle. This was especially important because these were the same people who were going out to sell the concept to their subordinates. Without practicing what they were preaching, they would not be credible.

Together with John Sharp, the vice president of operations (unrelated to Isadore), Isadore Sharp went out to each hotel in the Four Seasons chain to talk to the planning committee about the principle of the Golden Rule. Again, it was not a one-way communication channel. Sharp was interested in knowing if these same senior people were convinced by the principle. If the leadership did not believe in the Golden Rule, how would they communicate this central principle effectively to the people working under them?

This process of sharing the fundamental principle of the company took several years. As Sharp describes it himself, "You have to start at the tip of the triangle and get it down to the base of the triangle to make it work."[8]

Communicating principles is powerful. Everyone at Four Seasons, from the desk clerk to the bellboy, had a compass they could use regardless of the context that they found themselves in. No matter what happened, employees knew that their core business was to deal with others—not only hotel guests, but their fellow colleagues as well—in the same way that they wished to be treated.

Communicating priorities

Beyond communicating principles, senior management should also communicate its strategic priorities. When people know which outcomes are more important, they are able to make a conscious effort to focus on achieving those outcomes. Unless we have infinite amounts of money, energy or time, we will always be limited to doing a few things well. In a large and complex organisation, everybody needs to know how to tell the essential from the merely important.

Communicating with a common vocabulary

A common vocabulary needs to be used within the organisation. It is important that the vocabulary remain consistent when communicating principles and strategy. This ensures clarity and unity of the message being communicated. For execution to be effective, everyone—from the finance team to the production and planning team—has to be on the same page. If the vocabulary used is different, teams will end up talking past each other.

A common vocabulary also ensures that the different upstream and downstream processes are adequately coupled. For example, goals should be evaluated by the same set of indicators for the evaluation process to be meaningful.

How to communicate strategy effectively

Principles, priorities and a common vocabulary need to be communicated. But how should this happen?

First, understand that it is not about the frequency of communication. Rather, it is about how one goes about communicating strategy. For people to understand, retain and internalise the essence of your message, four essential factors are involved: managers need to be clear, concise, consistent and credible.

If the message is not clear, employees may become confused about the organisation's strategy.

If the message is not concise, people will not be able to keep track of the message. Do not overwhelm people with a deluge of information. Filter out the noise and focus on the most critical piece of information you wish to transmit.

Third, consistency matters. Variations in vocabulary lead to divergences in understandings of principles and strategies.

Finally and most crucially, be credible. Andy Grove describes how the chief executive officer of a potential partner company made a series of public statements about the strategic direction of the firm, only to retract his statements a day later.[9] This damaged the leader's credibility. How would his management team have felt upon hearing the contradicting statements? To make matters worse, these were done in a public setting. Without a clear understanding of the strategic direction set forth by the CEO, senior management would find it difficult communicating company policy to their employees.

Effective communication ensures organisational alignment. While this is necessary, however, it is insufficient for effective execution. An important but frequently overlooked factor is coordination. In the next section, we will look at the need for coordination, especially in large, complex organisations where there is a high degree of decentralisation and differentiation.

COORDINATION

At Intel, everyone had to be on board with the decision to shift from the memory industry to the microprocessor business. In Intel's case, coordination between different units and departments played a huge role in reorienting the direction taken by this mammoth organisation.

For example, the production planners and the finance team worked closely together to ensure that finances were adequately allocated to microprocessor plants, while monies were withdrawn from production lines that were financially unsustainable. Grove writes, "these people didn't have the authority to get [Intel] out of memories but they had the authority to fine-tune the production allocation process by lots of little steps."[10]

At FMG, one of our core operating principles is that of systems thinking.

In large complex organisations, systems thinking can be a challenge because of the many moving parts involved. Yet systems thinking is crucial. One useful analogy is the human body. If the brain sends a nerve signal to the left arm to swing upwards, the relevant muscles and nerve endings need to work together to ensure that the message is correctly processed and delivered. If any step within this process breaks down, the desired result is not achieved.

In fact, studies show that organisational alignment is less a problem than horizontal coordination. In a survey done by management professor Donald Sull, it was found that only 9% of managers could rely on their colleagues in other functions and units all the time. Half of the respondents said that they could rely on them most of the time. Considering that these people belong to the same organisation, this is an astonishingly low number.

In other words, commitments made by colleagues in these departments are only just slightly more reliable than commitments made by external partners.[11]

The same survey also found that the failure to coordinate frequently led to conflicts between functions and units. Two out of three times, these were badly handled.

The tendency to overemphasise alignment at the expense of coordination has led to what academics Donald Sull, Rebecca Homkes and Charles Sull (who is unrelated to Donald Sull) call the "alignment trap". When organisations overly focus on organisational alignment, micromanagement tends to take place, hindering the agility and peer-to-peer interactions that bolster coordination.[12]

Coordination improves organisational credibility. When an individual trusts that his or her colleagues in other departments and units are similarly committed to the larger goal, it inspires greater confidence. Coordination ensures that "all hands are on board".

This section introduces a framework to help large organisations better coordinate. This is called the coordination matrix (see Fig. 27). By comparing

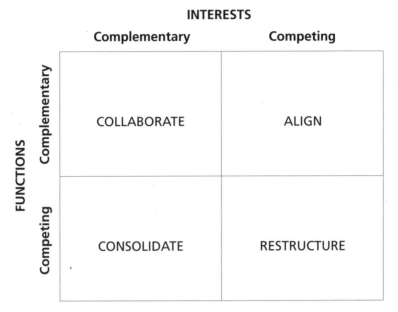

Figure 27: The Coordination Matrix

the interests of individual units and departments with their functions, the appropriate action steps can be identified.

Collaborate

When the functions and interests of different units are both complementary, there is strong alignment between the two, and collaboration becomes easy to achieve.

Take the production and finance departments at Intel, for example. Their functions were complementary—the production team relied on the finance department to disburse the required funds, while the finance team processed the revenue brought in by the production department.

Similarly, they shared complementary interests. Both departments were interested in ensuring that Intel continued to grow. The finance team was invested in ensuring that the production department was able to secure continued growth for the firm, while the production department had a stake in ensuring that the finance team was prudently managing the accounts.

When both functions and interests are aligned in a complementary fashion, collaboration becomes easy. When collaboration is difficult, it is usually due to personality factors. Then, senior management has to take interventionist measures to achieve greater organisational coordination.

Align

Sometimes, different departments may share complementary functions even as they possess competing interests. For example, a university administration faced with diminishing government funding and paltry alumni contributions may focus on reducing the faculty-to-student ratio to minimise costs. Such actions would not agree with the academic department interested in maintaining rigorous academic standards. Yet both departments are ultimately complementary in their functions. The administration needs the academic department to ensure that the academic standards are up to par, while the academic department requires the university administration to make sure that the university as a whole is running smoothly.

In such a scenario, competing interests need to be aligned according to what is being optimised under the strategy. In this case, both units have to be clear about the exact strategic priorities of the organisation. Perhaps the university president has decided to focus on raising academic standards in order to attract more out-of-state students to attend the university. Or perhaps the president has decided that costs should be managed, in order to keep tuition fees affordable so that students will continue to enrol.

In the case of the former situation, academic standards is the factor that is being optimised. In the latter, however, it is cost that is being optimised. In either case, a clarification of the variable being optimised is necessary to align the interests of the different departments. The administration could either work together with the academic department to improve academic standards, or it could work together with the academic department to implement cost-saving measures.

When alignment is required, structural processes can also be put in place to facilitate coordination. For example, performance matrices can be reformulated to give greater weight to collaboration.[13]

Consolidate

When the interests of different units are complementary but their functions are competing, consolidation needs to take place according to what is being optimised. It may be more effective if one of the units were absorbed into the other, or if one of the units were made redundant.

For example, an organisation may have an HR department and a training department. In many ways, their interests are complementary —they want to ensure that the human resources of the organisation are adequately developed, with the capacity for career development. However, their functions may clash. The HR department may believe that members' potential can be better developed by outsourcing training to external providers. The role of the training department, on the other hand, is to provide training to members within the organisation. There is a clear clash of functional roles here. In order to be more effective, senior management may want to look into making the training department redundant, or to have the HR department subsume the training department to ensure greater consistency.

Restructure

Finally, when the interests and functions of different units are both in competition with one another, some serious thought needs to be given as to how the organisation could be better restructured. This may entail eliminating one of the organisational units completely, or it may require reconstituting it as a separate entity independent of the parent organisation.

Whirlpool Corporation provides an interesting case study. A leading global manufacturer of home appliances, Whirlpool steadily began acquiring competitor brands during the second half of the 1980s. While this effectively eliminated the competition, Whirlpool had a strategic choice: because of the competing interests and functions brought about by the newly-acquired brands, it could either integrate these new product lines under its house brand, or it could work to continue differentiating the various brands under an overarching corporate brand. Initially, while Whirlpool did maintain brand differentiation among its new acquisitions, it centralised the running of its appliance groups.[14]

This, however, created problems, since the functions and interests of the different brands were ultimately competing. In 1987, David Whitwam came on board as president and CEO of Whirlpool. One of his first jobs was to reorganise Whirlpool's subsidiaries, such as the KitchenAid, Whirlpool and Roper brands, into separate and independent business units. This ensured that Whirlpool's multiple brands within the same product lines were able to de-conflict their commercial interests. At the same time, individual subsidiary brands were able to distinguish themselves more strongly from one another, while still enjoying the perks of being associated with the Whirlpool corporate brand.

For example, within the kitchen appliance business alone, Whirlpool Corporation hosts three different brands, each with its own specific target market. There is KitchenAid, an up-market brand that focuses on precision and accuracy. Then there is Whirlpool, a mass-market brand that targets families—in particular, the "supermom" who juggles the multifarious responsibilities of taking care of the family and the home. Products marketed under the Whirlpool brand tend to emphasise their durability and functionality. Finally, there is Roper, which caters to the bargain-loving crowd looking for the lowest price possible. Roper makes no qualms about its target demographics, stating unequivocally on its website that it provides the "sensible solutions for your family—simple, sturdy, affordable 'workhorse' appliances."

Yet even as Whirlpool treats its subsidiary brands as independent business units, these individual brands are still able to ride on the strength and brand recognition of the Whirlpool name. Because each brand is clearly differentiated from one another, consumers are able to distinguish between the niche areas of each brand, while recognising the overall quality that the Whirlpool corporate identity provides.[15]

Today, Whirlpool is the world's leading manufacturer of household appliances, with an annual revenue of more than US$19 billion and a market presence in nearly every country around the world.

Depending on the particular circumstances and conditions of the organisation, restructuring may look very different from the path that Whirlpool charted for itself. More importantly, organisations should be aware of the need for horizontal coordination and act accordingly to align their structures internally. Just as vertical alignment is important, we cannot neglect horizontal alignment. To ensure that execution can take place effectively, both planks need to be in place.

The final section of this chapter turns to the last C: commitment.

COMMITMENT

Intel's leadership consulted, communicated and coordinated. However, these actions would not have been sufficient without the commitment of resources. Here, commitment refers to the pouring of resources into a predetermined strategic direction at the expense of other possible options. In Intel's case, its senior management made a number of strategic commitments in terms of resource allocation.

Resource allocation often brings to mind the channelling of resources into specific avenues previously identified as being of strategic importance. However, what this also means is that resources are now being cut from areas no longer deemed as strategically relevant. This is the part that is often more difficult to do.

As Intel made the decision to transition from the memory business to microprocessors, it had to remove resources from areas that could not contribute to the strategic vision of the firm. Factories and manufacturing plants had to be shut down, and people laid-off. These were painful decisions with real consequences. Nevertheless, they were necessary to signal the leadership's commitment to their decision, and ultimately, to give the transition plan credibility.

Another aspect of resource allocation that is often neglected is the allocation of people. Where should the best people be allocated? Money and time are finite—how these are distributed reflects the choice of priorities more meaningfully than motherhood statements.

At Intel, there was often a conscious decision to shift key personnel from areas that were already doing well to areas where Intel was keen to develop as a strategic sector.

Of all the five Cs, the need for commitment should be the most intuitive, yet it is also the most overlooked. Without resources, strategy cannot leap from paper to reality. Commitment makes strategy real.

Commitment also promotes purpose and motivation. When people see that money and resources are being channelled into the communicated strategy, their sense of purpose becomes greater. People can see for themselves that the leadership is committed to the same strategy that they are promoting. In other words, commitment is ultimately the most important indicator of credibility. By putting money where your mouth is, you show that you are serious about pursuing the selected strategy. Your followers will be able to see this and feel assured that you are in it for the long haul.

According to a survey done by the Economist Intelligence Unit (EIU), only 50% of respondents agree that strategy implementation receives sufficient leadership attention in their respective organisations. An even lower percentage—28% of people—found that individual projects or strategy implementation initiatives do not receive the necessary amount of support from the leadership.[16]

Resources do not simply refer to money. It may refer to human capital, time, and in this case, attention. By channelling attention to the implementation of the strategy, senior management sends out very strong signals to its followers about its commitment.

At the end of the day, implementation is about doing. Without the necessary inputs, nothing will get done.

How to allocate resources

It is not difficult to see why commitment is important when it comes to execution. What is less intuitive however, is how leaders should go about allocating resources appropriately and adequately.

Two key ways of doing so are identified here.

The first is to revisit our first C: consultation. Consult the stakeholders involved. Who is creating the policy? Who is implementing the policy? And who will be affected by the policy? By consulting the stakeholders involved, it is possible to get feedback on how resources can best be allocated. People with operational experience in particular should be consulted on how resources should be allocated, given their experience on the ground.

While consultation is helpful, human judgement and experience can also be erroneous, sometimes even deliberately so. To guard against such tendencies, it is important to drill down to first principles. If we recall the story of Elon Musk and SpaceX from the previous section, we will remember how Musk used first principles to determine the amount of funding needed to build a rocket.

Musk did not base his resource allocation on analogous examples from other space shuttle manufacturers. Instead, he relied on first principles thinking. The SpaceX team did not look at industry norms; instead, they broke down the construction of a space shuttle into its most fundamental components—what were the necessary parts for a rocket? How much did these raw materials cost? In doing so, the team found out that they could build a rocket for around two percent of the typical price.

If the SpaceX team had relied solely on industry standards, they would never have realised that a more cost-efficient way of building a rocket existed. Even as strategy demands that we make that commitment by "putting money where our mouth is", we should also be prudent and careful in how we decide to allocate resources. Allocating resources to a particular initiative means fewer resources available elsewhere.

CREDIBILITY

Consultation, Communication, Coordination and Commitment all eventually culminate in the strategy being Credible. Yet, it takes a credible leader to effectively implement these four processes.

Credible leadership

In their book, *Credibility: How Leaders Gain and Lose It, Why People Demand It*, authors James Kouzes and Barry Posner talk about credibility as the foundation of leadership across both time and cultures.[17]

According to research conducted by the authors, people will only follow someone in whom they trust and believe. True loyalty is not something that can be demanded or forced.

Authority does not guarantee credibility. In the same way, compliance is not commitment. People may comply with the standards that you demand of them, but they may not be willing to fork out that little bit more of their time, energy, and capacity to achieve executional excellence.

Kouzes and Posner break down credibility into the four key qualities people want to see in their leaders: honesty, competency, inspiration and a forward-looking perspective. This requires time and effort—credibility is not built within a day.

The authors list out six steps to build up and sustain credibility.

First, discover yourself. Know the core values and beliefs that will guide your actions and decisions.

Second, appreciate your constituents. Build personal relationships, and be interested in what your constituents have to say.

Third, affirm shared values. Build consensus and commitment around shared values.

Fourth, develop capacity. Grow people's competencies and confidence, while fostering ownership and accountability.

Fifth, serve a purpose. Lead by example, and give meaning to your constituents.

Sixth, sustain hope. Keep the hope alive by taking charge and being optimistic and passionate in what you do.

A credible leader motivates people to give their best. A credible leader also gives credence to the strategy being formulated. If people trust their leader, they are more likely to trust the leadership's strategy. If people trust the strategy, they are also more likely to invest in it. It would be foolish to commit your time and energy to something you do not believe in.

Disruptive Implementation ultimately centres on being credible. In order for large, complex organisations to successfully overcome inertia and change their steering course, it is important to have a credible strategy, message, and organisational and leadership commitment. This are all strengthened through the 5Cs Action—Consultation, Communication, Coordination, Commitment and being Credible.

Effective execution does not end with implementation, however. After strategy has been implemented, it needs to be reviewed. The next section will look at the nuts and bolts of the post-implementation stage.

CHAPTER 22

REVIEWING PERFORMANCE

WHY REVIEWING STRATEGY IS IMPORTANT

Implementation is the most obvious portion of the Execution story. What is often neglected is the need to actively review strategy. There are three core reasons why organisations should take reviewing performance seriously.

First and most fundamentally, review permits the objective assessment of performance. This requires deciding which measures would adequately define the success and failure of any particular strategy.

Second, reviews are an expression of accountability. There is an obligation to the stakeholders involved, including those who contributed towards the implementation of the strategy, to know if the strategy is succeeding.

Third, and most crucially, well-timed reviews permit intervention. If the outcomes brought about by the implementation of the strategy can be assessed, improvements can also be identified.

But when is the right time to evaluate? And what are the criteria for a review?

The next section will look at when to review. We will then examine how outcomes can be evaluated more effectively, and how strategy can be judged to be working.

This chapter concludes by illustrating the importance of diagnosing performance. Once the outcome has been evaluated, the next step is to figure out what went wrong (or what went right).

WHEN TO REVIEW PERFORMANCE

Review is not only an end-state action. Evaluating results before the entire strategy runs its course allows for the problem to be diagnosed and for corrective action to be taken.

Reviews should thus be staged. Even as strategy is implemented, its performance should be regularly evaluated. Staging is helpful because it corrects problems early on, and adapts the strategy and mode of implementation along the way.

When staging reviews, it is helpful to adopt interim goals. Some strategies may be cumulative, where their effects increase rapidly rather than steadily across time. By adopting appropriate signposts, resources are not wasted in pushing the strategy all the way out, only to realise at the end that it is not working, or not working in the way intended.

Reviews should also be regularised. It is crucial that evaluation is performed at regular intervals according to the context in which the strategy is being implemented. This is because operating conditions do not remain stagnant—the environment is consistently changing, and it is important not to be caught unawares because you were so focused on implementing an irrelevant strategy in an already evolved environment.

Thirdly, reviews need to be followed through. Research shows that companies rarely track performance against long-term plans. This is wasteful because it creates a lot of redundancies, and does not allow for effective adaptation as operating conditions, assumptions or the internal environment changes.

According to the EIU's survey, less than 15% of companies religiously track their performance against how they thought they were going to perform.[1] What tended to happen was that only the initial year's goals were measured. This is problematic, because goals may be set low so as to make it easier to hit targets.

The absence of follow-up indicates a lack of conviction. It does not allow for the appropriate interventions to be taken. The organisation thus continues operating as per business-as-usual. Eventually however, the consequences of a plan that is not working catches up with it. When that happens, it seldom bodes well for the long-term survival of the company.

Having explained when strategy should be evaluated, the next section will look at how performance can be evaluated effectively.

HOW TO EVALUATE PERFORMANCE EFFECTIVELY
Reviews as making sense of outcomes

Reviews are about judging performance. This entails making sense of the results. The problem is, we are often confused as to what exactly should be measured. While evaluation should be about measuring the outcomes produced as a result of the strategy implemented, we often confuse outcomes with outputs, or worse, with the inputs committed.

Inputs refer to resources such as money or manpower that go into implementing a strategy. They form the starting point of strategy implementation, and do not measure the delta, or change effected, after the strategy has been implemented. For example, a company interested in broadening its market reach could look at the huge sums of money spent on publicity and judge its strategy a success. However, this merely measures the level of commitment and not the actual results of this commitment.

Outputs, on the other hand, refer to measurable activities produced by the strategy. They may not, however, relate directly to the intended effects of the strategy. For example, an advertising firm that has just rolled out a new campaign promoting a client's product may measure the number of people who have seen the ad. This figure is an example of an output. While it may be a result of the strategy, it does not necessarily mean that the ad was effective in raising sales numbers for the client.

The effectiveness of the campaign in raising brand awareness and product sales are what we call outcomes. Outcomes refer to the highest level of desired change from a strategy. They should be tightly coupled with the strategic perspective. When evaluating the success of a strategy, it is outcomes that you should be most concerned about.

Outcomes are often evaluated by measuring outputs. Because an outcome is ultimately a higher order indicator, multiple outputs may contribute to a single outcome. A government agency, for instance, may decide to implement a scheme where firms will receive government grants to introduce productivity-enhancing technology. The objective of this scheme is to increase productivity. The desired outcome thus takes its cue from the objective—an increase in the level of productivity across local firms.

But how should the government agency evaluate the success of this scheme? The agency can do so by first locating the right output indicators that correlate to the desired outcome. This may include the measurement of different indicators, such as the value-add of labour and capital.

An unrelated set of output indicators, on the other hand, may include the measurement of the number of grants distributed, or the number of companies taking up the grants. While it may be tempting to use such indicators exclusively—particularly given the ease of measurement—they do not gauge the extent to which the policy objective has been met.

The right outputs thus need to be chosen in order to ensure that the evaluation of outcomes is meaningful. The most challenging part of the evaluation process is to identify the relevant output indicators, and to make sure that these are adequately coupled with the outcomes desired.

Having identified the indicators for review, how does the process of evaluation work?

The need for objectivity

Most obviously, reviews need to be objective. In order for there to be objectivity, evaluation needs to be definable and measurable.

First, the desired outcome needs to be defined. Consensus needs to be reached, from the very beginning, on what constitutes success and failure.

Secondly, goals must be measurable. Even if the outcome is seemingly qualitative, the planning team should put in place a pre-determined formula to translate the goal into quantifiable aspects.

For example, the objective of a marketing strategy may be to increase brand awareness of a product. The output indicators chosen will not only have to be related to the desired outcome of increased brand awareness, they will also need to be measurable. One simple way of doing so is to compare the levels of public awareness before and after the marketing campaign was rolled out.

This can be done by measuring the number of times your brand name was searched for on the Internet, or by measuring the number of times your brand was mentioned on social media sites. Alternatively, surveys can also be carried out to understand what people are saying about your brand. Unlike the first two indicators, which are directly quantifiable, the third indicator has the potential to be highly qualitative. Nevertheless, it is still possible to measure brand awareness and brand perceptions. The simplest way could be by reducing responses to a simple matrix of positive and negative reactions, with anecdotes serving to reaffirm the data. This brings us to our third point.

The need to minimise bias

In order to be objective, reviews should ideally be bias-free. As tackled in a lengthy discussion in the earlier section on Understanding, several concrete steps can be put in place to mitigate the negative effects of biases.

One of the more pressing problems faced when evaluating outcomes is that of motivation bias. If the people evaluating the strategy are the same people who came up with the strategy, self-preservation may kick in and objectivity may be compromised. The most obvious measure then, would be to erect an independent process or "China wall", in which the people formulating and implementing the strategy are different from those evaluating its outcome.

This is also known as the Team B method. Gather a group of people who were not involved in the formulation process, and have them take a 360-degree view of the strategy and its resultant outcomes. Because Team B has no stake in formulating the strategy, they are able to provide an impartial assessment of the strategy and its implementation.

The need to declare assumptions

In the same way, it is crucial that assumptions in the strategy are declared. Using the previous example of measuring the outcomes of a marketing strategy, it is *assumed* that any increases in social media mentions or web searches are a direct causal result of the marketing strategy. While it may not be feasible, and in some cases, even possible to test and correct such assumptions, it is important to identify them from the onset.

The need for effective feedback loops

While evaluation should be deliberate and the consequence of a conscious decision taken by senior management, the first signs that the strategy is going or not going to plan are often uncovered by the people closest to the ground. One way of facilitating the evaluation process is to ensure that there are effective feedback loops in place so that ground feedback can be relayed accurately and efficiently to management.

Unsurprisingly, this is not always easy.

For one, managers may not be open to honest feedback, especially if they had a stake in formulating the policy or strategy (refer to motivation biases in the previous section).

Even when managers are open to feedback, they may not always receive it. This is particularly so in organisations with a strong bureaucratic hierarchy, where members at the lower end of the hierarchy feel stifled and disempowered to speak up. These biases extend to groupthink as well, where team members may feel the need to conform to prevailing opinion.

As author Tim Harford argued in his book *Adapt*, "We should not try to design a better world. We should make better feedback loops."[2]

There are three key ways to make this happen.

The first requires complicity at senior management level. A mind-set change needs to occur where management recognises the value of feedback and actively seeks it out, even if such opinion dissents from existing policies.

Harford attributes the disastrous outcome of the Iraq War to previous US Defense Secretary Donald Rumsfeld's refusal to listen to dissenting opinions from the ground. Time and time again, Rumsfeld steadfastly brushed off advice from his ground staff.

Before the Iraq War started, the US Army's chief of staff General Eric Shinseki had already warned a Senate committee that more troops would be needed to adequately deal with the aftermath of a US invasion. Yet Rumsfeld's deputy dismissed these remarks as being wildly off the mark and General Shinseki was subsequently shunned within the institution. General Shinseki's projections turned out to be spot-on.

This was not the only time where Rumsfeld dismissed dissenting opinions from his subordinates without even listening to what they had to say. Six days after the war started, Lieutenant General John Abizaid tried to speak to Rumsfeld about America's strategy in a post-Saddam Hussein Iraq. Abizaid was well-versed in the culture and politics of the Middle East, having lived in the region for over 30 years, and he knew from experience that simply purging the Ba'athist regime would not suffice; the US had to win over these same people who filled up the lower levels of Saddam Hussein's regime. Rumsfeld refused to listen.

Abizaid was not the only subordinate who tried to communicate sentiments from the ground to the higher-ups at the military headquarters. After Lieutenant General Abizaid's attempt, other military personnel tried repeatedly to convey to Rumsfeld the reality unfolding across Iraqi towns and cities. Rumsfeld remained deaf to their feedback. As far as he was concerned, the US military had worked out a strategy, and this strategy was going to be implemented regardless.

By the time Rumsfeld stepped down as Secretary of Defense in 2006, the massive sectarian civil war triggered by the American invasion of 2003 and its immediate post-war decisions was still raging. Today, long-term stability remains elusive. The divisive conflict between the Shia majority and the Sunni minority has, more frighteningly, allowed for the entrenchment of the transnational Sunni extremist group ISIS in northern Iraq. This has created a security threat that goes beyond anything that the US military could have conceived of back in 2003.

In contrast to Rumsfeld, however, there were other US military leaders who recognised the value of feedback and actively sought it out, even when (and especially if) these opinions were dissenting. While serving as an aide to the US Major General Jack Galvin, then-captain David Petraeus was firmly instructed that "it is not enough to tolerate dissent: sometimes you have to demand it."[3]

This lesson came in handy when Petraeus, who had by now been promoted to the rank of general, became a divisional commander during the Iraq War. During his term, not only did Petraeus seek out dissenting opinions within the closely-knit military community, he also ventured to look for opposing perspectives among other government agencies, the media and academia, as well as civil society. The feedback that he received allowed him to better understand realities on the ground; he was not merely obeying edicts being issued 6,000 miles away in the US Capitol.

A second way of creating better feedback loops is through organisational structure. This can take many different forms. For example, after the disastrous Bay of Pigs fiasco, President John F. Kennedy was careful never to allow the tragedy of groupthink to happen again. During the Cuban Missile Crisis, Kennedy broke up his advisory group to minimise the negative effects of groupthink. This helped people to be more comfortable in voicing dissenting opinions.

In organisations with a strict delineation of hierarchy, efforts may have to be made to shrink the space between top management and people on the ground. While this does not mean that organisations should be completely flat in their structure, there needs to be efficiency in the transmission of feedback from the bottom to the leadership.

The third way of improving feedback loops is to empower stakeholders by communicating relevant information. In the late 1990s, the Ugandan government started a newspaper campaign to strengthen schools' and parents' ability to monitor local officials' handling of government grants.[4] Within six short years, the amount of money that was illegally syphoned off was reduced dramatically from 80% in 1995 to less than 20% in 2001.

In this case, the stakeholders involved included schools—the recipients of the grants—as well as parents, whose children reaped the benefits of these grants. They were both actors with vested interests.

Prior to the newspaper campaigns, however, schools and parents were not aware of the mechanics of the grant programme. For example, they were less likely to know the rules involved; they were also not privy to the timing during which these grants were disbursed to the schools.

However, the communication of such relevant information via the news media meant that these stakeholders were now aware of the means of implementation. Armed with this information, they started looking out actively for kinks in the system—was there corruption going on or was the money being handled improperly? Because they now knew what to look out for, they could also better monitor and provide feedback on the implementation process.

There are thus three key ways to creating better feedback loops.

First, ensure that senior management are serious about implementing better feedback loops.

Second, adapt organisational structures in a way that encourages feedback.

Third, stakeholders should be empowered by disseminating relevant information in an effective fashion.

Diagnosing performance

Finally, reviews need to be book-ended by decisions. Without appropriate follow-up action, evaluation on its own does not achieve any real objective. Should the existing strategy be continued, modified or terminated?

Such a decision response is in turn contingent on the diagnosis of performance. This entails going one step further from merely judging the success of the strategy and its implementation, to dissecting why the strategy succeeded or failed.

It is important not to assume that a diagnosis of a successful strategy is unnecessary. If a strategy is successful, it needs to be successful for the right reasons. The causal factors need to be understood in order to ensure sustainability. Otherwise, you may be lulled into a false sense of security where you expect business to continue as usual, only to be thrown off guard when something goes wrong.

If a strategy is not meeting its desired outcomes, identify the reasons why it is not working so as to allow time for the appropriate remedy to be applied. If causation is incorrectly identified, the remedy will also be misdiagnosed. Hence it is absolutely vital that causation is carefully diagnosed.

Fig. 28 is an illustration of the IDE/A model. This provides a framework to thinking about performance diagnosis.

If it is an implementation problem, revise the implementation plan. Return to your operating considerations and revise them accordingly. For example, perhaps you had planned for a manpower force of five people to execute the strategy. However, the outcomes obtained were not desirable. When diagnosing the problem, you realised that your previous operating considerations of five people was overly ambitious and unrealistic. Perhaps

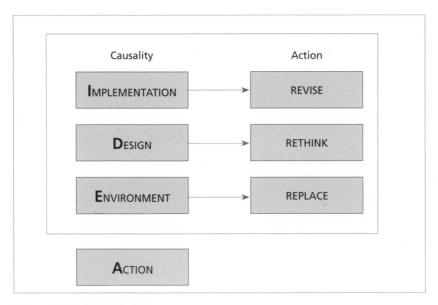

Figure 28: The IDE/A Model

the strategy required 10 implementing agents for it to be effective. In this case, you need to revise your implementation plan.

If it is a design problem, rethink your strategy. Re-examine the assumptions that underpin your strategy. Did you identify all the relevant assumptions? Are these assumptions valid? Once you have identified the mistaken assumptions, you can revise your strategy accordingly.

If it is the environment that has changed, replace your strategy. What worked previously may not work again, and if your strategy does not align with the new realities on the ground, it will not create the desired impact.

Action should follow diagnosis. If it is a design problem, rethink your assumptions. If it is an implementation problem, revise your operating considerations. If it is an environment problem, replace your strategy to cater to your new circumstances.

Be conscientious about diagnosing performance. This will facilitate the application of suitable remedies to enhance or improve outcomes.

CHAPTER 23
ADAPTING STRATEGY

In biological terms, adaptation happens when a mutation occurs in an organism that helps it to survive a changing environment. Because the mutation is useful, organisms with this genetic change are more likely to survive long enough to pass down their genetic makeup to their offspring. As time passes, more and more members of the organism will begin to possess this genetic mutation and eventually, the mutation becomes a typical characteristic among this species. When this happens, adaptation occurs.

Intel's move towards microprocessors in the 1980s was not exactly new. Even as they were concentrating on the memory business in the 1970s, they had started experimenting with microprocessors. As such, when the competitive environment for memories started to deteriorate rapidly during the 1980s, Intel was able to turn to another product that would not only survive, but thrive in the ensuing climate. Intel successfully changed its course of action amidst an evolving environment. It adapted.

Throughout the course of this book, we have repeatedly illustrated stories of companies that went from dominating their industries to being forced out of business completely.

These include Blockbuster, the movie-rental chain store that failed to adapt to a changing world where the Internet was increasingly giving the traditional bricks-and-mortar store a run for its money. Even as the world transited from the VHS tape to the higher quality DVD, Blockbuster was slow to adapt. More damningly, it never saw the online world as an opportunity to improve its market share. Instead, Blockbuster resisted adapting to a world where the most accessible storefront was increasingly one with an online presence.

The list of failed companies also includes Borders, the widely-loved bookstore that never caught up with the times. Even as the Internet became an increasingly popular place for people to buy books, Borders resisted the change. By the time it seriously considered online sales as a legitimate channel for generating revenue, it was too late. Borders also missed the boat when it came to the shift from print to digital. Even as the nature of books evolved, Borders was slow to adapt to such drastic shifts in the environment.

THE IMPORTANCE OF ADAPTATION

Adaptation is critical for two key reasons.

First, conditions change. Strategies and tactics that worked yesterday may be a liability in today's environment.

Second, local conditions may differ from the "big picture" view that strategy is usually formulated against. Implementing agents on the ground may have to adapt the strategy accordingly in order to produce the desired outcomes.

However, there are also two key reasons why adaptation is seldom easy.

First, there is the human tendency to be biased against change. Change is difficult. Be it at the organisational or individual level, inertia can be an effective force against pushing for the necessary changes.

Second, in hierarchical organisations, there may be an overemphasis on maintaining a strict chain of command, where people on the ground are not permitted the autonomy to adapt broad-based strategies to local conditions. This lack of flexibility leads to a lack of agility; eventually the organisation is slayed by its own rigidity.

HOW TO ADAPT EFFECTIVELY

How can we adapt more effectively?

This section presents an overview of two main techniques used in adaptive strategies. The first is called Management by Discovery (MBD), a change management framework pioneered by psychologist Gary Klein as a response to the conventional framework known as Management by Objectives (MBO). While MBO is used widely by organisations as a systematic way of resolving problems, in our increasingly complex world MBD is becoming more pertinent as a way of tackling wicked problems that have no simple answer.

A second technique is the Bayesian approach. Bayesian theory may have been around since the 1740s; however, it was not until recently that it gained mainstream acceptance as a scientific method of inquiry. Penalised by researchers and academics for its supposedly subjective and imprecise nature, Bayesian theory has nonetheless won over adherents by successfully solving difficult problems where the amount of available information was sparse.

Management by discovery

In 1954, management guru Peter Drucker introduced the term "Management by Objectives" in his seminal book *The Practice of Management*.[1] MBO is a highly systematic and organised approach with the aim of promoting managerial efficiency. As its name implies, it takes as its starting point the core objectives set out by management. MBO sets in place several systems to help increase organisational performance by aligning goals and objectives throughout the organisation.

In a nutshell, MBO can be summed up into five key steps:

1. Identify key objectives
2. Communicate these objectives to employees
3. Monitor the progress of the implementation of a plan
4. Evaluate performance
5. Reward performers

While this provides a helpful structural approach for organisations to move successfully towards key objectives, the problem is that it is often difficult to know what the exact objective should be. At the same time, MBO tends to create a situation where managers cling on to initial objectives even after such objectives become irrelevant or unrealistic.

While I have offered a framework for deriving objectives in an earlier section on Foresight, I have also repeatedly highlighted the rapidly evolving nature of the world. The status quo cannot be expected to last, and the reality may often be more complex than what we expect it to be—even after performing the most robust and comprehensive analysis possible.

In an uncertain world, we may simply lack the relevant information to make wise choices. When this happens, MBO fails.

A better framework to adopt, then, would be Klein's Management by Discovery. As its name suggests, MBD promotes a process of discovery where management expects to learn more about its goals even as the organisation pursues them actively.

One example of how MBD was successfully used in the corporate world was that of Xerox.[2] In the 1940s and early 1950s, the Xerox Corporation successfully developed a simpler and neater way of making photocopies. The initial objective was to sell the license for the technology to a larger firm that had the capability to manufacture and maintain complex devices.

However, Xerox machines were bigger and more expensive than the existing devices already on the market and Xerox soon found it almost impossible to persuade copying companies to take up its newly-developed technology.

Faced with a hostile reality, Xerox had to rethink its objective of selling the technology to copying firms. The management considered going into the business of selling the machines themselves, but they were worried that the high costs of the machines would deter potential sales.

As these discussions were taking place, a sales representative presented a new piece of information to the management. According to this representative, trial customers were making more copies per month than they had expected. Augmented by this new knowledge, the Xerox management decided to adopt a different model: rather than supplying machines to other copying companies, Xerox would enter the market as a copying service itself. The objective changed.

The concept behind MBD is thus simple: managers and leaders remain adaptive by learning more about their goals, even as they are pursuing them. This allows them to clarify goals and revise them accordingly.

However, MBD does not give leaders the license to become flippant in setting goals. At a talk given to military leaders in 2014, Klein highlighted an important caveat: "You don't want to change directions too often because then it's confusing to people and it's demoralising, but if you adhere rigidly to the original goals, that's just being insensitive."[3]

Even as you plan for the future to the best of your ability, you need to remain open and flexible to new information and changes in the external environment. The trick is to find the optimal balance between the two.

Bayesian approach

During the Great Depression of the 1930s, the famed British economist John Maynard Keynes purportedly said in response to criticisms that he had changed his position on monetary policy: "When my information changes, I alter my conclusions. What do you do, sir?"

This maxim is key to Bayesian theory. In an uncertain world, Bayes' rule states that beliefs must be updated when new evidence is presented. By conjoining new pieces of evidence to the old, a more complete set of evidence can be continuously updated. Instead of starting from scratch, prior evidence is acknowledged and weighted accordingly.[4]

Bayes' theorem takes the form of a mathematical formula used to calculate the likelihood of an event in the future based on prior experience and history. Because prior experience is not definitive, Bayes' theorem attempts to quantify probability as a measure of belief, or confidence of an event occurring. When new information arises, this is subsequently updated into the equation.

One famous example of a daunting problem that was solved using Bayes' theorem was the locating of the wreckage of Air France Flight 447, which disappeared over the Atlantic on the night of 31 May 2009.[5] When the crash happened, satellite records revealed a possible crash area of 6,500 square miles (16,800 sq km). This represented an undersea area the size of Switzerland.

A week after the crash occurred, floating debris and bodies were discovered about 45 miles (70 km) north of the plane's last reported position. An undersea search was instigated. Up to this point, the search for Air France Flight 447 represented the longest, most difficult, high-tech and expensive undersea search ever commissioned. No one believed that the airplane could be found. While underwater sonar was utilised, it failed to yield results: a 325 yard (297 metre) plane body is a needle in the haystack of large expanses of seabed.

One year after the search commenced, Bayesian consultants were brought in to help with the search. The team started off by first incorporating all of the known data from airplane flight dynamics and winds and currents in the area. The team also included information about previous flight crashes and data on debris drift, established in the early days of the search process. The uncertainty in the data was incorporated as probabilities to represent the degree of confidence researchers had about the credibility of the data.

Two years after the plane crashed, the search process began anew. The probability maps produced by Bayes' theorem identified a high-probability area that had not been previously searched. Within a week, the plane's engine, wing, fuselage panel and landing gear were found.

Bayesian theory provides a way for prior experiences to be taken into consideration even as new information augments previous knowledge.

While you need not be concerned with the mathematical aspects of the theorem, what is more important is understanding the core principle of Bayesian theory: arguments need to be updated and amended when there is new information and the strategy adapted accordingly.

In 1986, Hotel New World in Singapore collapsed, killing and trapping dozens of people. The ensuring emergency response was on a scale not seen before. Multiple agencies responded in accordance with their own plans. In the wake of the tragedy, the government gleaned several lessons that have continued to inform crisis response in Singapore. Retired Deputy Prime Minister Professor S. Jayakumar recounts the many lessons learned in his memoir.[6] Indeed, after each major international and local episode, Singapore makes a deliberate effort to identify, codify and assimilate new information and learning. This is in effect a form of Bayesian application.

Wargaming is a useful method for applying the Bayesian approach. Wargaming involves a table-top exercise built around a hypothetical scenario wherein different roles, including that of competitors, are played out in an interactive fashion. The object is to test strategies under dynamic, but controlled, conditions.

Wargaming allows for a Team B to serve as a sanity check against this newly adapted strategy. They should be testing against any existing or new assumptions, as well as the validity of the updated strategy. Team B includes staff hand-picked to question management's selected strategy. They should not have been involved in the development of the chosen strategy so they can take a "fresh eyes" look at the assumptions and plans. For the Team B to function effectively, they require the leader's protection from the bruised egos of departments and managers whose thinking is being critiqued.

Jayakumar recounts in his memoir an encounter with an Israeli counter-terrorism expert who gave him the advice to "rehearse, rehearse, rehearse!"[7] He tells of how in the Singapore government, practiced drills and table-top exercises of plans under different scenarios—often based on recent events elsewhere—are a norm. The plans are scrutinised and adapted with each new training experience.

Adaptation is about incremental improvements based on new information. It is a continual and conscious effort.

CONCLUSION

The ability to adapt as circumstances change and as information gets updated is crucial to the Execution process. Implementation is just the beginning. In order to obtain the desired outcomes on a sustainable basis, we need to adequately keep up with changes affecting our organisation and operating parameters. This may entail updating our objectives as more information becomes clear. It may also require us to revise prior information.

FUSE's emphasis on principles becomes even more important. By concentrating on principles—the core values that are non-negotiable —we avoid becoming bogged down by mechanistic and rigid frameworks in favour of action. At the individual level, there is more agency for adaptation within local settings. At the organisational level, there is more agility to change course when the external environment starts to transform.

In conclusion, the Execution process can be summarised into three key points.

First, credibility is central. When you carry out a strategy, ensure that both the strategy and its implementation are credible. This is the only way for implementation to be effective.

Secondly, evaluation and diagnosis are indispensable. Without evaluation and diagnosis, you will not know whether your plans are working. Importantly, you will not be able to understand why. This hinders making improvements, and in some cases, renders the entire plan unsustainable.

Finally, adaptation is necessary. Be on the constant lookout for factors that may signal a shift in tides. This brings us back to the first section on Foresight where the need for anticipation was emphasised. To facilitate responsive adaptation, maintain a degree of fluidity around a determinate core. Most importantly, be receptive towards the possibility of change.

By promoting greater effectiveness in the Execution process, you provide a foundation for success. Foresight, Understanding and Strategy are important, but without an effective Execution process, insights and plans cannot be translated into real outcomes.

THE EXECUTION PROCESS

1. **Effective Execution**
   - A successful strategy requires effective Execution. This demands:
     - Disruption
     - Review
     - Adaptation

2. **Disruption**
   - Foresight-led Execution requires the ability to disrupt oneself.
   - For disruption to be successful, the leadership and strategy should adopt the 5Cs Action.
     - Consult
     - Communicate
     - Coordinate
     - Commit
     - Be Credible
   - Consultation is important because it increases diversity of perspective, provides a sanity check, and increases the buy-in of stakeholders.
     - It can be carried out by performing a pre-mortem.
   - Communication is important because it promotes an understanding of the strategy to ensure organisation alignment.
     - Principles, priorities and a common vocabulary need to be communicated in a clear, concise, consistent and credible manner.
   - Coordination is important because it promotes organisational credibility.
     - Depending on the interests and functions of the different units, organisational coordination may be facilitated by collaboration, alignment, consolidation or restructuring.

    ○ Commitment is important because it translates strategy into tangible action.
- Stakeholders and first principles should be consulted when deciding on the allocation of resources.

3. Review

    ○ The review of performance is important because:
- It objectively assesses the performance of a strategy
- It is an expression of accountability
- It permits intervention

    ○ Reviews should be:
- Staged
- Regular
- Followed through

    ○ Performance can be reviewed effectively by:
- Evaluating outcomes, and not outputs or inputs
- Being objective
- Mitigating biases
- Declaring assumptions
- Providing for better feedback loops
- Identifying causation and locating the appropriate action to be taken

4. Adaptation

    ○ Adaptation is important because:
- Conditions change
- Local conditions may differ

    ○ There are two ways to adapt effectively:
- Management by Discovery promotes an adaptive process of learning about goals even as these goals are being pursued.
- Bayesian approach updates and amends arguments when new information is presented so that the strategy can be adapted accordingly.

SECTION 6
CONCLUSION

CHAPTER 24
THE JOURNEY TO FUSE

It is more conventional to begin a book with a personal story than to end with one. However, FUSE is about doing strategy differently, and hence it is fitting that the book concludes with the story of the FMG journey.

How were we conceived? How do we work? What are some of our projects? And importantly, where do we go from here?

These questions are relevant to the book because FUSE inspired the formation of FMG and FMG's operations paved the way for the refinement of the concept.

UNDERSTANDING

FMG has its beginnings in 2003. I had won an Open Fulbright Scholarship to read a Masters of Law and Diplomacy at the Fletcher School, Tufts University in Boston. It was a fascinating and enriching two years.

At Fletcher I had the chance to read a range of subjects and to work on a thesis in my second year. I chose to focus on understanding the reasoning behind strategic surprise. I identified cognitive rigidity as a causal agent for strategic surprise. My thesis was structured around case studies of infamous incidents of strategic surprise, including the 1968 Tet Offensive and the 1973 Yom Kippur War. I postulated that cognitive rigidity blinded analysts to signals and generated several models to explain how such rigidity could occur.[1]

My fundamental conclusion was that strategic surprise was essentially a failure to imagine a different world than convention suggested. Imagination and anticipation are intimately and intricately related.

My further thinking on the subject led me to explore Scenario Planning and other foresight methods. Recognising that we can assert control over the future by anticipating it and taking early action was both a revelation and an inspiration.

After graduate school, the time was ready for me to put my ideas into action. In 2005, I was appointed to my first operational command. I began having arrived at the first of the five principles that informs FUSE: **Imagination is key to thinking about the future**. The capacity to conceive of different possibilities for the future is essential to being a strategist.

ACTION

I served three years in command. First as the commanding officer of a police precinct, and later as head of operations of one of the six land divisions in Singapore.

I introduced tactics to anticipate, deter and interdict crime by careful study of intelligence, patterns and trends, and through developing a pathology of varied criminal behaviour. Over time, my command managed to bring about a sustained reduction in crime without overstretching our commitments. Indeed, resources became more freed up to attend to a diminishing amount of criminal activity, hence setting in place a virtuous cycle.

I was learning the lesson that outcomes have primacy over outputs. It was what actually changed—the delta—that determined whether a strategy was successful, and not the amount of resources invested or the volume of activity undertook. Only outcomes mattered.

Strategies and high-level goals should be the fixed reference points, but processes and tactics needed to be flexible and adaptable. It was critical that strategy and goal setting were carefully considered.

Practical policing experience taught me the importance of matching strategy to practical and flexible tactics. Policing is fundamentally about managing uncertainty. Bad things happen and police have to play catch up. This response was essentially geared at managing upwards the information threshold of what, who, when and why of whatever crime or accident that had occurred.

This upward push of the information envelope was inversely proportional to the downward compression of uncertainty. The object was to cross the two curves at a point of action where criminals would be identified, then apprehended and finally prosecuted.

Too often operational units were challenged to adopt intelligent-sounding strategies that were not grounded with a clear understanding of capabilities and capacities. Headquarters would become fixated on tactics, thus hampering innovation and adaptation to changing dynamic operating conditions.

It became viscerally clear to me that strategy had to have an internal as well as an external dimension. It was vital to identify a clear focal question to be answered with a logical strategy. But it was critical that strategy took into consideration the internal conditions of organisational culture, capability and capacity.

While the latter two could be quantified, the question of culture was harder to capture and define. Nevertheless, without this grounding in internal reality, strategy had little chance of impacting the external situation.

During the time I held command, the policing landscape of my area of jurisdiction was changing rapidly due to immigration. The population numbers were rising rapidly and new wealth was changing the residential infrastructure. These factors impacted policing priorities and called for a different set of relational skills. While it was possible to project forward these changes on a trend line, all around me people carried on BAU—business-as-usual.

I put together a presentation to show the shifts over the recent period and projected into the future to reframe mind-sets. While I could convince some, most were too preoccupied with present day concerns and a "don't rock the boat" attitude to be persuaded to take early action to better prepare the force for an evolving future.

This taught me the necessity of the second and third principles of FUSE.

Challenging assumptions is a deliberate act and not one that comes naturally. It is discomforting and disruptive. Recognising the discomfort as a positive indicator rather than a sign of trouble-making is the responsibility of good management. It should sanction the work of those charged with keeping the set of assumptions updated and tested. Without an explicit sanction, careers will inevitably suffer and it will become impossible to recruit quality strategists.

Next, it is vital to **reframe mind-sets** to drive changes in behaviour. People need to think differently in order to begin acting differently. Asking different questions will generate different answers from the norm. Reframing can be done through various modes—optically, numerically and with narrative. These are skill sets that need to be cultivated and honed. Investment has to be made in strategists so that they get better at communicating their insights and propelling a rethink of convention.

LEARNING

From 2008, I spent three-and-a-half years at two ministries taking on a range of strategy functions. I set up new experimental units in foresight. However, unlike foresight units that were proliferating across the public sector at the time, in both cases the units I established were toggled with active policy-making capabilities. This empowered futures thinking and gave traction to new ideas.

This brought me to the fourth and fifth principles of FUSE.

The global financial crisis of 2007–8 was disruptive and alarming. The Government of Singapore scrambled to put in place a response to a contracting economy and a worried citizenry.

During my time in the services, I had been part of the team managing the response to the domestic implications arising from the September 11, 2001 attacks in New York and later, the SARS crisis in 2003.

It struck me that all three crises—the financial crisis, the security crisis and the health crisis—called for a similar set of capabilities.

Foremost amongst them was the ability to adapt. **Adaptation** rather than sticking rigidly to BAU protocols or a pre-established, generic standard operating procedure is the correct response to a disruption which reconfigures the operating reality.

When the operating environment is violently changed, it is important to adjust to changing facts, rather than insist on the delusion that one can force circumstances to conform to a plan made obsolescent by events.

The Singapore government proved itself capable of rapid and effective crisis response in all these crises because it is adept at adaptation.

In the wake of the 2001 attacks it moved quickly to upgrade its counterterrorism capabilities, formed new networks with international security agencies and took swift action to interdict emergent threats encouraged by the bold actions of Al Qaeda.

During the SARS crisis, the government was quick to take bold measures to try to first contain and then break the infection. This called not only for rapid innovation in policies and protocols but new organisational relationships between agencies.

To cope with the global financial crisis, the government set a precedent by tapping into the national reserves to finance an extraordinary off-budget stimulus to cushion the impact of the crisis on firms and workers.

In all three cases, adaptation was premised on a willingness to face the facts as they occurred and not to cling to outdated ideas or indulge in wishful thinking. Importantly, adaptation also means not being imprisoned by a fixed idea or ideology but instead, being pragmatic and having a willingness to break rules.

In all these episodes, the managerial excellence of varied organisations was an important contribution to effective implementation of evolving policies and plans. However, left to itself, managerial excellence would not have been a catalyst for adaptation. **Leadership matters**.

Senior government leaders at both the political and policy levels worked with an outcome in mind. They separated the essential from the merely urgent. Taken together, this approach, fashioned by a pragmatic philosophy, gave licence to managers to unshackle themselves and take calculated risks in dealing with new and extreme situations. Without a new tone being set by high-level leadership, systems have a tendency, however professional and competent, to struggle on with BAU.

In 2010, I was hand-selected to lead the first foresight team at the Ministry of Finance and the first Whole-of-Government (WoG) strategic planning team. These new appointments arose out of a need to reconcile the many often conflicting demands and priorities from an increasingly complex government structure and governance space. As opposed to "blue-sky" thinking for its own sake, my teams had to focus on making a better future a practical realisation. We had to work difficult problems —sometimes wicked problems—to forge new and actionable solutions.

Wicked problems are those where the causation is distributed and there is no "silver bullet" solution. Public transport planning, labour market policy and land planning were prominent examples. It occasionally helped to break down the problem into smaller elements and tackle them piecemeal. But often, we needed to think "out of the box". This involved a willingness to invest in research and development to build new capabilities, generate new technology and to take managed risks with pilot projects.

This challenging experience taught me valuable lessons about the need to balance the trade-off between pragmatism and a capacity to stretch minds by thinking about how to do things differently. This has led me to focus on the idea of applied foresight as opposed to just futures-*thinking*.

The result—FUSE—thus places emphasis on future-*action*.

MAKING

I set up FMG in 2012 with the goal of creating an internationally successful Asian brand in the strategy arena. The long process of building a credible team, establishing a brand and earning a track record has been a journey filled with lessons and opportunities to apply and refine my thinking about FUSE.

In this journey FMG has done work across public and private sectors and in more than half a dozen countries. We have built a roster of high-profile clients and have proven ourselves through results.

When prospective clients have asked us to explain the value of our services, we clarify that our declared motto—*Move the Future*—is best explained by the phrase "we sell outcomes". Taking the FUSE approach, we work with clients to define goals, develop and apply strategy and in many cases to "get our hands dirty" with execution. This has built our credibility and enriched our experience and understanding of how to take "ideas to indicators"—that is, measurable performance improvements that matter.

This book is a not a culmination but another point in my own and FMG's journey into an exciting future. It is a future we have used FUSE to imagine, generate strategies and apply our resources towards actualising.

Let FUSE be your channel to move your future before the future moves you.

EPILOGUE

THE MAGIC TELEPHONE:
THE FUTURE-MOVES STORY

Today FMG is a thriving new company populated by enthusiastic and competent young people who are passionate about building a brand powered by principles. It is challenging for them to relate to the early period in the company's life when the client landscape was a barren desert with cold winds of despair blasting across the flatness and the horizon never seeming to come closer.

I started the company with a vision to build Singapore's, and Asia's, first internationally successful strategy consultancy. Full of vim and vigour, I sourced for premises to hang up my shingle.

I finally settled on a windowless office in Tagore Lane. It was what I could afford. Each day I would come to work and settle into my office and work on my plans.

I started to get requests for quotes for news reports. I felt that I was getting somewhere. Then one day a reporter sourcing for quotes relayed a question from her editor. She asked if I had been a "substantial" person in government. I did not understand the question. So she clarified that this meant if I had been high ranking enough for the political office holders to know me. I said that I had only been a humble cog in the vast machinery of government. She called back to explain sheepishly that, in which case, they could only use a small slice of my quote as I was not weighty enough a source.

It was humbling. It also made me more committed to show what I could do—I had always believed in a meritocracy of deeds and not one of patronage or mere academic results.

So I came to my office diligently and stared at the walls. I had the occasional invitation to speak or to showcase my work on a demonstration basis. But otherwise things were very quiet.

I had for company a shiny, many-buttoned phone. As time ticked by, I came to know this phone intimately. I had time to closely study its smooth, sleek shell and to run my hands over the tactile buttons. There were several clear plastic slashes, which I took to be lights. I did not know for sure for one simple reason: this was a "magic" phone. It never rang.

Day after day, as my mind spun with ideas for the business and I had the time to think through frameworks and do vast amounts of reading, the magic phone would stay unerringly silent. Little did I realise at the start the many lessons I would learn from this phone.

This silence created a cavern of mind space that I would fill not with hope but with a will. The phone will ring, I would will it to ring. Someday. Meanwhile, I had to leave my white-walled, windowless office periodically to avoid completely losing my mind.

I would wander the corridors, sit in the industrial *kopitiam* (local coffee shop) and take long walks along the tree-lined Upper Thomson Road. I began to slowly get to know some of the other people who had taken similar offices in the building. It turned out that there were five of us who were about the same age, in our thirties and early forties, who had recently started new businesses.

We shared our ideas and plans. The other four would give me strange looks—which looked disturbingly like pity. One evening we all had time on our hands and settled down to a couple of cold Tiger beers at the *kopitiam*. After the third round, one of my fellow aspirants asked us all to comment on what we thought of our respective chances of commercial success.

It was alarming to learn that the consensus was unanimous that I was considered the least likely to succeed. The reasoning was that as a former public servant I had no experience in the realities of doing business, and that consulting was a sector where the entrenched incumbents ruled the field.

In 2015, FMG is the only one of the five firms represented that evening still in business. I have asked myself why this is so, and have come to realise that the magic phone was much more than a phone—it was an origami of meanings.

First, it is critical to have a vision. To see beyond the challenge of the magic phone, one needs to have a picture of a desired future to focus on and work towards.

Second, it is vital to take action. The magic phone was a challenge to complacency—it was not going to ring if I just sat there and stared at it. I needed to move myself as urgently and as wilfully as possible.

Third, it is necessary to reach out. The magic phone may not have rung but I could use it to call out. So I spent part of each day calling contacts—to seek advice, to let people know what I was doing, and to set up meetings to go to, instead of expecting people to come to me. Many were not receptive, but a few were welcoming, and that was a start.

Fourth, the magic phone was a test of resolve. I needed to last long enough to get the business going. It was eight months before I got the first meaningful piece of work. The irony was that this long wait gave me the time to think about the business and to travel to gain a wider perspective of the market.

Fifth, realising the importance of working hard. The magic phone became a lesson in business development. There is no substitute for effort. My business grew from referrals from clients. FMG has earned a reputation for getting things done—we have an in-house saying, "We sell outcomes". If my phone was to ring, my contacts and clients needed to use theirs to ring others about me.

Sixth, understanding the need for humility. That was the final lesson of the magic phone—the need to be humble. Despite all my many accomplishments and experiences in the preceding 17 years, business was not going to walk through the door with a bouquet of flowers. I would have to learn to earn in the private sector. Old dogs can learn new tricks if they are willing to pay the price in effort and sacrifice.

The day finally came when I left my little cell for new digs. As I turned off the light, I looked back into the recess of this small room that had contained big hopes. My eyes stayed for a moment on the magic phone, still stubbornly silent. I said a silent "thank you" for the lessons it taught me.

I hope the young people who work for me today learn the lessons of the magic phone without having to pay the price I did. It is for them that I wrote this epilogue because it is they who can most ensure that FMG can meet the future challenges it sets for itself. My dream is now theirs, to own and share.

Somewhere in the virtual place of meaning, the magic phone is finally ringing.

END NOTES

Chapter 1: A Tale of Two Companies

[1] "Blockbuster Inc (BBI) IPO," Nasdaq; accessed October 24, 2014, http://www.nasdaq.com/markets/ipos/company/blockbuster-inc-10470-5223

[2] Greg Sandoval, "Blockbuster laughed at Netflix Partnership offer," *CNET*, December 9, 2010; accessed October 24, 2014, http://www.cnet.com/news/blockbuster-laughed-at-netflix-partnership-offer

[3] Jill Goldsmith, "Blockbusted: How technology and lack of vision took down Blockbuster," *Variety*, October 9, 2005; accessed October 24, 2015, http://variety.com/2005/biz/news/blockbusted-how-technology-and-lack-of-vision-took-down-blockbuster-1117930420/

[4] Christopher Harress, "The sad end of Blockbuster video: The onetime $5 billion company is being liquidated as competition from online giants Netflix and Hulu prove all too much for the iconic brand," *International Business Times*, December 5, 2011; accessed October 24, 2014, http://www.ibtimes.com/sad-end-blockbuster-video-onetime-5-billion-company-being-liquidated-competition-online-giants

[5] "Blockbuster closing all of its remaining retail stores," *Huffington Post*, November 6, 2013; accessed October 24, 2014, http://www.huffingtonpost.com/2013/11/06/blockbuster-closing_n_4226735.html

[6] Lucas Shaw, "Netflix looks to the Old World for new growth," *Bloomberg Business*, September 11, 2014; accessed October 24, 2014, http://www.businessweek.com/articles/2014-09-11/netflix-looks-to-europe-for-streaming-growth

[7] "Netflix's French connection," CNN Money, September 9, 2014; accessed October 24, 2015, http://money.cnn.com/2014/09/15/investing/netflix-france-media-cbs/

[8] Ryan Bushey, "Netflix CEO confesses he tried to sell the company to Blockbuster... But Blockbuster wasn't interested," *Business Insider Singapore*, February 1, 2014; accessed October 24, 2014, http://www.businessinsider.sg/blockbuster-missed-buying-netflix-2014-1/#.VE9aL_k7PUl

[9] Timothy Stenovec, "Netflix overtakes HBO in paid U.S. subscribers," *Huffington Post*, October 21, 2013; accessed October 24, 2014, http://www.huffingtonpost.com/2013/10/21/netflix-hbo_n_4138477.html

[10] Gail DeGeorge, *The Making of a Blockbuster: How Wayne Huizenga built a sports and entertainment empire from trash, grit, and videotape* (Wiley, 1997).

[11] Jeanine Poggi, "Blockbuster's rise and fall: the long, rewinding road," *The Street*, September 23, 2010; accessed October 24, 2015, http://www.thestreet.com/story/10867574/1/the-rise-and-fall-of-blockbuster-the-long-rewinding-road.html; DeGeorge, *The Making of a Blockbuster: How Wayne Huizenga built a sports and entertainment empire from trash, grit, and videotape.*

[12] Mae Anderson and Michael Liedtke. "Hubris – and late fees – doomed Blockbuster," *NBC News*, September 23, 2010, accessed October 2014, http://www.nbcnews.com/id/39332696/ns/business-retail/t/hubris-late-fees-doomed-blockbuster/#.VFHrSPk7PUk

[13] DeGeorge, *The Making of a Blockbuster: How Wayne Huizenga built a sports and entertainment empire from trash, grit, and videotape.*

[14] Alex Santoso, "Did you know that Blockbuster once had a chance to buy Netflix for a mere $50 million?", *Neatorama*, November 12, 2013; accessed October 24, 2014, http://www.neatorama.com/2013/11/12/Did-You-Know-That-Blockbuster-Once-Had-a-Chance-to-Buy-Netflix-for-a-Mere-50-Million/

[15] Alex Zambelli, "A history of media streaming and the future of connected TV," *The Guardian*, March 1, 2013; accessed October 24, 2014, http://www.theguardian.com/media-network/media-network-blog/2013/mar/01/history-streaming-future-connected-tv

[16] Michael V. Copeland, "Reed Hastings: Leader of the pack," *Fortune*, November 18, 2010; accessed October 24, 2014, http://fortune.com/2010/11/18/reed-hastings-leader-of-the-pack/

[17] Peter Cohan, "Invest in companies like Netflix that do the opposite of what Clay Christensen says," *Forbes*, July 14, 2014; accessed October 24, 2014, http://www.forbes.com/sites/petercohan/2014/07/14/by-disrupting-disruption-netflix-reveals-new-investing-strategy/

[18] Wendy Perez, "Online video will overtake TV by 2020, says John Farrell, Director of Youtube Latin America," Portada Online, February 14, 2013; accessed October 24, 2014, http://latam.*portada-online*.com/2013/02/14/online-video-will-overtake-tv-by-2020-says-john-farrell-director-of-youtube-latin-america/

[19] Amy Kuperinsky, "Binge-watching: How the hungry habit is transforming TV," *nj.com*, May 25, 2014; accessed October 24, 2014, http://www.nj.com/entertainment/index.ssf/2014/05/beau_willimon_house_of_cards_binge_watching.html

[20] Brian Stelter, "New way to deliver a drama: All 13 episodes in one sitting," *NY Times*, January 31, 2013; accessed October 24, 2014, http://www.nytimes.com/2013/02/01/business/media/netflix-to-deliver-all-13-episodes-of-house-of-cards-on-one-day.html?pagewanted=all&_r=0

[21] Kuperinsky, "Binge-watching: How the hungry habit is transforming TV."

[22] Michael Berliner, "*House of Cards, Breaking Bad* and binge viewing pull audiences online," *The Guardian*, August 7, 2014; accessed October 24, 2014, http://www.theguardian.com/media-network/media-network-blog/2014/aug/07/house-cards-breaking-bad-netflix-amazon-data

23 Rick Munarriz, "Netflix Inc. takes a bet on the box office," *The Motley Fool*, October 12, 2014; accessed October 24, 2014, http://www.fool.com/investing/general/2014/10/12/netflix-inc-takes-a-bet-on-the-box-office.aspx

24 "Q&A: Reed Hastings, Netflix," *Inc. Magazine*, December 1, 2005; accessed October 24, 2014, http://www.inc.com/magazine/20051201/qa-hastings.html

25 Elizabeth Rourke, Carrie Rothburd and Christina Stansell, "Blockbuster Inc.," *Encyclopedia. com*, 2006; accessed October 24, 2014, http://www.encyclopedia.com/topic/Blockbuster_Inc.aspx

26 Greg Satell, "The myth of the moron CEO, *Forbes*, August 1, 2013; accessed October 24, 2014, http://www.forbes.com/sites/gregsatell/2013/08/01/the-myth-of-the-moron-ceo/

27 Andrew Farrell, "Blockbuster's CEO ousted," *Forbes*, July 2, 2007; accessed October 24, 2014, http://www.forbes.com/2007/07/02/icahn-blockbuster-closer-markets-equity-cx_af_ra_0702markets36.html

28 Lauren Effron, "Netflix CEO Reed Hastings says company has 'sincere regret' over handling of service changes," *ABC News*, September 26, 2011; accessed October 24, 2014, http://abcnews.go.com/Business/netflix-ceo-reed-hastings-company-sincere-regret-customers/story?id=14608865&singlePage=true

29 Austin Carr, "Inside Netflix's project Griffin: The forgotten history of Roku under Reed Hastings," *FastCompany*, January 23, 2013; accessed October 24, 2014, http://www.fastcompany.com/3004709/inside-netflixs-project-griffin-forgotten-history-roku-under-reed-hastings

30 Ibid.

31 Ibid.

32 Copeland, "Reed Hastings: Leader of the pack."

33 Ibid.

34 Lauren Effron, "Netflix CEO Reed Hastings says company has 'sincere regret' over handling of service changes."

Chapter 2: Approaches to Strategic Planning

1 W. Cunninghan, Denys Freeman and Joseph McCloskey, "Of Radar and Operations Research: An Appreciation of A. P. Rowe (1898–1976)," *OR Forum* 32, 4 (July-August 1984): 958.

2 Harold Larnder, "The Origin of Operational Research", *OR Forum* 32, 2 (March-April 1984): 471.

3 Ibid.

4   Maurice Kirby, "Operations Research Trajectories: The Anglo-American Experience from the 1940s to the 1990s," *Operations Research* 48, 5 (September–October 2000): 662.

5   Larnder, "The Origin of Operational Research", 474.

6   Philip M. Morse, "The Beginnings of Operations Research in the United States," *Operations Research* 34, 1 (January-February 1986): 11.

7   Russell L. Ackoff, "Operations research," *Encyclopaedia Britannica*, n.d.; accessed November 13, 2014, http://www.britannica.com/EBchecked/topic/682073/operations-research/68171/History

8   Joseph B. Treaster, "Herman Kahn dies; Futurist and thinker on nuclear strategy," *NY Times*, July 8, 1983; accessed November 13, 2014, http://www.nytimes.com/1983/07/08/obituaries/herman-kahn-dies-futurist-and-thinker-on-nuclear-strategy.html

9   Louis Menand, "Fat man: Herman Kahn and the nuclear age," *The New Yorker*, June 27, 2005; accessed November 13, 2014, http://www.newyorker.com/magazine/2005/06/27/fat-man

10   Treaster, "Herman Kahn dies; Futurist and thinker on nuclear strategy."

11   Art Kleiner, "Mystics: Royal Dutch/Shell's scenario planners, 1967–1973," in *The Age of Heretics: A history of the radical thinkers who reinvented corporate management* (San Francisco: Jossey-Bass, 2008), 125.

12   Pierre Wack, "Scenarios: Uncharted Waters Ahead", *Harvard Business Review* (September–October 1985): 73.

13   William J. Worthington, Jamie D. Collins, Michael A. Hitt, "Beyond Risk Mitigation: Enhancing Corporate Innovation with Scenario Planning," *Business Horizons* 52, (2009): 441–450.

14   MG Siegler, "Eric Schmidt: Every 2 days we create as much information as we did up to 2003," *TechCrunch*, August 4, 2010; accessed November 13, 2014, 2010) http://techcrunch.com/2010/08/04/schmidt-data/

15   Jeff Kelly, "Big Data Vendor Revenue and Market Forecast 2013-2017," *Wikibon*, February 12, 2014; accessed November 13, 2014, http://wikibon.org/wiki/v/Big_Data_Vendor_Revenue_and_Market_Forecast_2013-2017

16   Louis Columbus, "Roundup of Analytics, Big Data & Business Intelligence Forecast and Market Estimates, 2014," *Forbes*, June 24, 2014; accessed November 13, 2014, http://www.forbes.com/sites/louiscolumbus/2014/06/24/roundup-of-analytics-big-data-business-intelligence-forecasts-and-market-estimates-2014/

17   Steve Lohr, "The Age of Big Data," *NY Times*, February 11, 2012; accessed November 13, 2014, http://www.nytimes.com/2012/02/12/sunday-review/big-datas-impact-in-the-world.html?pagewanted=all&_r=0

[18] Jordan Chariton, "Inside the new refresh of NBCNews.com six months after relaunch," *TVNewer*, August 11, 2014; accessed November 13, 2014, http://www.mediabistro.com/tvnewser/inside-the-new-refresh-of-nbcnews-com-six-months-after-relaunch_b234931; Malcolm Stewart, "Big Data's Big Mistake: Quantity over Quality," *DataInformed*, October 21, 2014; accessed November 13, 2014, http://data-informed.com/big-datas-big-mistake-quantity-quality/

Chapter 4: Introduction to Foresight

[1] Thomas Suddendorf and Michael C. Corballis, "The Evolution of Foresight: What is Mental Time Travel, and is it Unique to Humans?", *Behavioral and Brain Sciences*, Cambridge University Press (2007): 318.

[2] David Ingar, "Memory of the Future": An Essay on the Temporal Organization of Conscious Awareness, *Hum Neurobiol* 4,3 (1985): 127-136.

[3] Frederick L. Coolidge and Thomas Wynn, "Working Memory, its Executive Functions and the Emergence of Modern Thinking", *Cambridge Archaeological Journal* 15, 1 (2005): 17.

[4] "Moving Image Section – Motion Picture, Broadcasting and Recorded Sound Division," *The Library of Congress*, n.d.; accessed January 7, 2015, http://memory.loc.gov/ammem/awhhtml/awmi10/television.html

[5] "Statistics," *ITU*, 2015; accessed January 7, 2015, http://www.itu.int/en/ITU-D/Statistics/Pages/stat/default.aspx

[6] Donna Saunders, "September 2011 is the Final Chapter in the Story of Borders Books," *Examiner.com*, July 19, 2011; accessed January 7, 2015, http://www.examiner.com/article/september-2011-is-the-final-chapter-the-story-of-borders-books

[7] Peter Osnos, "What went wrong at Borders," *The Atlantic*, January 11, 2011; accessed January 7, 2015, http://www.theatlantic.com/business/archive/2011/01/what-went-wrong-at-borders/69310/

[8] Ben Austen, "The End of Borders and the Future of Books," *Bloomberg Business*, November 10, 2011; accessed January 7, 2015, http://www.businessweek.com/magazine/the-end-of-borders-and-the-future-of-books-11102011.html#p1

[9] Sean Lusk, "The Challenge of Foresight," *The Guardian*, June 10, 2010; accessed January 7, 2015, http://www.theguardian.com/public-sector-training/training-crisis-management-lusk

[10] Kim A. Kamin, Jeffrey J. Rachlinkski, "Ex Post =/= Ex Ante: Determining Liability in Hindsight," *Law and Human Behaviour* 19, 1 (1995): 89-104.

[11] Philip Tetlock, *Expert Political Judgment: How Good Is It? How Can We Know?* (NJ: Princeton University Press, 2005).

[12] M Nirmala, "Complexity: When 1 + 2 becomes 4," *AsiaOne News*, August 26, 2014; accessed September 17, 2014, 2014, http://news.asiaone.com/news/asian-opinions/complexity-when-12-becomes-4?page=0%2C1; September 2011 Newsletter, *VSA Capital;* accessed September 17, 2014, http://minesite.com/media/pub/var/release_downloadable_file/32863.pdf

Chapter 5: Locating a Focal Question

[1] Chris Palmer, "Gorillas in the Lung," *The Scientist*, July 18, 2013; accessed September 17, 2014, http://www.the-scientist.com/?articles.view/articleNo/36606/title/Gorillas-in-the-Lung/

[2] Ibid.

[3] John Kay, *Obliquity: Why Our Goals are Best Achieved Indirectly* (Profile Books, 2011).

Chapter 7: Identifying Assumptions

[1] Devadas Krishnadas, "Imagining Surprise: Locating the Causality of Strategic Surprise" (MA Thesis, Tufts University, 2005).

[2] Jeremy Dean, "The Availability Bias: Why people buy Lottery Tickets," *PsyBlog*, August 6, 2012; accessed January 8, 2015, http://www.spring.org.uk/2012/08/the-availability-bias-why-people-buy-lottery-tickets.php

[3] John Cassidy, "The Saliency Bias and 9.11: Is America Recovering?", *The New Yorker*, September 11, 2013; accessed January 8, 2015, http://www.newyorker.com/news/john-cassidy/the-saliency-bias-and-911-is-america-recovering

[4] Rolf Dobelli, "How Eye-Catching Details Render us Blind," *The Art of Thinking Clearly* (London: Sceptre, 2014), 254-255.

[5] Jill Krasny, "Malcolm Gladwell on What Really Makes People Disruptive," Inc., October 7, 2014; accessed September 17, 2014, http://www.inc.com/jill-krasny/malcolm-gladwell-on-the-one-character-trait-that-makes-people-disruptive.html?cid=sf01002

Chapter 8: Building Scenarios

[1] Adam Morris Kahane, "An Invention Born of Necessity," *Transformative Scenario Planning: Working Together to Change the Future* (San Francisco: Berrett-Koehler Publishers, 2012), 1–14.

[2] Adrian W.J. Kuah, "Foresight and Policy: Thinking about Singapore's Future(s)," *Social Space* (2013): 104-109.

[3] Ibid.

[4] Peter Schwartz, "The Pathfinder's Tale," *The Art of the Long View* (NY: Doubleday, 1996).

[5] Kees Van Der Heijden, "The Uncertain Environment," *Scenarios: the Art of Strategic Conversation* (West Sussex: John Wiley & Sons, 2005), 109.

[6] Van Der Heijden, "Scenario Development", 242.

[7] Joseph Voros, "A Primer on Future Studies, Foresight and the Use of Scenarios," *Prospect*, 6 (2001).

[8] Nassim Taleb, *The Black Swan*, 2nd ed. (NY: Random House, 2010).

[9] Thomas Suddendorf and Michael C. Corballis, "The Evolution of Foresight: What is Mental Time Travel, and is it Unique to Humans?", *Behavioral and Brain Sciences*, Cambridge University Press (2007): 299–313.

[10] "Foresight in Hindsight: Reinier de Graaf at TEDxHamburg City 2.0", *TEDx*, July 12, 2013; accessed September 17, 2014, http://tedxtalks.ted.com/video/Foresight-in-Hindsight-Reinier; "What was the Future of…"; accessed September 17, 2014, http://www.foresightinhindsight.com

Chapter 9: Inductive Scenario Building

[1] Van Der Heijden, "The Uncertain Environment," 103-107; "Scenario Analysis," 120.

[2] Van Der Heijden, "The Uncertain Environment," 104.

[3] Wack, "Scenarios: Uncharted Waters Ahead," 77.

[4] Schwartz, "Creating Scenario Building Blocks," 110–111.

[5] Ibid, 111–112.

Chapter 10: Deductive Scenario Building

[1] Thomas Reuter, "Reading the Future in Indonesia: Javanese Texts of Prophesy as a Popular Genre" (paper presented at the 17th Biennial Conference of the Asian Studies Association of Australia, Melbourne, July 1-3, 2008).

Chapter 11: Introduction to Understanding

[1] Quoted in John I. Beare, "Self-Knowledge," *Mind*, New Series 5, 18 (Apr., 1896): 229–230.

[2] Quoted in Roger Lipsey, "Know Thyself," in *Have You Been to Delphi?: Tales of the Ancient Oracle for Modern Minds* (Albany: State University of New York Press, 2001), 240–241.

3 Larry Huston and Nabil Sakkab, "Connect and Develop: Inside Procter & Gamble's New Model for Innovation," *Harvard Business Review*, March 2006; accessed January 16, 2015, https://hbr.org/2006/03/connect-and-develop-inside-procter-gambles-new-model-for-innovation

4 William C. Taylor and Polly LaBarre, "Innovation Inc.: Open Source Gets Down to Business," *Mavericks at Work* (NY: HarperCollins Publishers, 2006), 93.

5 Taylor and LaBarre, "Innovation Inc.: Open Source Gets Down to Business," 94.

6 Huston and Sakkab, "Connect and Develop: Inside Procter & Gamble's New Model for Innovation."

7 Ola Svenson, "Are We All Less Risky and More Skillful than Our Fellow Drivers?", *Acta Psychologica* 47 (1981): 143–148.

8 Caroline E. Preston and Stanley Harris, "Psychology of Drivers in Traffic Accidents," *Journal of Applied Psychology* 49, 4 (Aug 1965): 284–288.

9 "Aldous Huxley, *Ark in Time*, 2015; accessed January 16, 2015, http://thyselfknow.com/aldous-huxley/

10 David Dunning, Ann Leuenberger, and David A. Sherman, "A New Look at Motivated Inference: Are Self-Serving Theories of Success a Product of Motivational Forces?" *Journal of Personality and Social Psychology* 69, 1 (1995): 58–68.

11 D.T. Miller and M. Ross, "Self-serving Biases in the Attribution of Causality: Fact or Fiction?" *Psychological Bulletin*, 82, (1975): 213–225.

12 Cameron Anderson, Sebastien Brion et al., "A Status-enhancement account of Overconfidence," *Journal of Personality and Social Psychology* 103, 4 (October 2012): 718–735.

Chapter 12: Confronting Biases

1 Bin Gu, Prabhudev Konana et al., "Confirmation Bias, Overconfidence, and Investment Performance: Evidence from Stock Message Boards," *McCombs Research Paper Series No. IROM-07-10* (October 2010): 1-59.

2 L. Festinger and J.M. Carlsmith, "Cognitive consequences of forced compliance," *Journal of Abnormal and Social Psychology* 58, (1959): 203–210.

3 L. Festinger, *A Theory of cognitive dissonance* (Stanford, CA: Stanford University Press, 1957).

4 Ellen Langer, "The Illusion of Control," *Journal of Personality and Social Psychology* 32 (1975): 311–328.

5 Paul Lawrence and Jay Lorsch, "Differentiation and Integration in Complex Organisations," *Administrative Science Quarterly* 12, 1 (Jun. 1967): 1–47.

6 "The 9/11 Commission Report: Final Report of the National Commission on Terrorist Attacks Upon the United States," National Commission on Terrorist Attacks Upon the United States, 2004, accessed March 15, 2015, http://www.9-11commission.gov/report/911Report_Exec.htm

7 Irving Lester Janis, "The Bay of Pigs," in *Victims of Groupthink: A Psychological Study of Foreign-Policy Decisions and Fiascoes* (Houghton Mifflin Company, 1972), 14-49.

8 Barry Fischer, "Homes with pools use 49% more electricity per year, but it's not just because of the pool," *Outlier*, July 26, 2012; accessed March 15, 2015, http://blog.opower.com/2012/07/homes-with-pools-use-49-more-electricity-but-its-not-just-because-of-the-pool/

9 Daniel Kahneman and Amos Tversky, "Prospect Theory: An Analysis of Decision Under Risk," *Econometrica* 47, 2 (March, 1979): 263.

10 Daniel Kahneman and Amos Tversky, "The framing of decisions and the psychology of choice," Science 211, 4481 (1981): 453–458.

11 Thomas Barrabi, "After Air Algerie AH5017 Incident, a Stastical Look at the Probability and Chances of Dying in a Plane Crash," *International Business Times*, July 24, 2014; accessed March 15, 2015, http://www.ibtimes.com/after-air-algerie-ah5017-incident-statistical-look-probability-chances-dying-plane-crash-1638206

12 Olivier Dessaint and Adrien Matray, "Do Managers Overreact to Salient Risks?" (*Job Market Paper*, January , 2014), http://www.cbs.dk/files/cbs.dk/olivierdessaintpaper_1.pdf

13 Barry Staw, "Knee-Deep in the Big Muddy: A Study of Escalating Commitment to a Chosen Course of Action," *Organisational Behavior and Human Performance* 16, 1 (1976): 27–44.

14 Barry M. Staw and Ha Hoang, "Sunk Costs in the NBA: Why Draft Order Affects Playing Time and Survival in Professional Basketball," *Administrative Science Quarterly* (1995): 474–494.

Chapter 13: Mitigating Biases

1 Emily Pronin, Daniel Y. Lin and Lee Ross, "The Bias Blind Spot: Perceptions of Bias in Self Versus Others," *PSPB* 28, 3 (March 2002): 369-381; Emily Pronin and Matthew B. Kugler, "Valuing thoughts, ignoring behavior: The introspection illusion as a source of the bias blind spot," *Journal of Experimental Social Psychology* 43, 4 (2007): 565–578.

2 Pronin and Matthew B. Kluger, "Valuing thoughts, ignoring behavior: The introspection illusion as a source of the bias blind spot."

3 Ibid, 566.

[4]   Timothy D. Wilson, and Nancy Brekke, "Mental contamination and mental correction: unwanted influences on judgments and evaluations," Psychological Bulletin 116, 1 (1994): 117–142.

Chapter 14: Developing a Desired Vision of the Future

[1]   "Study Focuses on Strategies for Achieving Goals, Resolutions," Dominican University of California; accessed March 15, 2015, http://www.dominican.edu/dominicannews/study-highlights-strategies-for-achieving-goals/

Chapter 15: In-sighting

[1]   Donald O. Clifton and Paula Nelson, *Soar With Your Strengths* (NY: Dell Publishing, 1992).

[2]   Jean-Marie Dru, "The Agency," in *How Disruption Brought Order* (NY and Hampshire: Palgrave Macmillan, 2007), 98.

[3]   Jay B. Barney, "Looking inside for Competitive Advantage," *The Academy of Management Executive (1993-2005)* 9, 4 (November 1995): 49–61.

Chapter 16: Introduction to Strategy

[1]   L.D. Phillips, "What is Strategy?" *Journal of the Operational Research Society* 62 (2011): 926–929.

[2]   Alfred Chandler, *Strategy and Structure* (Cambridge, MA: MIT Press, 1962).

[3]   Kenneth Andrews, *The Concept of Corporate Strategy* (Homewood, IL: Irwin, 1971).

[4]   Michael E. Porter, "A Framework for Competitor Analysis," in *Competitive Strategy: Techniques for Analysing Industries and Competitors* (NY: The Free Press, 1980), 47–74.

[5]   Rich Horwath, "The Origin of Strategy," Strategic Thinking Institute, 2006; accessed March 2, 2015, http://strategyskills.com/Articles_Samples/origin_strategy.pdf

[6]   Igor Ansoff, "A Model for Strategic Decisions," in *Corporate Strategy* (London: Penguin, 1985): 18.

[7]   When there is a high market share and a high growth rate, the business unit is deemed a "star". When the business occupies a high market share in a market that is experiencing low growth rates, it is a cash cow. When a business unit occupies a small market share in a high growth market, this represents a question mark. Business units with a small market share in an already mature industry are considered "dogs".

[8]   Bruce D. Henderson, "The Origin of Strategy," *Harvard Business Review*, November-December 1989; accessed March 2, 2015, https://hbr.org/1989/11/the-origin-of-strategy

⁹ Michael E. Porter, "How Competitive Forces Shape Strategy," *Harvard Business Review*, March 1979; accessed March 2, 2015, https://hbr.org/1979/03/how-competitive-forces-shape-strategy; C.K. Prahalad and Gary Hamel, "The Core Competence of the Corporation," *Harvard Business Review*, May-June 1990; accessed March 2, 2015, https://hbr.org/1990/05/the-core-competence-of-the-corporation

¹⁰ Joseph L. Bower and Clayton M. Christensen, "Disruptive Technologies: Catching the Wave," *Harvard Business Review*, January-February 1995; accessed March 2, 2015, https://hbr.org/1995/01/disruptive-technologies-catching-the-wave

¹¹ Richard Whittington, "What is Strategy and Does it Matter?" in *What is Strategy – and Does it Matter?*, 2nd ed. (Cornwall: Thomson, 2002): 1–8.

Chapter 17: Leadership Matters

¹ Carl Hoffman, "Elon Musk, the Rocket Man with a Sweet Ride," *Smithsonian.com*, December 2012; accessed March 2, 2015, http://www.smithsonianmag.com/science-nature/elon-musk-the-rocket-man-with-a-sweet-ride-136059680/?page=1

² Nicole Litvak, "Is the SolarCity Model the Only Way to Scale Residential Solar?", *Greentech Media*, March 31, 2014; accessed March 2, 2015, http://www.greentechmedia.com/articles/read/is-the-solarcity-model-the-only-way-to-scale-residential-solar

³ Hoffman, "Elon Musk, the Rocket Man with a Sweet Ride."

⁴ Ibid.

⁵ Travis Hessman, "The World according to Elon Musk," *IndustryWeek*, October 7, 2013; accessed March 2, 2105, http://www.industryweek.com/technology/world-according-elon-musk?page=2

⁶ Hessman, "The World according to Elon Musk."

⁷ Elon Musk, "The Secret Tesla Motors Master Plan (just betwee you and me)," *Tesla Blog*, August 2, 2006; accessed March 2, 2015, http://www.teslamotors.com/blog/secret-tesla-motors-master-plan-just-between-you-and-me

⁸ Elon Musk, "All Our Patent Are Belong to You," *Tesla Blog*, June 12, 2014; accessed March 2, 2015, http://www.teslamotors.com/blog/all-our-patent-are-belong-you

⁹ Jeremy Hsu, "Strike Three for SpaceX's Falcon 1 Rocket," *NBCNews.com*, August 3, 2008; accessed March 2, 2015, http://www.nbcnews.com/id/25990806/ns/technology_and_science-space/t/strike-three-spacexs-falcon-rocket/#.VO7J9fnxKXx

¹⁰ Dolly Singh, "What is it like to work with Elon Musk?", *Quora*, November 2, 2013; accessed March 2, 2015, http://www.quora.com/What-is-it-like-to-work-with-Elon-Musk/answer/Dolly-Singh-8?srid=n2Fg&share=1

Chapter 18: Formulating Strategy

[1] Jim Collins and Jerry I. Porras, "More Than Profits," in *Built to Last: Successful Habits of Visionary Companies* (NY: HarperCollins Publishers), 46–79.

[2] Lucy Nicholason, "Elon Musk uses this Ancient Critical Thinking Strategy to Outsmart Everybody Else," *Business Insider*, January 6, 2015; accessed March 2, 2015, http://www.businessinsider.sg/elon-musk-first-principles-2015-1/#.VXKqg8_zrIU

[3] Chris Anderson, "Elon Musk's Mission to Mars," WIRED, October 21, 2012; accessed March 2, 2015, http://www.wired.com/2012/10/ff-elon-musk-qa/all/

[4] Jim Collins, "The Hedgehog Concept (Simplicity Within the Three Circles)", in *Good to Great, Why Some Companies Make the Leap... And Others Don't* (NY: HarperCollins Publishers, 2001), 90-119.

[5] "U.S. Births Decline, Baby Business Grow," *Sarasota Herald-Tribune*, September 9, 1974; accessed March 2, 2015, http://news.google.com/newspapers?id=D_wjAAAAIBAJ&sjid=62YEAAAAIBAJ&pg=6866%2C3789354

[6] John Gorman, "Gerber Isn't Kidding about Diversification," *Chicago Tribune*, December 9, 1985; accessed March 2, 2015, http://articles.chicagotribune.com/1985-12-09/business/8503250237_1_baby-food-grocery-vinyl

[7] Erika Andersen, "21 Quotes From Henry Ford on Business, Leadership and Life," *Forbes*, May 31, 2013; accessed March 2, 2015, http://www.forbes.com/sites/erikaandersen/2013/05/31/21-quotes-from-henry-ford-on-business-leadership-and-life/

[8] Collins and Porras, "The Best of the Best," 1–21.

[9] Collins, "From Good to Great to Built to Last," 188–210.

[10] Manny Garcia-Tunon, "Conform or Transform: The Choice is Yours," *Miami Herald*, February 22, 2015; accessed March 2, 2015, http://www.miamiherald.com/news/business/biz-monday/article10788944.html

[11] John Kay, "Drug Companies are built in Labs, not Boardrooms," *Financial Times*, May 6, 2014; accessed March 2, 2015, http://www.ft.com/intl/cms/s/0/413557b4-d162-11e3-81e0-00144feabdc0.html#axzz3SjS6mr5X

[12] "Vioxx Death Estimate Revised Upwards," *Vioxx, Celebrex, Bextra Recall News*, January 2, 2005; accessed March 2, 2015,http://www.mynippon.com/vioxx/2005/01/vioxx-death-estimate-revised-upwards.html

[13] JS Ross, et al., "Guest authorship and ghostwriting in publications related to Rofecoxib: A Case Study of Industry Documents from Rofecoxib Litigation," *JAMA* 299, 15 (April 2008): 1800-1812.

14 Milanda Rout, "Vioxx Maker Merck and Co drew up Doctor Hit List," *The Australian*, April 1, 2009; accessed March 2, 2014, http://www.theaustralian.com.au/news/drug-company-drew-up-doctor-hit-list/story-e6frg6n6-1225693586492

15 "Arizona gets $2.3 million from Vioxx Settlement," *KTAR.com*, May 20, 2008; accessed March 2, 2015, http://ktar.com/?nid=6&sid=842595&r=1

16 Judith Rehak, "Tylenol made a hero of Johnson & Johnson: The recall that started them all," *NY Times*, March 23, 2002; accessed March 2, 2015, http://www.nytimes.com/2002/03/23/your-money/23iht-mjj_ed3_.html

17 Therese Poletti, "What Really Keeps Airbnb's CEO up at night," *MarketWatch*, February 13, 2015; accessed March 2, 2015, http://www.marketwatch.com/story/what-really-keeps-airbnbs-ceo-up-at-night-2015-02-13; Jordan Crook, "A Brief History of Airbnb," *TechCrunch*, June 20, 2014; accessed March 2, 2015, http://techcrunch.com/gallery/a-brief-history-of-airbnb/; Burt Helm, "Airbnb is Inc.'s 2014 Company of the Year," *Inc.*, December 2014; accessed March 2, 2015, http://www.inc.com/magazine/201412/burt-helm/airbnb-company-of-the-year-2014.html

18 "Travel Like a Human With Joe Gebbia, Co-founder of AirBnB," *Allentrepreneur*, August 26, 2009; accessed March 2, 2015, https://allentrepreneur.wordpress.com/2009/08/26/travel-like-a-human-with-joe-gebbia-co-founder-of-airbnb/

19 Brian Chesky, "Airbnb," *Airbnb*, July 16, 2014; accessed March 2, 2015, http://blog.airbnb.com/belong-anywhere/

20 Burt Helm, "Airbnb is Inc.'s 2014 Company of the Year."

21 Austin Carr, "Inside Airbnb's Grand Hotel Plans," *Fast Company*, March 17, 2014; accessed March 2, 2015, http://www.fastcompany.com/3027107/punk-meet-rock-airbnb-brian-chesky-chip-conley

22 Burt Helm, "Airbnb is Inc.'s 2014 Company of the Year."

23 Austin Carr, "Inside Airbnb's Grand Hotel Plans."

24 Burt Helm, "Airbnb is Inc.'s 2014 Company of the Year."

Chapter 19: Stress-testing Strategies

1 Nick Greene, "Challenger Explosion – A NASA Tragedy," About.com, 2015; accessed March 2, 2015, http://space.about.com/cs/challenger/a/challenger.htm

2 Richard Bookstaber, "Cockroaches and Hedge Funds," in *A Demon of Our Own Design: Markets, Hedge Funds and the Perils of Financial Innovation* (NJ: John Wiley & Sons, 2007): 207–242.

Chapter 20: Introduction to Execution

[1] "Intel Corporation History," Funding Universe, n.d.; accessed April 27, 2015, http://www.fundinguniverse.com/company-histories/intel-corporation-history/

[2] Andrew Grove, "Why Not Do It Ourselves?", in *Only the Paranoid Survive* (NY: Crown Business, 1999), 79–98.

[3] "Intel Annual Report 2014," Intel Corporation, n.d.; accessed April 27, 2015, http://www.intc.com/intel-annual-report/2014/

[4] "Qualcomm Annual Report 2014," Qualcomm, n.d.; accessed April 27, 2015, http://investor.qualcomm.com/secfiling.cfm?filingID=1234452-14-320&CIK=804328

[5] Brian Cleere, "Are you doing what you said you would?", Curo, March 11, 2015; accessed April 27, 2015, http://www.curo.ie/are-you-doing-what-you-said-you-would/

[6] EIU, "Why Good Strategies Fail: Lessons for the C-Suite," *The Economist Intelligence Unit*, 2013.

[7] Robert S. Kaplan and David Norton, "The Balanced Scorecard – Measures that Drive Performance," *Harvard Business Review*, January-February 2002; accessed April 27, 2015, https://hbr.org/2005/07/the-balanced-scorecard-measures-that-drive-performance

Chapter 21: Disruptive Implementation

[1] Donald Sull, Rebecca Homkes, and Charles Sull, "Why Strategy Execution Unravels – and what to do about it," *Harvard Business Review*, March 2015; accessed April 27, 2015, https://hbr.org/2015/03/why-strategy-execution-unravelsand-what-to-do-about-it

[2] Grove, "'Signals' or 'Noise'?", 99–120.

[3] Michael C. Mankins and Richard Steele, "Turning Strategy into Great Performance", *Harvard Business Review*, July-August 2005; accessed April 27, 2015, https://hbr.org/2005/07/turning-great-strategy-into-great-performance

[4] Gary Klein, "How to Spot Problems Before They Get Out of Hand," in *The Power of Intuition: How to Use Your Gut Feelings to Make Better Decisions at Work* (NY: Doubleday, 2003), 96–118.

[5] Grove, "Rein in Chaos," 137–164.

[6] " Founder and Chairman: Isadore Sharp," *Four Seasons*, n.d.; accessed April 27, 2015, http://www.fourseasons.com/about_four_seasons/isadore-sharp/

[7] Isadore Sharp, "The Golden Rule," *Four Seasons: The Story of a Business Philosophy* (London: Penguin, 2009), 103–108.

[8] "In Conversation with Isadore Sharp, Founder and Chairman, Four Seasons Hotels and Resorts," *Knightsbridge*, 2014; accessed April 27, 2015, http://www.knightsbridge.com/sitecore/content/Knightsbridge/home/ThoughtLeadership/onPeopleNewsletter/Articles/2014_ICW_IsadoreSharp.aspx

[9] Grove, "Rein in Chaos."

[10] Grove, "'Signal' or 'Noise'?"

[11] Donald Sull, Rebecca Homkes, and Charles Sull, "Why Strategy Execution Unravels – and what to do about it."

[12] Ibid.

[13] Ibid.

[14] "KitchenAid – Company Profile, Information, Business Description, History, Background Information on KitchenAid," *Reference for Business*, n.d.; accessed April 27, 2015, http://www.referenceforbusiness.com/history2/40/KitchenAid.html

[15] Leonor Ciarlone, "Building a House of Brands: Whirlpool Corporation's Blueprint for Success," *The Gilbane Report*, August 2005.

[16] EIU, "Why Good Strategies Fail: Lessons for the C-Suite."

[17] James M. Kouzes and Barry Z. Posner, *Credibility: How Leaders Gain and Lose It, Why People Demand It* (San Francisco: Jossey-Bass, 2011).

Chapter 22: Reviewing Performance

[1] EIU, "Why Good Strategies Fail: Lessons for the C-Suite."

[2] Tim Hartford, "Finding what Works for the Poor or: Variation," in *Adapt: Why Success Always Starts with Failure* (London: Abacus, 2011), 115-153.

[3] Hartford, "Conflict or: How Organisations Learn," 37-79.

[4] Ritva Reinikka and Jakob Svensson, "The Power of Information: Evidence from a Newspaper Campaign to Reduce Capture," *World Bank Policy Research Working Papers*, December 2003.

Chapter 23: Adapting Strategy

[1] Peter Drucker, *The Practice of Management* (NY: Harper, 1954); G.S. Odiorne, *Management by Objectives: A System of Managerial Leadership*, (NY: Pitman Publishing, 1965).

[2] Gary Klein, "Management by Discovery: Revisiting Goals Through Insight," *Realbusiness*, March 14, 2014; accessed 24 April, 2015, http://realbusiness.co.uk/article/26019-management-by-discovery-revising-goals-through-insight

3   U.S. Army, "Scientist shares Insights on Decision Making," *Army.mil* July 22, 2014; accessed April 24, 2015, http://www.army.mil/article/130337/Scientist_shares_insights_on_decision_making/

4   Jon Butterworth, "Belief, Bias and Bayes," *The Guardian*, September 28, 2014; accessed April 27, 2015, http://www.theguardian.com/science/life-and-physics/2014/sep/28/belief-bias-and-bayes

5   Sharon Bertsch McGrayne, "Applying Bayes' Rule," *The Theory That Would Not Die: How Bayes' Rule Cracked the Enigma Code, Hunted Down Russian Submarines, and Emerged Triumphant From Two Centuries of Controversy* (New Haven; London: Yale University Press, 2011): 259-270.

6   S. Jayakumar, "Twelve Years in the Ministry of Home Affairs (1981–1994)," *Be at the Table or Be on the Menu: A Singapore Memoir* (Singapore: Straits Times Press, 2015), 124–160.

7   Jayakumar, "Other Roles," 161–174.

Chapter 24: The Journey to FUSE

1   Krishnadas, *Imagining Surprise: Locating the Causality of Strategic Surprise.*

BIBLIOGRAPHY

Ackoff, Russell L. n.d. "Operations research." *Encyclopaedia Britannica*. Accessed November 13, 2014. http://www.britannica.com/EBchecked/topic/682073/ operations-research/68171/History.

Allentrepreneur. 2009. "Travel Like a Human with Joe Gebbia, Co-founder of AirBnB." Allentrepreneur. August 26. Accessed March 2, 2015. https:// allentrepreneur.wordpress.com/2009/08/26/travel-like-a-human-with-joe-gebbia-co-founder-of-airbnb/.

Andersen, Erika. 2013. "21 Quotes From Henry Ford on Business, Leadership and Life." *Forbes*. May 31. Accessed March 2, 2015. http://www.forbes.com/sites/ erikaandersen/2013/05/31/21-quotes-from-henry-ford-on-business-leadership-and-life/.

Anderson, Cameron, Sebastian Brion, Don A. Moore, and Jessica A. Kennedy. 2012. "A Status-enhancement Account of Overconfidence. *Journal of Personality and Social Psychology* 103 (4): 718-735.

Anderson, Chris. 2012. "Elon Musk's Mission to Mars." *WIRED*. October 21. Accessed March 2, 2015. http://www.wired.com/2012/10/ff-elon-musk-qa/all/.

Anderson, Mae, and Michael Liedtke. 2010. "Hubris – and late fees – doomed Blockbuster." *NBCNews.com*. September 23. Accessed October 24, 2014. http:// www.nbcnews.com/id/39332696/ns/business-retail/t/hubris-late-fees-doomed-blockbuster/#.VFHrSPk7PUk.

Andrews, Kenneth. 1971. *The Concept of Corporate Strategy*. Homewood, IL: Irwin.

Ansoff, Igor. 1985. "A Model for Strategic Decisions." In *Corporate Strategy*, by Igor Ansoff, 17-26. London: Penguin.

Ark in Time. 2015. "Aldous Huxley." *Ark in Time*. Accessed January 16, 2015. http:// thyselfknow.com/aldous-huxley/.

Austen, Ben. 2011. "The End of Borders and the Future of Books." *Bloomberg Business*. November 10. Accessed January 7, 2015. http://www.businessweek.com/ magazine/the-end-of-borders-and-the-future-of-books-11102011.html#p1.

Barney, Jay B. 1995. "Looking Inside for Competitive Advantage." *The Academy of Management Executive* (1993–2005) 9 (4): 49-61.

Barrabi, Thomas. 2014. "After Air Algerie AH5017 Incident, A Statistical Look at the Probability and Chances of Dying in a Plane Crash." *International Business Times.* July 24. Accessed March 15, 2015. http://www.ibtimes.com/after-air-algerie-ah5017-incident-statistical-look-probability-chances-dying-plane-crash-1638206.

Beare, John I. 1896. "Self-knowledge." *Mind* New Series 5 (18): 229-230.

Berliner, Michael. 2014. "*House of Cards, Breaking Bad* and binge viewing pull audiences online." *The Guardian.* August 7. Accessed October 24, 2014. http://www.theguardian.com/media-network/media-network-blog/2014/aug/07/house-cards-breaking-bad-netflix-amazon-data.

Bookstaber, Richard. 2007. "Cockroaches and Hedge Funds." In *A Demon of Our Own Design: Markets, Hedge Funds and the Perils of Financial Innovation*, by Richard Bookstaber, 207-242. NJ: John Wiley & Sons.

Bower, Joseph L., and Clayton Christensen. 1995. "Disruptive Technologies: Catching the Wave." *Harvard Business Review.* January–February. Accessed March 2, 2015. https://hbr.org/1995/01/disruptive-technologies-catching-the-wave.

Bushey, Ryan. 2014. "Netflix CEO confesses he tried to sell the company to Blockbuster... But Blockbuster wasn't interested." *Business Insider Singapore.* February 1. Accessed October 24, 2014. http://www.businessinsider.sg/blockbuster-missed-buying-netflix-2014-1/#.VE9aL_k7PUl.

Butterworth, Jon. 2014. "Belief, Bias and Bayes." *The Guardian.* September 28. Accessed April 27, 2015. http://www.theguardian.com/science/life-and-physics/2014/sep/28/belief-bias-and-bayes.

Carr, Austin. 2014. "Inside Airbnb's Grand Hotel Plans." *Fast Company.* March 17. Accessed March 2, 2015. http://www.fastcompany.com/3027107/punk-meet-rock-airbnb-brian-chesky-chip-conley.

—. 2013. "Inside Netflix's project Griffin: The forgotten history of Roku under Reed Hastings." *Fast Company.* January 23. Accessed October 24, 2014. http://www.fastcompany.com/3004709/inside-netflixs-project-griffin-forgotten-history-roku-under-reed-hastings.

Cassidy, John. 2013. "The Saliency Bias and 9/11: Is America Recovering?" *The New Yorker.* September 11. Accessed January 8, 2015. http://www.newyorker.com/news/john-cassidy/the-saliency-bias-and-911-is-america-recovering.

Chandler, Alfred. 1962. *Strategy and Structure.* Cambridge, MA: MIT Press.

Chariton, Jordan. 2014. "Inside the new refresh of NBCNews.com six months after relaunch." TVNewswer. August 11. Accessed November 13, 2014. http://www.mediabistro.com/tvnewser/inside-the-new-refresh-of-nbcnews-com-six-months-after-relaunch_b234931.

Chesky, Brian. 2014. "Airbnb." *Airbnb*. July 16. Accessed March 2, 2015. http://blog.airbnb.com/belong-anywhere/.

Ciarlone, Leonor. 2005. "Building a House of Brands: Whirlpool Corporation's Blueprint for Success." *The Gilbane Report*, August.

Cleere, Brian. 2015. "Are you doing what you said you would?" *Curo*. March 11. Accessed April 27, 2015. http://www.curo.ie/are-you-doing-what-you-said-you-would/.

Clifton, Donald O., and Paula Nelson. 1992. *Soar With Your Strengths*. NY: Dell Publishing.

CNN Money. 2014. "Netflix's French connection." *CNN Money*. September 15. Accessed October 24, 2014. http://money.cnn.com/2014/09/15/investing/netflix-france-media-cbs/.

Cohan, Peter. 2014. "Invest in companies like Netflix that do the opposite of what Clay Christensen says." *Forbes*. July 14. Accessed October 24, 2014. http://www.forbes.com/sites/petercohan/2014/07/14/by-disrupting-disruption-netflix-reveals-new-investing-strategy/.

Collins, Jim. 2001. "The Hedgehog Concept (Simplicity Within the Three Circles)." In *Good to Great: Why Some Companies Make the Leap... And Others Don't*, by Jim Collins, 90-119. NY: HarperCollins Publishers.

Collins, Jim, and Jerry I. Porras. 2002. *Built to Last: Successful Habits of Visionary Companies*. NY: HarperCollins Publishers.

Columbus, Louis. 2014. "Roundup of Analytics, Big Data & Business Intelligence Forecasts and Market Estimates, 2014." *Forbes*. June 24. Accessed November 13, 2014. http://www.forbes.com/sites/louiscolumbus/2014/06/24/roundup-of-analytics-big-data-business-intelligence-forecasts-and-market-estimates-2014/.

Coolidge, Frederick L., and Thomas Wynn. 2005. "Working Memory, its Executive Functions and the Emergence of Modern Thinking." *Cambridge Archaeological Journal* 15 (1): 5–26.

Copeland, Michael V. 2010. "Reed Hastings: Leader of the pack." *Fortune*. November 18. Accessed October 24, 2014. http://fortune.com/2010/11/18/reed-hastings-leader-of-the-pack/.

Crook, Jordan. 2014. "A Brief History of Airbnb." TechCrunch. June 20. Accessed March 2, 2015. http://techcrunch.com/gallery/a-brief-history-of-airbnb/.

Cunninghan, W., Denys Freeman, and Joseph McCloskey. 1984. "Of Radar and Operations Research: An appreciation of A.P. Rowe (1898–1976)." OR Forum 32 (4): 958–167.

Dean, Jeremy. 2012. "The Availability Bias: Why People buy Lottery Tickets." *PsyBlog*. August 6. Accessed January 8, 2015. http://www.spring.org.uk/2012/08/the-availability-bias-why-people-buy-lottery-tickets.php.

DeGeorge, Gail. 1997. *The Making of a Blockbuster: How Wayne Huizenga built a sports and entertainment empire from trash, grit, and videotape*. Wiley.

Dessaint, Olivier, and Adrien Matray. 2014. "Do managers overreach to salient risks?" *Job Market Paper*. January.

Dobelli, Rolf. 2014. "How Eye-catching Details Render us Blind." In *The Art of Thinking Clearly*, by Rolf Dobelli, 254–255. London: Sceptre.

Dominican University of California. n.d. "Study Focuses on Strategies for Achieving Goals, Resolutions." *Dominican University of California*. Accessed March 15, 2015. http://www.dominican.edu/dominicannews/study-highlights-strategies-for-achieving-goals.

Dru, Jean-Marie. 2007. *How Disruption Brought Order*. NY: Palgrace Macmillan.

Drucker, Peter. 1954. *The Practice of Management*. NY: Harper.

Dunning, David, Ann Leuenberger, and David A. Sherman. 1995. "A New Look at Motivated Inference: Are Self-Serving Theories of Success a Product of Motivational Forces?" *Journal of Personality and Social Psychology* 69 (1): 58-68.

Effron, Lauren. 2011. "Netflix CEO Reed Hastings says company has 'sincere regret' over handling of services changes." *abcNEWS*. September 26. Accessed October 24, 2014. http://abcnews.go.com/Business/netflix-ceo-reed-hastings-company-sincere-regret-customers/story?id=14608865&singlePage=true.

Elkind, Peter. 2014. "Inside Elon Musk's $1.4 Billion Score." *Fortune*. December 1. Accessed March 2, 2015. http://fortune.com/inside-elon-musks-billion-dollar-gigafactory/.

Farrell, Andrew. 2007. "Blockbuster's CEO Ousted." *Forbes*. February 7. Accessed October 24, 2014. http://www.forbes.com/2007/07/02/icahn-blockbuster-closer-markets-equity-cx_af_ra_0702markets36.html.

Festinger, L. 1957. *A Theory of Cognitive Dissonance*. Stanford, CA: Stanford University Press.

Festinger, L., and J.M. Carlsmith. 1959. "Cognitive Consequences of Forced Compliance." *Journal of Abnormal and Social Psychology* 58: 203–210.

Fischer, Barry. 2012. "Homes with Pools use 49% more Electricity per year, but it's not because of the pool." *Outlier*. July 26. Accessed March 15, 2015. http://blog. opower.com/2012/07/homes-with-pools-use-49-more-electricity-but-its-not-just-because-of-the-pool/.

Four Seasons. n.d. "Founder and Chairman: Isadore Sharp." *Four Seasons*. Accessed April 27, 2015. http://www.fourseasons.com/about_four_seasons/isadore-sharp/.

Funding Universe. n.d. "Intel Corporation History." *Funding Universe*. Accessed April 27, 2015. http://www.fundinguniverse.com/company-histories/intel-corporation-history/.

Garcia-Tunon, Manny. 2015. "Conform or Transform: The Choice is Yours." *Miami Herald*. February 22. Accessed March 2, 2015. http://www.miamiherald.com/news/business/biz-monday/article10788944.html.

Goldsmith, Jill. 2005. "Blockbusted: How technology and lack of vision took down Blockbuster." *Variety*. October 9. Accessed October 24, 2014. http://variety.com/2005/biz/news/blockbusted-how-technology-and-lack-of-vision-took-down-blockbuster-1117930420/.

Gorman, John. 1985. "Gerber Isn't Kidding About Diversification." *Chicago Tribune*. December 9. Accessed March 2, 2015. http://articles.chicagotribune.com/1985-12-09/business/8503250237_1_baby-food-grocery-vinyl.

Greene, Nick. 2015. "Challenger Explosion – A NASA Tragedy." *About.com*. Accessed March 2, 2015. http://space.about.com/cs/challenger/a/challenger.htm.

Grove, Andrew. 1999. *Only the Paranoid Survive*. NY: Crown Business.

Harress, Christopher. 2013. "The sad end of Blockbuster video: The onetime $5 billion company is being liquidated as competition from online giants Netflix and Hulu prove all too much for the iconic brand." *International Business Times*. December 5. Accessed October 24, 2014. http://www.ibtimes.com/sad-end-blockbuster-video-onetime-5-billion-company-being-liquidated-competition-online-giants.

Hartford, Tim. 2011. *Adapt: Why Success Always Starts with Failure*. London: Abacus.

Heijden, Kees Van Der. 2005. *Scenarios: The Art of Strategic Conversation*. 2nd. West Sussex: John Wiley & Sons.

Helm, Burt. 2014. "Airbnb is Inc.'s 2014 Company of the Year." Inc. December. Accessed March 2, 2015. http://www.inc.com/magazine/201412/burt-helm/airbnb-company-of-the-year-2014.html .

Henderson, Bruce D. 1989. "The Origin of Strategy." *Harvard Business Review*. November–December. Accessed March 2, 2015. https://hbr.org/1989/11/the-origin-of-strategy.

Hessman, Travis. 2013. "The World According to Elon Musk." *IndustryWeek*. October 7. Accessed March 2, 2015. http://www.industryweek.com/technology/world-according-elon-musk?page=1.

Hoffman, Carl. 2012. "Elon Musk, the Rocket Man with a Sweet Ride." *Smithsonian. com*. December. Accessed March 2, 2015. http://www.smithsonianmag.com/science-nature/elon-musk-the-rocket-man-with-a-sweet-ride-136059680/?page=2.

Horwath, Rich. 2006. "The Origins of Strategy." *StrategicThinking Institute*. Accessed March 2, 2015. http://strategyskills.com/Articles_Samples/origin_strategy.pdf .

Hsu, Jeremy. 2008. "Strike Three for SpaceX's Falcon 1 Rocket." *NBCNews.com*. August 3. Accessed March 2, 2015. http://www.nbcnews.com/id/25990806/ns/technology_and_science-space/t/strike-three-spacexs-falcon-rocket/#.VO7J9fnxKXx.

Huffington Post. 2013. "Blockbuster closing all of its remaining retail stores." *Huffington Post*. November 11. Accessed October 24, 2014. http://www. huffingtonpost.com/2013/11/06/blockbuster-closing_n_4226735.html.

Huston, Larry, and Nabil Sakkab. 2006. "Connect and Develop: Inside Procter & Gamble's New Model for Innovation." *Harvard Business Review*. March. Accessed January 16, 2015. https://hbr.org/2006/03/connect-and-develop-inside-procter-gambles-new-model-for-innovation.

Inc. Magazine. 2005. "Q&A: Reed Hastings, Netflix." *Inc. Magazine*. December 1. Accessed October 24, 2014. http://www.inc.com/magazine/20051201/qa-hastings. html.

Ingar, David. 1985. "Memory of the future: An essay on the temporal organisation of conscious awareness." *Hum Neurobiol* 4 (3): 127–136.

Intel Corporation. n.d. "Intel Annual Report 2014." *Intel Corporation*. Accessed April 27, 2015. http://www.intc.com/intel-annual-report/2014/.

ITU. 2015. Statistics. Accessed January 7, 2015. http://www.itu.int/en/ITU-D/ Statistics/Pages/stat/default.aspx.

Janis, Irving Lester. 1972. "The Bay of Pigs." In *Victims of Groupthink: A Psychological Study of Foreign-Policy Decisions and Fiascoes*, by Irving Lester Janis, 14–49. Houghton Mifflin Company.

Jayakumar, S. 2015. *Be at the Table or Be on the Menu: A Singapore Memoir*. Singapore: Straits Times Press.

Kahane, Adam Morris. 2012. "An Invention Born of Necessity." In *Transformative Scenario Planning: Working Together to Change the Future*, by Adam Morris Kahane, 1-14. San Francisco: Berrett-Koehler Publishers.

Kahneman, Daniel, and Amos Tversky. 1979. "Prospect Theory: An analysis of Decision under Risk." *Econometrica* 47: 263–291.

Kahneman, Daniel, and Amos Tversky. 1981. "The Framing of Decisions and the Psychology of Choice." *Science* 211 (4481): 453–458.

Kamin, Kim A., and Jeffrey J. Rachlinski. 1995. "Ex Post =/= Ex Ante: Determining Liability in Hindsight." *Law and Human Behavior* 19 (1): 89-104.

Kaplan, Robert S., and David Norton. 2002. "The Balanced Scorecard – Measures that Drive Performance." *Harvard Business Review*. January-February. Accessed April 27, 2015. https://hbr.org/2005/07/the-balanced-scorecard-measures-that-drive-performance.

Kay, John. 2014. "Drug Companies are built in Labs, not Boardrooms." *Financial Times*. May 6. Accessed March 2, 2015. http://www.ft.com/intl/cms/s/0/413557b4-d162-11e3-81e0-00144feabdc0.html#axzz3SjS6mr5X.

—. 2011. *Obliquity: Why our Goals are Best Achieved Indirectly*. Profile Books.

Kelly, Jeff. 2014. "Big Data Vendor Revenue and Market Forecast 2013-2017." *Wikibon*. February 12. Accessed November 13, 2014. http://wikibon.org/wiki/v/Big_Data_Vendor_Revenue_and_Market_Forecast_2013-2017.

Kirby, Maurice. 2000. "Operations Research Trajectories: The Anglo-American experience from the 1940s to the 1990s." *Operations Research* 48 (5): 661–670.

Klein, Gary. 2003. "How to Spot Problems Before they get out of Hand." In *The Power of Intuition: How to Use Your Gut Feelings to Make Better Decisions at Work*, by Gary Klein, 96–118. NY: Doubleday.

—. 2014. "Management by Discovery: Revisiting Goals Through Insight." *Realbusiness*. March 14. Accessed April 24, 2015. http://realbusiness.co.uk/article/26019-management-by-discovery-revising-goals-through-insight .

Kleiner, Art. 2008. "Mystics: Royal Dutch/Shell's scenario planners, 1967-1973." In *The Age of Heretics: A history of the radical thinkers who reinvented corporate management*, by Art Kleiner, 121–154. San Francisco: Jossey-Bass.

Knightsbridge. 2014. "In Conversation with Isadore Sharp, Founder and Chairman, Four Seasons Hotels and Resorts." *Knightsbridge*. Accessed April 27, 2015. http://www.knightsbridge.com/sitecore/content/Knightsbridge/home/ThoughtLeadership/onPeopleNewsletter/Articles/2014_ICW_IsadoreSharp.aspx.

Kouzes, James M., and Barry Z. Posner. 2011. *Credibility: How Leaders Gain and Lose It, Why People Demand It.* San Francisco: Jossey-Bass.

Krasny, Jill. 2014. "Malcolm Gladwell on What Really Makes People Disruptive." *Inc.* October 7. Accessed September 17, 2014. http://www.inc.com/jill-krasny/malcolm-gladwell-on-the-one-character-trait-that-makes-people-disruptive.html?cid=sf01002.

Krishnadas, Devadas. 2005. "Imagining Surprise: Locating the Causality of Strategic Surprise." Tufts University.

KTAR.com. 2008. "Arizona gets $2.3 million from Vioxx Settlement." *KTAR.com.* May 20. Accessed March 2, 2015. http://ktar.com/?nid=6&sid=842595&r=1.

Kuah, Adrian W.J. 2013. "Foresight and Policy: Thinking about Singapore's Future(s)." *Social Space* 104-109.

Kuperinsky, Amy. 2014. "Binge-watching: How the hungry habit is transforming TV." nj.com. May 25. Accessed October 24, 2014. http://www.nj.com/entertainment/index.ssf/2014/05/beau_willimon_house_of_cards_binge_watching.html.

Langer, Ellen. 1975. "The Illusion of Control." *Journal of Personlity and Social Psychology* 32: 311–328.

Larnder, Harold. 1984. "The origins of Operational Research." *OR Forum* 32 (2): 465–476.

Lawrence, Paul, and Jay Lorsch. 1967. "Differentiation and Integration in Complex Organisations." *Administrative Science Quarterly* 12: 1–47.

Lipsey, Roger. 2001. "Know Thyself." In *Have You Been to Delphi? Tales of the Ancient Oracles for the Modern Mind*, by Roger Lipsey, 229–258. Albany: State University of New York Press.

Litvak, Nicole. 2014. "Is the SolarCity Model the Only Way to Scale Residential Solar?" *Greentech Media*. March 31. Accessed March 2, 2015. http://www.greentechmedia.com/articles/read/is-the-solarcity-model-the-only-way-to-scale-residential-solar.

Lohr, Steve. 2012. "The Age of Big Data." *NY Times*. February 11. Accessed November 13, 2014. http://www.nytimes.com/2012/02/12/sunday-review/big-datas-impact-in-the-world.html?pagewanted=all&_r=0.

Lusk, Sean. 2010. "The Challenge of Foresight." *The Guardian*. June 10. Accessed January 7, 2015. http://www.theguardian.com/public-sector-training/training-crisis-management-lusk.

Mankins, Michael C., and Richard Steele. 2005. "Turning Strategy into Great Performance." *Harvard Business Review*. July-August. Accessed April 27, 2015. https://hbr.org/2005/07/turning-great-strategy-into-great-performance.

McGrayne, Sharon Bertsch. 2011. *The Theory That Would Not Die: How Bayes' Rule Cracked the Enigma Code, Hunted Down Russian submarines, and Emerged Triumphant from Two Centuries of Controversy*. New Haven; London: Yale University Press.

Menand, Louis. 2005. "Fat Man: Herman Kahn and the nuclear age." *The New Yorker*. June 27. Accessed November 13, 2014. http://www.newyorker.com/magazine/2005/06/27/fat-man.

Miller, D.T., and M. Ross. 1975. "Self-serving Biases in the Attribution of Causality: Fact or Fiction?" *Psychological Bulletin* 82: 213-225.

Morse, Philip M. 1986. "The beginnings of *Operations Research* in the United States." Operations Research 34 (1): 10–17.

Munarriz, Rick. 2014. "Netflix Inc. takes a bet on the box office." *The Motley Fool*. October 12. Accessed October 24, 2014. http://www.fool.com/investing/general/2014/10/12/netflix-inc-takes-a-bet-on-the-box-office.aspx.

Musk, Elon. 2014. "All Our Patent Are Belong to You." *Tesla Blog*. June 12. Accessed March 2, 2015. http://www.teslamotors.com/blog/all-our-patent-are-belong-you.

—. 2006. "The Secret Tesla Motors Master Plan (just between you and me)." *Tesla Blog*. August 2. Accessed March 2, 2015. http://www.teslamotors.com/blog/secret-tesla-motors-master-plan-just-between-you-and-me.

Nasdaq. n.d. BLOCKBUSTER INC (BBI) IPO. Accessed October 24, 2014. http://www.nasdaq.com/markets/ipos/company/blockbuster-inc-10470-5223.

National Commission on Terrorist Attacks Upon the United States. 2004. "The 9/11 Commission Report: Final Report of the National Commission on Terrorist Attacks on the United States." *National Commission on Terrorist Attacks Upon the United States*. Accessed March 15, 2015. http://www.9-11commission.gov/report/911Report_Exec.htm.

Nicholason, Lucy. 2015. "Elon Musk uses this Ancient Critical Thinking Strategy to Outsmart Everybody Else." *Business Insider*. January 6. Accessed March 2, 2015. http://www.businessinsider.sg/elon-musk-first-principles-2015-1/#.VXKqg8_zrIU.

Nirmala, M. 2014. "Complexity: When 1+2 becomes 4." *Asiaone News*. August 27. Accessed January 7, 2015. http://news.asiaone.com/news/asian-opinions/complexity-when-12-becomes-4?page=0%2C1.

Odiorne, G.S. 1965. *Management by Objectives: A System of Managerial Leadership*. NY: Pitman Publishing.

Osnos, Peter. 2011. "What went wrong at Borders." *The Atlantic.* January 11. Accessed January 7, 2015. http://www.theatlantic.com/business/archive/2011/01/what-went-wrong-at-borders/69310/.

Palmer, Chris. 2013. "Gorillas in the Lung." *The Scientist.* July 18. Accessed September 17, 2014. http://www.the-scientist.com/?articles.view/articleNo/36606/title/Gorillas-in-the-Lung/.

Park, Jae-Hong, Prabhudev Konana, Bin Gu, Alok Kumar, and Rajagopal Raghunathan. 2010. "Confirmation Bias, Overconfidence, and Investment Performance: Evidence from Stock Message Boards." *McCombs Research Paper Series* No. IROM-07-10 1-59.

Perez, Wendy. 2013. "Online video will overtake TV by 2020, says John Farrell, Director of YouTube Latin America." *Portada Online.* February 2. Accessed October 2014, 2014. http://latam.portada-online.com/2013/02/14/online-video-will-overtake-tv-by-2020-says-john-farrell-director-of-youtube-latin-america/.

Phillips, LD. 2011. "What is Strategy." *Journal of the Operational Research Society* 62: 926-929.

Poggi, Jeanine. 2010. "Blockbuster's rise and fall: The long, rewinding road." *The Street.* September 23. Accessed October 24, 2014. http://www.thestreet.com/story/10867574/1/the-rise-and-fall-of-blockbuster-the-long-rewinding-road.html.

Poletti, Therese. 2015. "What Really Keeps Airbnb's CEO up at Night." *MarketWatch.* February 13. Accessed March 2, 2015. http://www.marketwatch.com/story/what-really-keeps-airbnbs-ceo-up-at-night-2015-02-13.

Porter, Michael E. 1980. "A Framework for Competitor Analysis." In *Competitive Strategy: Techniques for Analysing Industries and Competitors*, by Michael E. Porter, 47-74. NY: The Free Press.

—. 1979. "How Competitive Forces Shape Strategy." *Harvard Business Review.* March. Accessed March 2, 2015. https://hbr.org/1979/03/how-competitive-forces-shape-strategy.

Prahalad, C.K., and Gary Hamel. 1990. "The Core Competence of the Corporation." *Harvard Business Review.* May-June. Accessed March 2, 2015. https://hbr.org/1990/05/the-core-competence-of-the-corporation.

Preston, Caroline E., and Stanley Harris. 1965. "Psychology of Drivers in Traffic Accidents." *Journal of Applied Psychology* 49 (4): 284–288.

Pronin, Emily, and Matthew B. Kugler. 2007. "Valuing thoughts, ignoring behavior: The introspection illusion as a source of the bias blind spot." *Journal of Experimental Social Psychology* 43 (4): 565–578.

Pronin, Emily, Daniel Y. Lin, and Lee Ross. 2002. "The Bias Blind Spot: Perceptions of Bias in Self Versus Others." *PSPB* 28 (3): 369–381.

Qualcomm. n.d. "Qualcomm Annual Report 2014." Qualcomm. Accessed April 27, 2015. http://investor.qualcomm.com/secfiling.cfm?filingID=1234452-14-320&CIK=804328.

Reference for Business. n.d. "Company Profile, Information, Business Description, History, Background Information on KitchenAid." *Reference for Business.* Accessed April 27, 2015. http://www.referenceforbusiness.com/history2/40/KitchenAid.html.

Rehak, Judith. 2002. "Tylenol made a Hero of Johnson & Johnson: The Recall that Started Them All." *NY Times.* March 23. Accessed March 2, 2015. http://www.nytimes.com/2002/03/23/your-money/23iht-mjj_ed3_.html.

Reinikka, Ritva, and Jakob Svensson. 2003. "The Power of Information: Evidence from a Newspaper Campaign to Reduce Capture." *World Bank Policy Research Working Papers.*

Reuter, Thomas. 2008. "Reading the Future in Indonesia: Javanese Texts of Prophesy as a Popular Genre." *17th Biennial Conference of the Asian Studies Association of Australia.* Melbourne.

Ross, JS, KP Hill, DS Egilman, and HM Krumholz. 2008. "Guest authorship and ghostwriting in publications related to Rofecoxib: A Case Study of Industry Documents from Rofecoxib Litigation." *JAMA* 299 (15): 1800–1812.

Rourke, Elizabeth, Carrie Rothburd, and Christina Stansell. 2006. "Blockbuster Inc." *Encyclopedia.com.* Accessed October 24, 2015. http://www.encyclopedia.com/doc/1G2-3483400030.html.

Rout, Milanda. 2009. "Vioxx maker Merck and Co drew up doctor hit list." *The Australian.* April 1. Accessed March 2, 2015. http://www.theaustralian.com.au/news/drug-company-drew-up-doctor-hit-list/story-e6frg6n6-1225693586492.

Sandoval, Greg. 2010. "Blockbuster laughed at Netflix partnership offer." *CNET.* December 9. Accessed October 24, 2014. http://www.cnet.com/news/blockbuster-laughed-at-netflix-partnership-offer/.

Santoso, Alex. 2013. "Did you know that Blockbuster once had a chance to buy Netflix for a mere $50 million?" *Neatorama.* November 12. Accessed October 24, 2014. http://www.neatorama.com/2013/11/12/Did-You-Know-That-Blockbuster-Once-Had-a-Chance-to-Buy-Netflix-for-a-Mere-50-Million/.

Sarasota Herald-Tribune. 1974. "U.S. Births Decline, Babay Business Grow." *Sarasota Herald Tribune.* September 9. Accessed March 2, 2015. https://news.google.com/newspapers?id=D_wjAAAAIBAJ&sjid=62YEAAAAIBAJ&pg=6866,3789354&hl=en.

Satell, Greg. 2013. "The myth of the moron CEO." *Forbes.* August 1. Accessed October 24, 2014. http://www.forbes.com/sites/gregsatell/2013/08/01/the-myth-of-the-moron-ceo/.

Saunders, Donna. 2011. "September 2011 is the Final Chapter in the Story of Borders Books." *Examiner.com.* July 19. Accessed January 7, 2015. http://www.examiner.com/article/september-2011-is-the-final-chapter-the-story-of-borders-books.

Schwartz, Peter. 1996. "The Pathfinder's Tale." In *The Art of the Long View*, by Peter Schwartz, 3-15. New York: Doubleday.

Sharp, Isadore. 2009. "The Golden Rule." In *Four Seasons: The Story of a Business Philosophy*, by Isadore Sharp, 103–108. London: Penguin.

Shaw, Lucas. 2014. "Netflix looks to the Old World for new growth." *Bloomberg Business.* September 11. Accessed October 24, 2014. http://www.businessweek.com/articles/2014-09-11/netflix-looks-to-europe-for-streaming-growth.

Siegler, MC. 2010. "Eric Schmidt: Every 2 days we create as much information as we did up to 2003." *TechCrunch.* August 4. Accessed November 13, 2014. http://techcrunch.com/2010/08/04/schmidt-data/.

Singh, Dolly. 2013. "What is it like to work with Elon Musk?" *Quora.* November 2. Accessed March 2, 2015. http://www.quora.com/What-is-it-like-to-work-with-Elon-Musk/answer/Dolly-Singh-8?srid=n2Fg&share=1.

Staw, Barry. 1976. "Knee-Deep in the Big Muddy: A Study of Escalating Commitment to a Chosen Course of Action." *Organisational Behavior and Human Performance* 16 (1): 27–44.

Staw, Barry M., and Ha Hoang. 1995. "Sunk Costs in the NBA: Why Draft Order Affects Playing Time and Survival in Professional Basketball." *Administrative Science Quarterly* 474-494.

Stelter, Brian. 2013. "New way to deliver a drama: All 13 episodes in one sitting." *NY Times.* January 31. Accessed October 24, 2014. http://www.nytimes.com/2013/02/01/business/media/netflix-to-deliver-all-13-episodes-of-house-of-cards-on-one-day.html?pagewanted=all&_r=0.

Stenovec, Timothy. 2013. "Netflix overtakes HBO in paid U.S. subscribers." *Huffington Post.* October 21. Accessed October 24, 2014. http://www.huffingtonpost.com/2013/10/21/netflix-hbo_n_4138477.html.

Stewart, Malcolm. 2014. "Big Data's big mistake: Quantity over Quality." *DataInformed.* October 21. Accessed November 13, 2014. http://data-informed.com/big-datas-big-mistake-quantity-quality/.

Suddendorf, Thomas, and Michael C. Corballis. 2007. "The Evolution of Foresight: What is mental time travel, and is it unique to humans?" *Behavioral and Brain Sciences* (Cambridge University Press) 30 (3): 299–313.

Sull, Donald, Rebecca Homkes, and Charles Sull. 2015. "Why Strategy Execution Unravels – and what to do about it." *Harvard Business Review.* March. Accessed April 27, 2015. https://hbr.org/2015/03/why-strategy-execution-unravelsand-what-to-do-about-it.

Svenson, Ola. 1981. "Are we all less risky and more skillful than our fellow drivers?" *Acta Psychologica* 47: 143–148.

Taleb, Nassim. 2010. The Black Swan. 2nd. NY: Random House.

Taylor, William C., and Polly G. LaBarre. 2008. *Mavericks at Work: Why the Most Original Minds in Business Win.* NY: HarperCollins Publishers.

TEDx. 2013. "Foresight in Hindsight: Reinier de Graaf at TEDxHamburg City 2.0." *Tedx.* July 12. Accessed September 17, 2014. http://tedxtalks.ted.com/video/Foresight-in-Hindsight-Reinier.

Tetlock, Philip. 2005. *Expert Political Judgment: How Good Is It? How Can We Know?* NJ: Princeton University Press.

The Library of Congress. n.d. "Moving Image Section – Motion Picture, Broadcasting and Recorded Sound Division." *The Library of Congress.* Accessed January 7, 2015. http://memory.loc.gov/ammem/awhhtml/awmi10/television.html.

Treaster, Joseph B. 1983. "Herman Kahn dies; Futurist and thinker on nuclear strategy." *NY Times.* July 8. Accessed November 13, 2014. http://www.nytimes.com/1983/07/08/obituaries/herman-kahn-dies-futurist-and-thinker-on-nuclear-strategy.html.

U.S. Army. 2014. "Scientist shares insights on Decision Making." *Army.mil.* July 22. Accessed April 24, 2015. http://www.army.mil/article/130337/Scientist_shares_insights_on_decision_making/.

Vioxx, Celebrex, Bextra Recall News. 2005. "Vioxx death estimate revised upwards." *Vioxx, Celebrex, Bextra Recall News.* January 2. Accessed March 2, 2015. http://www.mynippon.com/vioxx/2005/01/vioxx-death-estimate-revised-upwards.html.

Voros, Joseph. 2001. "A Primer on Future Studies, Foresight and the Use of Scenarios." *Prospect* (Swinburne University of Technology) (6).

VSA Capital. n.d. *September 2011 Newsletter.* Accessed September 17, 2014. http://minesite.com/media/pub/var/release_downloadable_file/32863.pdf.

Wack, Pierre. 1985. "Scenarios: Uncharted waters ahead." *Harvard Business Review* 73–89.

n.d. *What was the Future of.* Accessed September 17, 2014. http://www.foresightinhindsight.com/static/1.

Whittington, Richard. 2002. *What is Strategy – and does it matter?* 2nd. Cornwall: Thomson.

Wilson, Timothy D., and Nancy Brekke. 1994. "Mental contamination and mental correction: unwanted influences on judgments and evaluations." *Psychological Bulletin* 116 (1): 117-142.

Worthington, William J., Jamie D. Collins, and Michael A. Hitt. 2009. "Beyond Risk Mitigation: Enhancing Corporate Innovation with Scenario Planning." *Business Horizon* 52: 441–450.

Zambelli, Alex. 2013. "A history of media streaming and the future of connected TV." *The Guardian.* March 1. Accessed October 24, 2014. http://www.theguardian.com/media-network/media-network-blog/2013/mar/01/history-streaming-future-connected-tv.

ABOUT THE AUTHOR

Devadas Krishnadas is the founder and CEO of Future-Moves Group. Prior to founding Future-Moves Group, Devadas played a leading role in developing Singapore's fiscal and social policy where he led efforts in long-term planning and strategic thinking.

He is the author of *Sensing Singapore: Reflections in a Time of Change*, and has been cited and published in international publications on foresight and strategy.

ABOUT FUTURE-MOVES GROUP

Future-Moves Group is an international consultancy founded in 2012. It is Southeast Asia's first strategy consultancy using foresight tools to complement conventional analysis. Headquartered in Singapore, Future-Moves Group's practice is international and multi-sectoral.